UNBOUND

POLICE CHIEF
ANTHONY V. BOUZA (RET.)

UNBOUND

CORRUPTION, ABUSE, AND
HEROISM BY THE BOYS IN BLUE

Prometheus Books

59 John Glenn Drive
Amherst, New York 14228-2197

Published 2001 by Prometheus Books

Inquiries should be addressed to
Prometheus Books
59 John Glenn Drive
Amherst, New York 14228–2197
VOICE: 716–691–0133, ext. 207
FAX: 716–564–2711
WWW.PROMETHEUSBOOKS.COM

04 03 02 01 00   5 4 3 2 1

Library of Congress Cataloging-in-Publication Data

Bouza, Anthony V.
    Police unbound : corruption, abuse, and heroism by the boys in blue / by Anthony V. Bouza.
        p. cm.
    Includes bibliographical references and index.
    ISBN 1–57392–877–1 (alk. paper)
    1. Police—United States. I. Title.

HV8138 .B596 2001
363.2'0973—dc21

00–065316

Printed in Canada on acid-free paper

For Cynthia, Tony George, and August 23rd

CONTENTS

ACKNOWLEDGMENTS

The impetus for this book comes from editor Linda Regan, who also labored mightily to refine and improve the text. In writing it I tried to follow the urgings and suggestions of my dear friend Dr. Peter Marchant, who pressed me for years to do it.

My son Dominick revised and typed the manuscript. Marilyn Mason and Constance Caplan were good enough to read the draft and offer suggestions and guidance.

Inspiration flowed from Doctors George A. Kateb and Lawrence W. Sherman.

My wife, Erica, always helps, but this time she offered specific pointers and anecdotes that proved rich source material.

I owe a debt I can never repay to the cops—in three departments—whose heroics and devotion to duty instructed and inspired my awe.

The flaws are my fault alone.

INTRODUCTION

What's going on here?

Chances are that even the best-informed people, looking at seemingly straightforward cases of police actions, will come to quick—and almost certainly wrong—conclusions.

No insider expected the cops in the Amadou Diallo shooting to be convicted of murder, yet outsiders—the press and general public—were shocked by the Albany, New York, jury's acquittals.

Some observers will wonder why the cops didn't arrest the violent demonstrators at the Seattle, Washington, protests in December 1999. They will equate the Louima and Diallo New York Police Department (NYPD) cases as being similar examples of street justice tinged with racism and wonder why the court outcomes differed so radically. Readers will wonder why a highly regarded, well-educated, if mentally disturbed, man had to be shot and killed in a celebrated case involving a Jewish Sect in Brooklyn. Why not disabled? Why not have the weapon shot out of his hand?

Whole industries have grown around popular misunderstandings of the street realities cops face and general confusion has attended the public's appreciation of the appropriateness of police responses.

11

Invoking such emblematic images as Waco, Rodney King, the Oklahoma City Murrah Federal Building explosion, Seattle's World Trade Organization conference, or lesser-known but repeatedly surfacing incidents in your hometown, or touching someone known to you, will inspire a knowing raising of the eyebrows. Yet cops know that this flash of insight is very likely to be off the mark.

What appear to be uncomplicated sagas conceal complex and often—to a public derisively dismissed as "citizens" or "civilians" by the police—fatally fragmented truths and misconceptions that serve to conceal or distort much larger and unseen verities. Cops, immersed in these kinetic, violent, and confused street encounters not only come to appreciate the ambiguities and complexities but also develop a scorn for the quick judgments of unknowing observers.

There is a yawning chasm between police reality and public perception.

Indeed, in civil suits alleging police wrongdoing, it is critical to employ credible individuals with insiders' knowledge to lead jurors to a sense of what really happened. It is no exaggeration to say that, absent the knowing guidance of a police expert witness on the stand, juries are more likely than not to miss the crux of meaning in a lot of police operations.

Experts may, of course, also engage in distortions, but they at least offer a view that contrasts with the cops' "official version."

Distinguishing between proper and improper police procedures—the legitimate use of force from police brutality and the use of appropriate or inappropriate standards and policies—has spawned a cottage industry of consultants, usually former police executives, serving as these expert witnesses.

Ours is a very complex society, but the difficulties rise exponentially when trying to fathom the truth of a police action on the street.

Look about you and how you spend your day. The transactions, the interactions, the interdependences. You understand them, despite their complexities, because you're experiencing them. Outsiders may well be puzzled by what is, to you, a perfectly straightforward matter. The same is true of cops, only their actions appear on the front pages.

We don't try to understand all of it; yet, in the main, the events of our lives are pretty predictable and graspable. This transparency and our involvement lead us to conclude we understand the seas in which we sail. And we mostly do.

The world of cops, though, is an unfathomable Atlantis—and most of us are clueless to that reality.

The larger society still, in its power centers—mainly white, male, and middle-class—transmits assignments and messages to its institutions. Most of these directives, tacit and explicit, are pretty clear, logical, and direct. We want our media to tell the truth, our scholars to educate our young, our banks to look after our treasure, and our services to function as expected.

Society's message to the police, as reflected in laws, charters, policy statements, public pronouncements, and other verifiable documents, is both clear and unambiguous—protect and serve.

So, where does this dissonance between the media's description of an egregious act of wrongdoing by the cops and the cops' sense of betrayal and hurt originate? And how could the rest of us possibly be complicit in such atrocities?

There is a clear, yet subliminal, message being transmitted that the cops, if they are to remain on the payroll, had better obey.

The overclass—mostly white, well-off, educated, suburban, and voting—wants the underclass—frequently minority, homeless, jobless, uneducated, and excluded—controlled and, preferably, kept out of sight. Property rights are more sacred than human lives. And some lives are more precious than others.

Over the years, we've seen the evolution of the unspoken message to go after the underclass, much in the manner of the NYPD's attacks on "quality of life in street conditions," into sanitized versions that have become acceptable. The understanding has to be the tacit agreement as to who the target is, as well as what's to be done about it. This usually means creating a wilderness and calling it peace—Pax Romana on America's streets.

And yet to define it all in the hysterical, neo-Marxist terms of class struggle is to invite a dismissive shrug. Who wants to hear how they're part of the oppression? And how many victims seek to learn how they contributed to their own victimization?

Heavy, heady stuff.

I started out as an immigrant from Spain, grateful for the certitudes of civil service—a steady salary and the glories of a pension at sundown.

I ended up a desiccated sociologist of sorts whose unpopular notions no one wants to hear.

Gilbert and Sullivan had it right—"When constabulary's duty's to be done, to be done, a policeman's lot is not a happy one." Today, political correctness and constitutional necessity would transpose "police officer" for the less androgynous "policeman." But it makes the rhyming tougher. Indeed, indeed.

Sure, there are a brace of TV shows, movies, and a flow of novels granting verisimilitude to our appreciation of police reality, but these are mere concentrates that avoid the really hard questions of internal rot and external abuses. And, of course, they have to omit the long passages of boredom between the spikes of action or risk putting audiences to sleep. There are exceptions such as *Serpico*, *Cop Land*, and *Prince of the City*, but it's hard to think of any that speak to the subtler and less penetrable questions of class and race.

So, why, in my seventh decade and gratefully in debt to police institutions that fed, educated, and enriched me and my family, should I stir the shit, in the colorful police vernacular I hope to employ in this effort?

I love cops. They do heroic and noble things every day. Policing as an institution is flawed and can be made a lot better. I don't want to pass up a chance to serve those cops in the best way I can, by making their departments cleaner and stronger. It is the least they deserve from me.

I want this to be a breezy, personal, subjective narrative rather than a scholarly treatise. Sociologists and criminologists have the bookshelves groaning under the weight of their police tomes. Yes, there are the occasional self-congratulatory memoirs and the recitations of boring war stories, but mostly, the insiders have provided zilch to the reader. I thought a ruminative, reflective, anecdotal approach might shed a shaft of light on one of society's darker corners—the world of cops.

And, yes, there is a greater loyalty than the one we owe to the institutions that nurtured us: the one to the great nation that mothers us all.

The challenge is to tell the unvarnished truth. Have I the courage?

That is the real question.

I hope so.

1
POLICE WORK

W hat is police work?

We all know the answer. We've seen the cop shows and the dramas on what we once called the "silver screen." Short of the comings and goings of Bat Masterson, Wyatt Earp, or Billy the Kid, is there any line of work we know—or think we know—more about than the cop's world?

The conceit of this effort is to prove this supposition bankrupt, and dangerously so.

Outwardly, the functions of America's urban police are straightforward—to combat street crime, respond to emergencies, and regulate traffic. We don't have a uniformed national police. Sophisticated depredations such as those of bankers, Mafiosi, international terrorists, and brokers are left to specialized federal and sometimes state agencies.

By street crime we mean muggings, break-ins, assaults, murder, car theft, rape, drug offenses, other thefts, and the myriad acts we encounter, usually on our streets, that have been officially proscribed. We are codified—which, as a practical matter, means that if you can find an act that, while hideously offensive, has not yet been formally legally forbidden, you can perform it with impunity. Good luck. We do have thousands and thousands of codes and the odds are good they will, like Procrustes' bed, find one to fit your circumstances.

I learned, early on, just how encompassing the law could be.

On a bleak November Sunday in 1955 my partner and I received a report of a DOA found on the deserted beach in Coney Island. The case came to us because the dead lady's address was in our precinct, the Chelsea section of Manhattan.

There were no signs of violence on the well-dressed, meticulously made-up young woman—white and in her thirties.

Our investigation led to an apartment the deceased shared with two other young women, one of whom was named Eroica, after Beethoven's Third Symphony. We separated them and lied that we were investing the case as a homicide and hinted darkly at their implication; the two women hastily explained what happened.

They'd returned home Friday to discover their roommate dead, apparently of a drug overdose. Pursuing a busy social schedule, they went out Friday and Saturday, leaving the corpse to rest. On Sunday they enlisted a male friend to carry the body to a car and drove her to Brooklyn, where they dumped the now dressed and carefully cosmeticized friend on the beach.

The autopsy confirmed the cause of death so all we had was a simple DOA. The facts, though, were egregious and shocking.

We consulted an assistant district attorney who, sure enough, found—in the Medical Examiner's Section of the Administrative Code—the offense "it shall be unlawful to transport a dead human body without a permit." It was a misdemeanor punishable by up to a year in jail and/or a $500 fine. This was do doubt a vestigial trace of the days when grave robbers furnished medical schools with cadavers.

The three—two roommates and the glom they'd impressed into service—were charged. They hired a lawyer.

Every court appearance was much the same—a bored judge called the trivial issue up and his or her eyes would widen at the recitation of the facts. Not wanting to resolve such a serious case too frivolously, judge after judge continued the case. At last, one judge resolved it—finding the three guilty and sentencing them to six months in jail.

The Third Symphony became the first classical recording I'd buy.

The operative principle was that, if it looked seriously wrong, the chances were good that an arcane law could be found to match the transgression.

Service, as in the national formula of "To Protect and To Serve," basically encompasses the panoply of reasons for which we call 911. And I grew up, halfway at least, in a system that had never, until early 1967, even heard of an easily remembered three-digit number to use in emergencies. Now 911 needs only its invocation to produce total familiarity with its promise. Everyone knows what it is.

Controlling traffic flow is easier to understand, at least until such complexities as "driving while black" and its related racial profiling are thrown into the mix.

It develops then, or it will, that such edifying and chiseled pursuits as chasing muggers, responding to injuries, and regulating traffic, the police department's mandate ought to be reasonably simple to direct and carry out.

Why, then, the terrible controversies and public hand-wringings attending so many areas in our lives in which the police are concerned?

INITIATION

It is kind of remarkable how cops take a callow youth and transform him into a compliant member of the cult.

It starts with graduation from a police academy that basically serves as an apprenticeship for the development of the essential skills needed to function. Once acquired, the acolyte is turned over to a "hairbag" (in the NYPD, a wizened pro) to teach him the ropes.

Acculturation invariably starts with a slogan that rarely varies by a syllable, "Forget about the bullshit they taught you at the academy, kid; this is the real world." Next comes an introduction into a universe whose existence is not suspected—not even by the recruit. The values are transmitted and reinforced, in an endless series of proddings, hints, examples, and nods.

"Stand-up guys," who protect the brethren, keep quiet, and back you up, are proudly pointed out; and pariahs among the force come in all shapes, sizes, and levels of opprobrium, sharing only the visceral contempt of their associates.

It's okay to be a little weird. Deviance can be tolerated, if it doesn't threaten the group.

"Rats" are scorned, shunned, excluded, condemned, harassed, and, almost invariably, cast out. No back-up for them. They literally find cheese in their lockers. Unwanted items are delivered to their homes. The phone rings at all hours—followed by menacing silences, anonymous imprecations, or surprisingly inventive epithets. The police radio crackles with invective. The message is eloquent and pervasive.

Remarkably, the brass joins in.

It soon becomes clear that, just as threats to authority are put down with swift and sure punishments (e.g., uniform violations such as wearing some unallowed item or doffing a hat, or challenging a superior, or other forms of truculence), violations against group cohesion and protection, for whatever motive, are snuffed out quickly even when—actually, especially when—they carry the offensive odor of reform or attempts to uncover wrongdoing in the ranks.

The Mafia never enforced its code of blood-sworn omerta with the ferocity, efficacy, and enthusiasm the police bring to the Blue Code of Silence.

Stand-up guys and gals have balls. This includes silence or support. It does not include contradiction or exposure.

Cops are physically brave. Cowardice is an unthinkable option and an unmentionable word. It is as if it is so unacceptable as to be unacknowledged as a possibility. In thirty-six years in that world, I saw only one certifiable instance of cowardice—when a cop abandoned a partner in a close-encounter gun battle, and was fired.

Very often the "thumpers," the quick-fisted, violent cop leaders on the street, are the first through the door, the first to show up to give blood to a fallen mate, the loudest in asserting group interests, and the untitled vanguard setting the tone within the ranks. They sometimes achieve titles, too, but usually in union posts.

We are accustomed to equating courage with nobility but, in the police world, the bravest are often the most brutal. And, because of their willing immersion in the sometimes awful realities of policing, they are widely admired by others in the ranks. Ask any cop to define a "great cop" and, if he or she gives you an honest answer, it will be laced with adjectives that, to an uninitiated ear, might prove borderline cruel or even shockingly aggressive.

"Active cops," or the cops who make the most collars and get the most action on the street, often have records marked by troubling signposts of brutality, productive arrest and citation records, and medals for heroism. These cops communicate a mixed and even incomprehensible message to the civilian world. They can be either heroes or sadists—or both.

It has been said that policing offers a ringside seat on the greatest show on earth.

What is that show?

It is the human animal in dishabille—drunk, violent, battered or battering, sexually exposed (in such resplendent variety as to impoverish the imagination), and at his worst, lowest, meanest, most vulnerable, and revealing. Policing provides a fascinating look at the real animal beneath the patina of civilization we conceitedly assume to be our true nature. The cops are society's charnel house cleaners and are privy to *our* goriest secrets.

Cops come into secret knowledge by being admitted into our secret acts. Cops don't bother to speculate whether this or that person could possibly kill another; they see that, rubbed hard enough, anyone could—and often does—kill.

Cops learn that psychos are dangerous and frequently possessed of superhuman strength fueled by manic-driven adrenaline rushes—and the power of even small, slight people under its influence can reach incredible levels. When they try explaining this they are usually met with uncomprehending stares. The cops think, Well, fine, you go and respond to the knife-wielding maniac in the corridor and I'll go home. But they can't.

Cops know that fans at a ballpark can turn into rioters, and parade watchers can transform into manhandlers of women.

So they learn to act, cover their asses, back each other up, and say nothing.

CYNICISM[1]

The underbelly of the human beast reveals not only insights that produce profound cynicism, but oftentimes even black humor. The enduring hallmark of every cop's character is, in fact, the very antithesis of the contemptible naïf—cynicism. There are many strange birds in the police world, but no naive turkeys. There have been learned studies of police cynicism, which is the one characteristic unfailingly transmitted by the experience of policing.

Cops, by learning just how very thin the veneer of civilization is over every human's psychic skin, know what that animal is capable of. Cops come in all shapes, sizes, and attitudes—in a wild profusion of varieties— but they share one quality: the sobering knowledge of human possibilities, and this cannot be observed without engendering a profound skepticism, caution, or suspicion. This soon, unfortunately, changes into cynicism.

Cynicism, in this hard world, frequently finds its expressions in black humor that may feature body parts, sexual functions, or other rough passages.

Young cops excitedly share their thrilling discoveries with those near to them and are silently appalled when they discover that "civilians" don't get it. Even loved one are outsiders. Their laughter comes, if at all, in the wrong places. The flow of questions reveals the gap between their worlds, and the judgments offered can be harsh and unexpected.

Quickly, a cop learns that only other cops understand. This bond brings them closer. Soon they are vacationing together, bowling, eating, and, sometimes, sleeping together. Shared excitement and danger tightens the connection.

There are few more unifying experiences than sharing a moment of risk in the early morning hours and depending on your buddies to cover your back. It is something understood also by men and women in combat.

Gradually and through repeated reinforcements or sanctions, the young cop is shaped into an acceptable member of a very insular fraternity. The pressures to conform are inexorable, the pleasures of membership exhilarating, and the pains of exclusion excruciating.

ACCULTURATION[2]

The entire process of acculturation takes a few years of responding to calls, encountering the dangerous or unpredictable spikes that dot the often boring landscape, and shared moments that form the basis for bedrock attachments.

Ask any cop who his best friend is and if the answer is anything but "my partner" you are looking at a troubled worker. Cops' wives recite the complaint that their husbands care more for their partners than they do for their spouses.

The advent of women in the ranks has changed the inner reality in some ways. They are now, after a quarter century of entering in numbers, often a civilizing presence in a harsh, formerly all-male environment. A few have also given literal expression to the love cops feel for their partners, in acceptable forms. There is a bit of "friggin' in the riggin'," in the words of the late Admiral Elmo Zumwalt.

Such a thing as "the police character" exists uniquely because of the power of the institution to shape and condition its members. This is the process of inuring the psyche to gore and repulsiveness, overcoming the inhibitions normally applied to the use of violence, and drawing on cynicism as a way of assessing the human animal's potential to wreak havoc.

A suspicious nature leads to the discovery of the evil behind innocent appearances. It is a useful tool. Cops evolve into veterans by developing the mechanisms essential to their effective functioning, even as these approaches strike dissonant chords with the larger community.

Although cops are shaped into cynics, it is indisputable that, in general, a certain identifiable segment is attracted to police work and this might be described as the more macho segment of the blue-collar population.

The masculine police world is aggressively libidinous. What this means is that contacts with women—at traffic stops, for example—have to be monitored and controlled. It also means a higher-than-normal level of sensitivity is essential to combat sexual harassment or exploitation within the ranks. Like the military, the world of cops is too often given to the excesses of sexual predators—at all levels and ranks.

In the end, the result—the formation of the hardened cop—occurs from the hundreds of blows struck and caresses bestowed by an organization endlessly reinforcing the messages that insure its survival and which protect the secrets essential to that viability.

Cops also learn that moral courage is not prized.

A thumper declaims, "*The job* (surprisingly this is the universal appellation the cops give their profession, as if no other form of employment could be contemplated) sucks; the chief is a psycho; we're going to hell in a handbasket and morale has never been lower than at this precise minute." These are among the usually accepted internal verities. It would be unthinkable for any other cop in the room to contradict such assertions, even if a contrary view is deeply felt and possible to demonstrate.

The moral courage to stand up and disagree or to point out wrongdoing or to remonstrate when someone is committing a brutal or corrupt act has been systematically exorcised from the body. Nothing is rarer than dissidents publicly disagreeing with their colleagues about the codes of conduct, as is clearly evident from the cover-ups and studied silences accompanying serious acts of wrongdoing. Whistle blowers, reformers, and other troublemakers are "snitches and rat finks" and all ranks are to close against these menaces.

Not one of the scores of LAPD cops witnessing or participating in the assault on Rodney King,[3] a black male, in March 1991, interceded to stop the brutality or volunteered to come forward to testify against colleagues who were clearly involved in an egregious criminal act.

Frank Serpico[4] peddled his case against corruption within the ranks of the NYPD, first to the very authorities charged with attacking such problems. He was a plainclothes cop assigned to enforce vice, gambling, and liquor violations in 1971 and—remarkably and uniquely—apalled to discover corruption in the ranks. He was shocked to discover the studied indifference of NYPD executives who had carefully nurtured reputations as the very nemeses of rogue cops.

Serpico then took his case of gambling payoffs and other crimes to the NYPD's superiors at City Hall but, unwilling to rile the cops with another long, hot summer in the offing, with its threat of more riots in Harlem, got sloughed off again.

It was not until he went to the *New York Times'* ace police reporter, David Burnham, and the story appeared on page one, that officialdom was reluctantly galvanized into real action.

The mayor appointed the Knapp Commission. He named Patrick V. Murphy the one and only *reform* police commissioner in the department's recent history; he, incidentally lasted only thirty months. Murphy was given the peg on which to hang a series of sweeping changes that, by his exit in May 1973, had the NYPD at unprecedented levels of cleanliness in terms of systemic brutality and corruption. Individual, ad hoc acts would continue to bedevil the agency, as they do all organizations, but the worst connections had been shattered. The department thereafter lived off these dramatic changes as it drifted back into such behaviors, as we will explore anon.

ROTTEN AND OTHER APPLES

So what is a citizen to make of all of this?

A scandal breaks and the chief trots out the favored litany, "The vast majority of our cops are honest, dedicated public servants. These guys [the accused] are just a few rotten apples in an otherwise healthy barrel." This hoary phrase has served police execs faithfully since Bobby Peel started the bobbies.

The truth, however, is otherwise.

The overwhelming majority of cops are dedicated, noble workers, but the unstated truth is that they are all complicit in the code of silence. This includes the determination to cover up for each other, at least for as long as the charges don't include organizational "betrayals," as we will see, and which others might call "whistle blowing."

As the rookie is conditioned he has to be offered a menu of choices. He can stay reasonably clean and uninvolved and continue to function or he can partake of the goodies. The great majority choose noninvolvement in the raunchier pursuits but get along by going along with the demand for silence and, sometimes, backing up the accused cop. In the latter case the preferred strategy is blissful ignorance: "I wasn't there," or "I didn't see it," or some variation thereof. To the degree possible, associates are supported but in no case are they to be contradicted.

And therein lies the problem. The Code of Silence[5] demands full and total participation. It is the price of admission and by accepting it, as all do—even those destined to rise in the ranks or who are already there—they become tainted. Even the cops who stay totally out of the seamier aspects, who wouldn't even accept a free cup of coffee, must be a part of the code of silence or risk the scorn—and worse—of all the members.

Thus policing becomes a sort of permanent, floating conspiracy of insiders against the larger public without. The clean and the unclean can

be described as the "grass eaters" and the "meat eaters" (the more fero-
cious and aggressive members).

One curious artifact of this culture is that court records abound with
sworn assurances from countless cops and chiefs that they'd never heard
of a code of silence and that it doesn't exist. No judge in America, however, is free of the knowledge of this unspoken code and a host of other
brazen police mendacities.

THE CODE AND TESTILYING

I received a call recently from a federal judge who interrupted a trial
midway through its course when three cops testified, one after the other,
that they'd never heard of the code and that it didn't exist.

A search warrant for drugs was being executed on an apartment
when a black woman walked by on the sidewalk in front of the building.
She was swept up and roughly rushed into the apartment, strip-searched,
and after an hour reluctantly released. She, to everyone's surprise, sued.
No one expected a "street person" to complain.

Now the cops, under oath, described the textbook perfection of the
warrant's execution and justified the detention of the woman as reasonable and good police practice. When they added the palpable fiction that
no such code of silence existed, the judge "just lost it." He stopped the
proceedings and called to see if I'd testify in the case as a neutral expert
witness. I accepted.

I met with the lawyers immediately.

The city attorney for the cops had been perfectly content to have a
compliant jury, very likely mostly white, sop up the police fictions. He
knew that white America loves and trusts its cops, whatever the police
protestations to the contrary. Now he blanched visibly as I described the
gravamen of my forthcoming testimony.

The next day the judge called to thank me and to tell me to stop my
work on the case. The cops' lawyer had hied to the city rulers and spelled
out what is, in another euphemism, artfully described as the city's "potential exposure." The city decided to settle lest they be depicted in the
media as racists. I was sure the settlement would be a high figure. The

judge told me the city was giving the woman a quarter of a million dollars and paying her legal fees, as well as mine. I received $1,233 for my efforts.

So much for the sanctity of the cops' sworn testimony.

The cops call this "testilying." Clearly they feel no shame in it.

Yes, it turns out to be true—the barrel does contain mostly healthy apples but these are content to live in uneasy symbiosis with the rotten.

MESSAGES TO COPS

Cops work within a social context that, while dry and dull as dust, needs to be described and analyzed if the police are to be understood.

The police enforce laws (which are nothing more than the written expressions of societal values) in a society that divides with increasing sharpness along age, race, and wealth fault lines.

The chasm between rich and poor widens by every measure and the attempts to erase the graduated income tax constitute the elite's most formidable Trojan horse in this effort. Eliminating the "death tax" is another blatant attempt at accelerating the widening chasm.

Although many black citizens are making it, any statistical analysis demonstrates that the vast majority are sinking deeper into the slough of poverty and despondency. Measures of wealth distribution and poverty reflect a bifurcating society, along both money and race lines.

A study released in August 2000 by the National Center for Children in Poverty at Columbus University revealed that child poverty is higher, in all but a few states, than it was twenty years ago. More than 13 million children live in homes where the income, for a family of four, is under $17,050. This is three million more children than in 1979, or about the time when we decided the war on poverty had indeed been lost.

Seniors vote and juniors don't, which is why poverty centers on the young. The presence of females as single heads of poverty-stricken households, disproportionately in this population of the underclass, also speaks to their persistent plight. The result is social security, Medicare, and lower death taxes at the geriatric level and homelessness at the *jejune*. Blacks appear prominently in all statistics reflecting social, economic, and even political distress. Were they, for example, to vote with the same enthusiasm as white seniors, their victimization would be sharply reduced.

Travel the Sun Belt and observe an army of seniors in carefree repose on the quest for pleasure in caravans of recreational vehicles. There, state income taxes are low to nonexistent; senior athletic programs, with cultural facilities, are ubiquitous and cheap; real estate taxes are low amidst a general air of care for their well-being. Sales taxes, however, which strike with disproportionate ferocity at the poor—are uniformly high. Gambling, a sort of stealth tax on the poor and uneducated, can be found everywhere.

The other side of the coin are inadequately funded schools, a dearth of public housing, inferior medical care for the poor, harsh welfare policies, and a general scorn for "socialist" measures. The ultimate payers are the juniors and the blacks. There is not a single advanced nation—whether Denmark, Canada, Japan, or Australia—that offers its citizens the paucity of government support and programs that we do.

The transfer of wealth, from young to old, can be seen and heard in the debates over school funding and the other services provided by governments. The fewer the services, the more citizens get to keep of their money. Who can object? The result, however, is to consign the underclass to further depths of despair.

Even the attacks on welfare rolls accelerate the transfer of wealth from the underclass to the overclass. Surpluses induced by savings from shrinking welfare costs get transferred to the wealthier in the form of tax cuts. And if there weren't enough breaks for the haves, among the more popular ideas in Washington is the elimination of capital gains and death taxes, or the elimination of the federal income tax altogether. In 1998, a Republican Congress trotted out "victims" of IRS harassment and bullying in a highly publicized series of hearings.

If ever an agency was demonized it was the tax collector.

Two years later, the audit by Treasury's inspector general revealed that claims of abuse were bogus—mainly—and the politicians reluctantly granted they had overreacted. Enforcement, however, declined and IRS employees were described as demoralized. It had been another attempt at killing this federal program. In the end the clear winners were the tax dodgers.

The unprecedented boom of the nineties and the welfare reforms that accompanied it produced some salutary effects. Unemployment among black males was reduced to about 7 percent, or about triple that of white males. Yet in 2000, the jail and prison populations reached a record of 2 million—an undreamed-of total only a decade ago.

The economy itself mirrored the wider society in the contrasts it created and exacerbated. High-end jobs further enriched the top 5 percent, and low-skilled jobs mired the bottom 20 percent in poverty. The chasm of economic disparity widened, reflecting an educational inequality that featured, at one end, the world's busiest and most competitive institutions and, on the other, disgraceful warrens of ignorance and neglect.[6]

Reducing capital gains taxes and increasing estate exemptions and profits from the sales of residences (every two years and one day, an interesting incentive to "serial builders" of their own homes) greatly aided the elite. It is possible in twenty-first-century America to build a residence, live in it for two years and one day, and sell it—pocketing up to a $500,000 gain with no tax liability. It is one yummy tax shelter and it can be repeated without limit. The principal benefit for the working poor was the "earned income tax credit" that largely exempted the first $25,000 or so of salary from federal income taxes. They still had to face the social security tax.

Welfare time limits postponed the reckoning and served as a ticking time bomb within the body politic.

While external, if no longer existent, threats were met with lavish and increasing expenditures on defense, the more serious problems of internal danger—from crime, riots, and other violence—received very short shrift. It wasn't even an item of serious discussion during the 2000 presidential campaign.

The surface was deceptively becalmed but the forces of social dissolution waxed, unseen, unattended, and unchecked, below the surface.

Less than half our eligibles vote, even in presidential elections, and the majority of these are suburbanites and elderly, as well as white. The vote of an elite in this diminished landscape gives their ballots twice the weight. Less than a quarter of potential voters decide our presidents—and the better-educated, richer, older, and whiter Americans are well aware of this fact.

Something that looks suspiciously like nascent class struggle is being played out in our public life, and the special interests aren't lobbying for the shirtless.

Much as it clashes with our egalitarian myths and ambitions, America has a growing underclass amidst unparalleled prosperity and, of course, a rarely named overclass provides the marching orders for the police. According to the United States Treasury, the distribution of net worth from 1983 to 1998 went from 33.8 percent to 38.1 percent for the top 1 percent of America's earners. The median net worth of families rose to over $80,000 for whites and to $10,000 for blacks.

Cops know that property rights are sacred. Attend any neighborhood rally in which any police concern is expressed and you'll soon hear the totemic "property values" concern expressed. The NIMBY (not in my backyard) factor is a variation of this theme.

The overclass wants—rightly, it must be said—order, but it also wants tidiness. It does not want to encounter unappetizing or threatening visions. Messages are transmitted in evolving and usually carefully woven euphemisms. "Law and order" gave way to "those people," and currently the threat is "gangs and outsiders." The cops get it. They'd better.

The overclass will not admit that its practices of privilege and exclusion create pressures for the underclass that drive it to revolt. This takes the form of street crime and, occasionally dotted over our history, riots. Unable to escape the ghetto's oppressions, some of its denizens succumb to drugs and alcohol.

The cops love what they do and they swallow the bitter pills, protect and serve, and stay and stay. Policing is about the stablest career imaginable, notwithstanding the police unions' periodic invocation of the myth of the exodus, the notion that cops are hard to hire and those in the ranks are on the verge of leaving—en masse.

Police work means being given a front row seat in the great drama of life. Any human would find such a privileged perch fascinating.

2
A POLICE CAREER

Policing is very decidedly a career. Entrants don't leave or quit. Civil service tenure makes them virtually firing-proof. And so they stay and stay—a minimum of twenty years. Policing is an extended calling. It isn't as easy to enter as outsiders think, nor is it as onerous as the insiders claim. And it isn't anything like as dangerous as farming or mining.

SCREENING

A concerned citizen learns of a cop's prior history and wonders why he hadn't been screened out upon entering. Later, his records and actions are egregious enough to have certainly shown up earlier, which should have called for dismissal. A cop looks at the same record and thinks, Active, aggressive guy who may have gone a bit far this time.

The reason seemingly sociopathic cops aren't filtered out is that too many are made, not born. It is the institution that not only shapes them but that affords tempting opportunities to pursue submerged predilections for violence and worse.

In fact, the employment of cops is as much shrouded in mist as their actions prove incomprehensible to outsiders. The public and media reactions to the Diallo case's acquittals demonstrated the chasm between public and police perceptions.

Most onlookers think becoming a cop is easy. It isn't.

There is a daunting gauntlet to be run.

Cops are recruited from the upper reaches of the un-colleged working class, which considers civil service its property and guards the preserve jealously. Despite this narrow focus, there is a very lively competition for the posts.

It would not be an exaggeration to hold that cities could get all the truly qualified applicants they want, fully representative racially and in gender, if they raised their requirements to include a bachelor's degree.[1] In fact, a few smaller cities have done this successfully, but it hasn't been widely aped.

Requiring a bachelor's degree among entering cops would ensure a pool of better-educated applicants and hasten achieving the Holy Grail of professionalization, yet the opportunity is widely eschewed. Requiring a B.A. would shift the job from the working class (meaning the upper reaches of the lower class) to the lower rungs of the more-educated middle class. The specter of a subtle form of class warfare emerges from this speculation.

In any event, by the time officialdom decides on the one in three applicants it wants to hire (civil service offers three qualified candidates, as a rule, for every job and the hirers can winnow out the less-desirable applicants and skim the cream off the top, at least in theory), it has developed about a half-inch file of data on the would-be cop. The rookie experiences a period of about a year of probation, during which he or she may be fired for any reason. After that comes tenure. It would be easy to spot the thumpers early, if they were shaped before, not after, entering.

The file contains information on every facet of the applicant's life—school, military, work, driving, criminal, and, yes, personal history. By the time the hiring moment is reached the reviewer is likely to know more about the recruit than the parents of that youth. Doubts—given the one in three rule—can be conveniently resolved in favor of the agency, and are. Since the hirer must take one of every three qualified candidates offered, the agency has a lot of leverage in the hiring decision.

Personal contretemps are sifted through and relationships examined. Even minor acts are viewed as harbingers of future performance.

The entering recruit is certifiably squeaky clean—that he or she is also malleable proves grist to the mills of the veterans waiting to shape him or her.

Do not doubt, however, that the next account of an officer's depredations will be greeted by eloquent demands that such undesirables be excluded at the employment gate.

"How could they have hired that maniac?" "Why wasn't he screened out before being hired?" The answer is easy—he wasn't a monster coming in and the action may even have been justified by the circumstances on the street. Armchair second-guessers are no better at police matters than they are at quarterbacking. The thumpers may have hidden predilections, on entering, but these are encouraged and surface as a result of the organizational structure.

ENTRANCE

People who've encountered me in the last several years—after a lot of success and luck—often ask why I chose a police career.

The question always strikes me as odd, with the jarring and indisputably presumptuous supposition that I, like they, had a choice. I didn't. I was a feckless, impoverished immigrant without prospects. As a firmly embedded member of the working poor I saw civil service in terms of only one word—escape.

I'd been working in the Garment Center sweeping, packing, and then graduating to selling, especially to visiting Latin Americans. Strangely, it was the selling that bothered me.

The rag industry is based on lies.

I was told to sell the dregs of leftovers to unknowing and gullible visitors from Spanish-speaking countries and call them our hottest items. I was to visit buyers' offices that hadn't given our firm any business in years. On the very odd breakthrough, when I managed an order from these dead leads, the boss's brother-in-law would simply take over the account. I didn't bring in much business but what little I did snare was credited to others.

I was sometimes drafted into taking the daughters of visiting buyers to dinner and the theater. While escorting our biggest client's daughter to see *Death of a Salesman*, I was transfixed and horrified to see myself on the stage in the person of Willie Low-man (*sic*). There I was, on the stage, thirty years later, an empty, broken vessel. I suddenly had an explanation for my headaches, stomach cramps, and foot problems.

Never more, thereafter, could anyone convince me that art is a societal frill for the cognoscenti and well-off. I adopted the view from the marrow of experience that artists are prophets. They define the meaning of our lives and point the way. Arthur Miller had shown me where my life was going. We ignore their message—I speak of the true, as opposed to the prophets manqué—at our peril.

I went home and announced to my mother that I was going to take the sanitationman's test and become a garbage man. It seemed to me the apex of human ambition.

Although we came to America precisely midway through Spain's civil war, in December 1937, we were not refugees but immigrants.

Ours was a simple transition. In our poor part of Spain—Galicia, in the northwest—young men left for jobs in America. My father, a coal stoker on ships, worked in the U.S. Merchant Marine from around 1920 and returned to Spain to find a wife and have children—my sister and me.

Since Franco was born nearby, our family mostly supported his insurrection and it was many years before I discovered what a mistake this had been. My memories of the war centered on the trucks carrying Italian troops, zooming through our town at night; a large harbor full of captured ships and hauling enormous crates from Nazi Germany and silvery specs, droning lazily high in the sky, followed by the sight of uprooted trees far off. Altogether not much to flee from. Our elderly next-door neighbor was carted off to prison one day and his wife, after a week of bringing him lunches, was told he'd been shot as a spy.

Our lives were surrounded by a host of relatives and friends and we led a secure and comfortable existence as a result of my father's meager salary—which translated into a lot of pesetas.

Our arrival in Brooklyn was a rude awakening to real poverty—a psychically unsettling process, I was to discover. Suddenly we were poor, living in tenements and scrounging to get enough to eat. I was nine. My mother, sister, and I all worked at home clipping lace. My mother embroidered and soon had to become a sewing machine operator, a job she held for thirty-five years.

My sister contracted rheumatic fever at sixteen and was bedridden for many months, dropping out of school, never to return.

Helping the family and working were highly prized virtues; education was not.

My father died in 1944, when I was fifteen. I'd spent a a calculated total of thirty-six hours in his company during myentire life, yet fathers matter a lot. I still think long and hard about a simple, humble, limited man whose existence was hard. He called me into our darkened living room, where he'd been sitting alone, knowing he was dying of stomach cancer.

"Tucho"—my Spanish nickname—"you're going to be the man of the house now." I nodded, and that was about it.

I've had to wonder why my mother left the security of home, parents, sisters, uncles, aunts, family, and country for America. I concluded that her feisty and independent spirit was simply smothered in our small town's confines. She needed to breathe.

And so, around Christmas in 1937, our struggle began—and continues.

What I remember most clearly is the overwhelming power of American culture—language, music, cinema, comic books, radio, and baseball. It led me to scorn my roots, returning only many years later.

America, we found, really is a great country.

My sister had married a Spaniard while in her teens and this liaison shaped my future. He was a cop whose two brothers had preceded him into the ranks and my mother said, "If he can be a cop, so can you." My course was set and, while I didn't know it then, I was taking a well-traveled route to the uniform, since so many of the entrants had connections to the ranks.

With the fury of an escaping convict, for the first time in my life, I really studied, trained, and prepared for the effort.

DELEHANTY

At twenty-one, this was the very first time in my life I seriously focused on anything. I sat in the ass-splintering benches of Delehanty Institute,

listening to mind-numbing lectures on the arcana of municipal government in a cavernous hall, surrounded by unknowable rivals vying with
me at about 6-to-1 odds.

I left pools of sweat in the worthy institute's gym and heavily lugged
a bag loaded with the additional weight of the alien perspiration of my
predecessors around rickety tracks on the school's roof.

The insecurity of the competition was conveyed by the sight of
5' 7½" men, who'd spent the night lying—sleep was pretty much out of
the question, given the angst and discomfort—on hardwood floors and
were carried in on wooden slats, by four sturdy friends, for a measurement
they hoped would stretch them to reach the required 5' 8" limit.

The tests were usually in three parts—a medical to check you out; an
eliminating one-hundred-question, multiple-choice exam on laws and
police procedures; and a grueling, graded physical, including running,
climbing, and lifting. These weeded out the less qualified, but the real
crucible came with a thorough background check that usually produced
a file a half inch thick.

Little has changed since then, except for the lawsuits (many of which
I participated in as an expert witness decades later) brought by women,
to make certain that the physical, especially, was a bona fide occupa-
tional qualification (BFOQ)—which meant that the test had to relate to
the actual requirements of the job.

Over twenty-five thousand took the test for four thousand jobs and,
after a faltering start, I made it onto the list high enough to be reached,
even without veteran's preference. I was drafted, served two years in the
Army, and was sworn in by Mayor Vincent Impelliteri on January 1,
1953. It was the greatest and happiest achievement of my life.

It might have looked to some as if I'd jumped into the fire but even
a systemically brutal and corrupt police agency contained enough oases
of honesty to make the comparison with my previous job a nonstarter.
The NYPD was my salvation.

When I'm asked to advise youngsters on a police career I always
strongly urge them to do so—whatever their prospects, education, or
economic status. I make a special plea to women and blacks because
they're needed, especially African Americans. It's great to see the long
march of women into police ranks.

In another illustration of the chasm between the public's under-standing, or lack thereof, and the inner police reality, most would-be entrants who don't have a connection in the police world feel timid about their ability to perform: Will I be brave enough and tough enough?

The question cannot encompass two important truths—the accul-turation process will gradually inure you to the dangers and those TV dramatized heroics are so rare and unique, albeit true, as to make their consideration unnecessary. And those dangerous spikes tend to be attended by lots of back-up and help, in any case.

Policing provides the chance to serve and that brings the psychic income that only those who devote their lives to such pursuits can experience.

Herman Melville described a whale ship as his Harvard and Yale; the NYPD was mine.

When I left policing decades later I took with me an abiding affec-tion and respect for cops, an appreciation of the managerial limitations impeding their progress, and a thorough disgust for the silent messages transmitted to them by a hypocritical society.

Cops are brave and caring. They devote decades to a calling they adore. They can also be narrow and cruel. Cynicism becomes a central feature of their acculturation.

Cops are never more impressive than when combating violent crime on the street. This is the trench warfare of America's war on crime.

3
STREET CRIME

The street criminal is a familiar stereotype. Unlike the white-collar criminal or the Mafiosi, or even the Mediterranean terrorist, the street criminal is male, young (fifteen to twenty-five), uneducated, unemployable (often because of a criminal record), a drug or alcohol abuser, frequently born of an incompetent teenage mother whose hopeless boyfriend sees no prospect in acknowledging his responsibilities, and unfortunately, due to society's abandonment of responsibility and safety nets, disproportionately black.

Victimization surveys by the Bureau of Justice Statistics, corrections data from all the elements of the criminal justice system, and even homicide rates all attest to the large involvement of young black males in street crime.

That racism makes many of them unemployable and withholds educational opportunities—while extending the tempting escapes of drugs and alcohol—becomes the central factor white America refuses to confront. Blacks are, far and away, the principal victims of murder, violence and street crime in America.

A 1999 study held that the decline in street crime in the nineties could—on the basis of statistical analyses—be attributed to the number of "at risk" males aborted, as a result of *Roe* v. *Wade*, since 1973. The scholars' findings were based on their analysis of the experience in states, like New York, that adopted legal, widely practiced abortions a few years earlier.[1]

The finding, when formally published, offers to launch a very heated debate, likening the statistics to the Nazi assertions of improving society through eugenics.

Amid the decline of violence, police chiefs rush to claim the credit while a growing body of academics might respond, "It's the demographics." The ugly reality is that it is very likely a combination of known and unknown factors.

Our indifference to social, economic or racial justice continue to fuel the fires of street crime, whatever our genteel and self-congratulatory sense of today's "progress." Are those fires banking?

It would appear so, judging from fairly reliable crime statistics across the country, whatever the levels of police efficiency. Street crime, at least for the present, and until a cohort of teenagers in the "at-risk population" arrives in a few years, really is declining dramatically across the national landscape.

In the fifties and sixties New York City had about a murder a day. With the same population, it had almost six a day in the early nineties. By the turn of the century the numbers more nearly reflected the sixties than the early nineties, and other cities could boast similar figures. A demographic wave of "at-risk" teenagers, however, is approaching.

Since the underlying conditions for street crime are not ameliorating—witness our tolerance of poverty as reflected in welfare, housing, medical care, education, jobs, and so on—we can look forward to a swelling population of the disaffected. The widening economic chasm is bound to exacerbate class tensions.

While we marvel at the brilliance of our police executives, let's also recognize just how incognita the terra of street crime can be. Its level might have been affected by a peaking crack epidemic in the mideighties and a decline thereafter. That epidemic, for a time, almost destroyed the lives of too many disaffected black mothers, the cohesive heart and soul of the ghetto community. The toll on the white community was high, too, but masked by the factors that protect the overclass.

But who can predict the impact of such new drugs as Ecstasy or some as yet unknown attraction?[2]

The crime rate might also be easing because of a subtle and as yet imperceptible shift in attitudes among the underclass.[3] Certainly lower unemployment and general prosperity help, but ours is a lock rather than a tidal economy, and the rising waters of a booming gross domestic product mainly benefit only the privileged boats in the special locks.

It's not hard to list reasons for the current decline of street crimes but the harsh truth is that no one knows for sure. The answers will come with the passage of years and many analyses, and they will include predictable as well as surprising factors.

But, in lower or higher crime tides, the message from the overclass is clear, if often subliminally offered—keep the underclass under control.

This, cops come to sense, is an unreasonable request—and even an unfair one—but they want to stay employed, so they swallow hard and do what they can. It is in response to such pressures that practices like racial profiling are spawned.

The cops believe they know what the car-stealing, drug dealing criminal looks like and instead of waiting for justifiable and articulable grounds, they pounce on the stereotype. Why do they do this?

Strangely enough, cops mostly love what they do. They glory in going after the bad guys. They're the good guys. In their minds it's a forties film. And occasionally they score and nab a really bad guy with lots of contraband. They live for that rush and in the process they create the unintended category that makes every black male wince. The cops unfairly and disproportionately single out cars driven by black men for their attentions. And ambitious mayors, pressing for a public facelift, pressure the chiefs to go after the "bad guys."

Cops feel the unreasonableness of being punished for carrying out the elite's wishes. The overclass is shocked, *shocked*. Middle-class blacks are outraged and ghetto blacks see the police as an occupying army.

Forgotten in all this is the importance and compelling force of the intended, if unarticulated, message of the white overclass. Does anyone in their right mind think that Henry II explicitly ordered his nobles to massacre Thomas A. Becket in 1170? Or that anyone is going to find a signed order from Adolf Hitler calling for the extermination of the Jews?

Not bloody likely.

More likely than explicit orders calling for oppression of "street people" are bitter complaints about hectoring pests and, "Isn't there anyone man enough to acknowledge his devotion to his king by doing the right thing?" And, "Couldn't the 'final solution' have been explained away as a work or repatriation scheme?"

"Plausible deniability" has served as a euphemism for evil acts committed by our own government.

We certainly understand such verbal gymnastics; yet somehow find it difficult to apply to our situations. Maybe we're too immersed in the waters to notice our own evasive directives.

STRIVING FOR UNDERSTANDING

On some level we understand what's going on even if we are, on a subliminal basis, ordering outrages. Yet we are the sort of people who want to know. America is nothing if not a raging, continuous series of public debates. That's how we get from here to there. We don't want to believe that some of the egregious police abuses on the street are really the cops' attempts to keep "those people" under control or out of sight.

What is the police role, if any, in the dramatic declines in street crime in the nineties?

Are the police better today than they were yesterday?

What's going on in the black community in the middle of all this?

The ugly truth is that Americans refuse to seriously examine the economic, racial, and social sources of street crime, or even how we might best cope with rising tides of violence, as occurred in the early nineties, being content to hire more police officers and pass stricter laws.

COPS AS CRIME FIGHTERS

By the time a cop encounters the criminal, the crime has occurred and the offender has been shaped. Those reassuring cops in uniform, one of which most citizens would like in front of their homes, rarely make important arrests. Felony and other sexy busts are usually made by plainclothes or undercover investigators. The commonly held notion—one invariably reinforced by chiefs—that today's police are more aggressive and talented than their forebears is only half true. The current crop is, for very good reasons, flaccid in its approaches to street crime, even if the corps is generally somewhat better educated and trained. Although still short of requiring college degrees, some police agencies have raised entering requirements a bit: a grudging concession to the educational realities in contemporary America.

Even the vaunted claims of superaggressive policing, as were made by New York City Mayor Rudolph Giuliani,[4] will be seen to be nonsense on real examination. As crime declined precipitously, leaders rushed in to display their "successful" programs and claim the credit. But when every city reported declining violence rates—whether they had a nifty plan or not—the claims began to ring hollow. Why did crime decline precipitously and broadly in the late nineties? It may be years before the economic, social, and cultural forces at work reveal their influence.

The idea of police as crime preventers is rubbish. By the time the cop appears the criminal has been formed and the crime has been committed.

The truth is that police agencies displace crime and they can be very good at finding ways to detect and arrest the criminals—but they've had to give up a lot of their most promising strategies because of political realities no one will discuss.

Whew!

Can any of that be true?

Such cherished myths . . .

But that, of course—that you, the reader, are burdened by fairy tales—is the point of this effort.

Our Founding Fathers never intended the Constitution as a protective mantle for the criminal, whatever rock-hard conservatives might say. The Constitution allows aggressive policing even as it insists on preserving individual rights. It just doesn't allow invasions, roundups, torture, or any of the other cruelties its framers fled and fought.

While commanding all Bronx forces from 1973 to 1976,[5] I ran the most aggressive police operation in the nation, continued that for three years in the transit police as number two, and deepened and extended the effort in my nine years as police chief in Minneapolis. Yet even as ardent a believer in constitutional and forceful tactics as I could not, for example, use stake-out units in any but the most demanding circumstances.

I banned sap gloves and blackjacks because they are illegal—and rightly so.

Police chases are hugely controversial. They often result in the deaths of innocent onlookers. Who would not be outraged at the image of a child's broken body following these colorful events?

Hollywood loves chases. Some police departments have virtually banned them by creating hamstringing restrictions. But if cops don't chase the bad guys, who will? How ingenuous can we be to think that most villains won't run off if they can be confident that no chase will ensue?

Cops must chase, but these can be controlled through rules that require supervisory involvement, radio discipline, and orders that forbid caravanning (the Keystone Kops chases involving a train of vehicles behind the bad guys) and cowboying (the sort of heroic antics movie-makers adore). Interceptions, speed limitations, and a graduated scale of priorities in chase scenarios are also needed. Tire-disabling devices and even barricades (a hugely controversial factor) need to be available for extreme cases. Placing obstacles in the path of an escaping vehicle is certain to produce a violent result.

The LAPD's use of "Big-Brother-in-the-sky" helicopters, shining dazzling lights in the eyes of ghetto residents, were intrusive forays into the "hood." This was more infatuation with technology and an attempt to intimidate than aggressive policing.

By the late eighties my aggressive policing approach was viewed as a dangerously impolitic tactic, even if no one would argue its constitutionality.

I used decoys, stings, monitoring of recidivists, very aggressive traffic enforcement that focused on drivers with warrants outstanding, and a host of other strategies that swelled the arrest statistics impressively. Political pressures led to the declining use of such aggressive tactics as decoys, stings, and stake-outs after I left policing.

We started the arrests, on a wide scale, of batterers of women and focused on bucket-of-blood bars, troublesome locations, and dysfunctional families that repeatedly showed up on our response statistics. We literally exploded fortresslike iron doors in crack houses to gain entrance.

We did all that and more while punctiliously observing constitutional strictures. We still failed miserably at controlling crime. Midway through my term, and for thirty-six awful months, the incidence of street crime in Minneapolis looked like the chart of an Internet company.

Nothing we did worked.

We were in the middle of a devastating crack cocaine epidemic that was hooking men and boys and a lot of women and mothers. The few frayed strands of stability and cohesion in the ghetto were snapping.

The outlines of this disaster became clear only more than a decade after its peak, through analyses of overdoses, drug deaths, polls and surveys, drug-related crimes, drug seizures, and other data. Nothing that I did then led me to this discovery, but I'd learned to suspect that not always readily identifiable forces could be at work in the poor neighborhoods that bred street crime and violence.

At that time I thrashed about, nevertheless, looking for answers. In my meetings with fellow chiefs—and they were frequent and extensive— I knew I had the most, in the fashionable word of the time, proactive anticrime operation in the nation. Why, I was even training officers in the use of the carotid choke hold to induce fainting in obstreperous miscreants, long after the George S. Patton of American policing, Daryl Gates, had been forced to abandon the practice in Los Angeles.

These may sound inhumane, but when the cop has been trained and uses it appropriately, the choke hold becomes a method of control, preferable to bludgeoning or shooting, and more likely killing, a raging, out-of-control person. There has been the rare fatality, but any violent act can produce severe injury or death.

Of a piece with the agressiveness of the Minneapolis Police Department to crime was our approach to service and traffic. We responded to genuine 911 emergencies within six minutes.

Traffic enforcement quadrupled, with the additional result of arrests for motorists wanted on warrants.

It was a direct consequence of my experience with aggressive tactics—in the Bronx and Minneapolis—that I became a thorough skeptic of the claims of latter-day wizards that their "tough tactics" had controlled crime.

PRODUCTIVITY AND QUOTAS[6]

So who can object to an insistence on better performance, greater productivity, more efficient management?

Actually, the police union can.

Sophists taught mankind that the inventive mind can find arguments to refute or support any position. Call for productivity and the union responds, "quotas."

What do they mean?

That cops will be required mindlessly to produce a number of enforcement actions, whether a problem exists or not, within the time frame. Quotas demand action where none is objectively required by circumstance.

Quotas are simply demands for production, irrespective of the impact of the actions on problems—or which are required even when no problem exists.

Productivity involves analyzing a real, serious problem and directing enforcement actions to its solution. An example would be a high-accident location, involving the running of red lights, in which cops ticket offenders until the violations cease and the accidents measurably decline or disappear.

Tied into these actions is the enormous field of discretion in which cops operate. They can arrest, detour, summons, or ignore. They have a sea of laws, ordinances, traffic regulations, and even sanitary or health codes from which to choose or disdain action and move on.

The problems, however, cry out for productivity and enforcement measures. Citizens are safer when cops respond to more calls, faster and more skillfully. Accidents decline when their causes are attacked. A city functions more smoothly when obstacles are removed. Even public morale is affected by the presence of absence of rotting metal carcasses or defiant graffiti on our landscapes.

Attacking quality-of-life violations makes great sense, but as adjuncts to aggressive police tactics, not as their replacements.

Cops need to be productive and their performance can and must be measured.

I was advised that a cop in a Minneapolis precinct didn't believe in issuing traffic citations because he couldn't see the point of them. Recognizing his wide discretion, he felt free to pursue other activities. Traffic safety, however, was a high priority of mine—third in fact to dealing with street crime (first) and responding to citizen emergencies (second)—and a quadrupling of traffic enforcement had had a dramatic impact on accidents.

I could not have such defiance, yet I understood that the realm of discretion available to him could be used as an excuse to do other things. I hit upon a simple plan. I ordered him out of the car and gave him a busy post to patrol on foot. Additionally, a supervisor would accompany him on his rounds, point out traffic violations, and order him to issue a citation. Failing to comply would be a sanctionable refusal to obey a direct order. I relished the chance to bring the matter to a head. The officer, however, got the message and began enforcing the traffic laws vigorously. We monitored his actions and he did just fine. He retained the discretion to pick and choose, but not the discretion to fail to act.

The insurrection was snuffed and everybody got the message. The notion of having a sergeant accompany you all day, every day—which I fully intended to see through—was too unappetizing to consider. I insisted on productivity and debated the quota issue with the union energetically. I drove the agency to higher productivity with all the zeal of a CEO facing stockholders.

We started a gun squad to work with the Feds to reduce the carnage. They concentrated on making "gun collars" and tracing illegal shipments and generally working to reduce the number of firearms on the street. We had a task force with the Drug Enforcement Administration that made large and frequent seizures and important arrests. They focused on the big players. We were late to the party on this one but started a gang unit to monitor youth violence. The reality was that we didn't have rumbles, or colors, or turf, but we did have gangs actively engaged in drug-related violence. I'd been attacking this as a drug problem, rather than a gang problem, and received a bit of criticism for seeming to pooh-pooh gangs.

Still, the maddening dance of climbing crime numbers rolled merrily on.

Chastened by my Bronx experience—a borough in social dissolution and ablaze during my four years there—I knew better than to claim any credit during the brief, sporadic periods of decline in crime. This modesty preserved me from press barbs about failed programs and refuted promises when the upward spiral began.

I desperately needed answers and sought them everywhere. I consulted experts, pored over the statistics, and read extensively. Ultimately I happened upon a Minnesota state demographic analysis that pinpointed the problem's source.

I had been lulled as to demographics by the fact that Minneapolis had been closing and consolidating high schools due to a rapidly declining teenage population. Since males in this cohort contributed mightily to street crime, I had been reassured by the dip, but I was to learn the error of my hubris. I should have been looking for a subset of the teenage population.

What the state's study revealed was that, while the population of fifteen- to twenty-year-old males was, indeed, declining in Hennepin County (of which Minneapolis was the largest unit), the population of "at-risk males" (poor; uneducated; on welfare; born of single, teenaged mothers; unemployable; drug or alcohol addicted, among other disabilities; and largely African American or Native American) was exploding.

So it proved a figure within a figure that revealed the awful truth, that it was the demographics after all. When combined with the crack epidemic that became clear years later, it was still easier to see the cause of the tsunami of crime we'd been at a loss to stem. It proved a sobering insight into the limitations of the police in impacting street crime levels.

But what could be done about this?

The police would have to keep on truckin'—and energetically—but the underlying causes—racism, poverty, jobs, education, and general hopelessness—had to be pointed out in the futile hope that the dominant society would awaken to its injustices. Which is not to say the cops are irrelevant to the effort, only that their limits must be recognized. The police can, in a rare exception of the limits of crime prevention, arrest domestic abusers and interrupt a spiral of violence that often escalates into murder. This might be labeled a homicide prevention program.

But such crimes as car theft, for instance, are importantly influenced by manufacturers' security improvements, legislative measures requiring identification numbers on all parts, and a national directory listing such data. Clever thugs learn to circumvent the security innovations, but it is a treadmill on which the manufacturers must be forced to keep running. Police tactics help, but they need to be buttressed by a support system.

Altogether not a popular message.

I served my term in Minneapolis and left, never having experienced success as a crime fighter and, much worse, never having been heard by the people I'd been lecturing about racial, social, and economic policies that doomed the underclass to desperate acts.

So when the chiefs trot out their community policings, charts, graphs, and other props, you'll pardon my skeptical yawn.

DECOYS[7]

There is no doubt but that the NYPD and many others will strenuously object to the characterization that they've abandoned decoys and point to concrete examples to prove their point. The fact is, except in drug cases—where rigorous action is still politically acceptable—decoy use is declining rapidly nationwide. It's in examining one situation that we see the bankruptcy of the assertion that they still use them.

Seven livery/cab drivers were killed by robbers the first three and a half months of 2000 in New York City. Eleven were murdered in all of 1999. Such an appalling statistic should be a spark to action—the most effective form of which would be to have cops precisely replicate the victimization patterns and take the role of the victims.

Such tactics involve risks. Being a decoy is dangerous work but police departments nationwide demonstrated devilish inventiveness in meeting precisely such challenges in the seventies and eighties.

In this case, however, the NYPD—responding to pressures from the drivers and their representatives and new outrage at the carnage—created the new Livery Task Force in February 2000 and expanded it to more than three hundred officers around April 10, 2000. Three hundred! That is more cops than the overwhelming majority of police departments in the nation. And, yes, they hastened to reassure that they were employing decoys.[8] Really? This is literally throwing cops at the problem, without developing an effective decoy strategy.

The department announced the purchase of two autos to be used as decoys. Two. And these would no doubt be employed in carefully measured situations to minimize both the risk and the possibility of interdictions. Almost a year later the only announced arrests came from the heroic and sometimes foolhardy actions of the livery drivers themselves.

The crisis was a perfect example of the true flaccidity of the NYPD's approach to street crime as the twenty-first century began and, given the lack of political popularity of aggressive tactics, who could blame them? But it was an unmentionable factor in any case.

What might they have done?

First, they have to realize cops are very brave and ready to run big risks to catch the bums and killers out there. And they can be rewarded with medals and promotions to detective. It is the duty of police commanders to devise strategies, even those that endanger cops' lives, to cope with violence.

Next, you can depend on cops' ingenuity to create imaginative approaches. For example, since most of the murders occurred in liveries without partitions, this could be replicated with a concealed partition that would spring up with the push of a button and that would also lock the doors and perhaps even release tear gas into the passenger's compartment, disabling and imprisoning these murderers. There would be coordinated back-up teams nearby. These would be employed in a larger fleet of decoy cabs, which wouldn't require three hundred officers and which would result in arrests and at least get the criminals thinking the driver could be a cop—an effective deterrent.

Cops who worked for me were regularly mugged and assaulted in the service of catching robbers. Indeed, in one notable case, a female officer went to the media, objecting to my removing her from decoy work because I wanted to spread the risk among other female cops. She loved the excitement of decoy work and had been mugged two hundred times. I thought it my job to insert other officers—all women—into this dangerous work, whether they wanted it or not. Decoys are dangerous, but police work involves danger and the public must be protected. Some grumbled, but even the unhappiest saw the essential fairness of spreading the risks. Nobody quit.

The NYPD's response to the systematic decimation of livery/cab drivers was little more than a very expensive public relations effort.

Fate, as if to make a mockery of this puny program, decreed the tragic hold-up death of still another livery driver on April 24, following the announcement of the police's ballyhooed measures. In this case the victim was shot and killed but his cab veered out of control and slammed into a wall, trapping the four teenage robbers and enabling the police not only to make some arrests, but even recover the handgun that might easily be tied to other such crimes.

A ghastly, tragic, lucky stroke.

With characteristic empathy, the police and mayor obliquely but clearly blamed the victim. Guarded references were made to the risks he took, how much better protection bullet-resistant dividing panels provide, and other very unhelpful observations.

The police do have valuable roles to play—in fighting crime as well as responding to emergencies and traffic enforcement—but they also have to recognize the limits and they must report the need for societal reforms that are so evident to them in their daily rounds.

But New York wasn't the only place abandoning such tactics. My successor quickly folded the decoy tent in Minneapolis and proceeded to more welcoming political waters.

That there are vigorous political pressures applied to eliminate aggressive—and perfectly legal—police operations is not a popular subject for public discussion. But the one area of enforcement in which there is virtual unanimity as to the use of decoys and other aggressive police tactics is in drug enforcement.

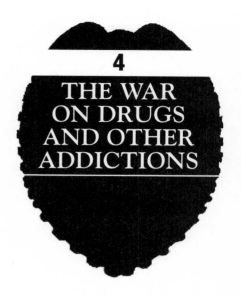

4

THE WAR ON DRUGS AND OTHER ADDICTIONS

Having achieved a rough chiaroscuro consensus on the need to aggressively combat drugs, legislatures, inspired by Governor Nelson Rockefeller's 1973 laws in New York State, went into overdrive in framing draconian measures.[1]

The principal features were increasing punishments for decreasing amounts of drugs in the suspect's possession and, just to make certain that woolly headed liberal judges couldn't surrender to their predilections for softness, imposition of mandatory sentences.

The jails filled quickly with the nonviolent "junkies" who took up the room that might have been better reserved for the more violent, dangerous, and repeating criminal offenders. The response to the growing crush was a binge of prison construction, but the escalating crack epidemic filled the new spaces faster than prisons could be built. By the year 2000 the astonishing total of two million prisoners had more than tripled the population in custody since 1980. The greater folly was that these were the wrong men. Muggers, rapists, and murders slipped through the net in the rush to lock up the druggies.

The war—and the very title given the effort ensures an overweighting of enforcement—was waged at the expense of prevention, education, and treatment strategies. Governments of grower countries, as well as those of the transit points in between, railed over America's unwillingness or inability to attack demand. America railed at the other governments for their flabby crop interdiction efforts, corruption, or disinterest.

By contrast, our concerns over the AIDS epidemic, and the very eloquent and organized demands of the gay community, prodded us, rightfully, to deal with it as a public health issue rather than as a moral crisis rooted in unsafe and possibly illegal sexual practices. We are content to incarcerate endless numbers of addicts while abandoning, correctly, our obsessive concerns over the ridiculously labeled crime of sodomy. The absence of public health figures in the war on drugs—as well as on a host of other criminal justice issues, like guns, that ought to be at the center of their concerns—has led to the abandonment of the field to mindless enforcement activists.

Since the black community is only too aware of the devastatingly debilitating effects of addiction on its members, it has been content to go along with the war wagers, even while harboring suspicions about the white community's motives in allowing drugs and alcohol to flow so freely in the ghetto.

The thirty years or so during which the war on drugs has been vigorously waged, the impact has been nil. Supplies are plentiful and cheap! A kilogram of cocaine sold for the wholesale price of $40,000 in 1980 and $20,000–$25,000 in 2000. A gram of cocaine, on the streets of New York, sold for $100 in 1990 and $50 ten years later.

The dimensions of the problem can be seen in the national statistics. In 1999 about 450,000 people died of smoking-related illness, 150,000 from alcohol diseases, and another 100,000 by legally prescribed drugs. Only around 5,000 deaths could be attributed to heroin or cocaine. Yet 1.5 million people are arrested for drug-related crimes every year.

What does this suggest?

For one thing, criminalizing hard drugs probably greatly reduces deaths in this area. Secondly, decriminalizing alcohol and tobacco has had fearful consequences. Studiously ignored are the suicides occasioned by compulsive gambling.

America's battle proves hideously complex. It continues.

Hard drugs proved the classical market paradigm of capitalism: entrepreneurs weighed the risks and profits, adjusted, and dealt. So much for the heralded seizures, masses of arrests, and long sentences. Only the prices of computers fared better.

A curious anomaly surfaced in an evolutionary manner as police agencies began to lose interest in enforcing violations involving minor amounts of marijuana. Except for cases they couldn't ignore, America's cops effectively decriminalized the few cigarettes or roaches and mostly blithely ignored pungent odors at rock concerts. Or at least they had, until caught up in the wash of the enthusiasm for enforcing "quality-of-life violations" in New York City.[2] It is perfectly sensible to go after these conditions, but not as replacement for much more aggressive tactics against street crime.

In New York, under the rubric of a philosophy that held that allowing signs of social dissolution to flourish encouraged lawlessness generally, the police energetically pursued enforcement of laws against graffiti and squeegee men and flooded areas with cops enforcing narcotics laws. These efforts proved a potemkin village type of approach, serving to conceal the rot of inaction behind a facade of activism. It looked a lot like an NYPD version of three-card monte.

The usual claims of miraculous results followed these mass visitations into ghetto areas by hordes of cops, on expensive overtime, which resulted in floods of low-level arrests. Predictably, the sensible evolution of the policy of neglect toward small amounts of marijuana was halted and reversed. It made sense to attack even small problems that, through their toleration, communicated both despair and an "anything goes" attitude. These must not be undertaken as substitutes for really aggressive assaults on muggers, burglars, and car thieves.

Narcotics Division arrests in New York City for the first eighty days of 2000 experienced the not-unexpected shifts, greatly increasing those for misdemeanors or minor violations by 68 percent and reducing arrests for felonies or serious crimes by 9 percent.

Such "carpets of blue"—the equivalent of sweeps and roundups—produce impressive arrest totals that mask more complex realities. It is of more than passing interest that these saturations don't occur in white neighborhoods. They also, in one notable case, clearly endangered the black community's support for antidrug operations when white and Hispanic cops shot and killed an unarmed black male they had approached to ask if he had marijuana for sale. Patrick Dorismond, an innocent passerby, was angered and insulted and paid for the encounter with his life.[3]

Mayor Giulani came to the cops' defense, a melee between mourners and police attended the man's funeral, and the black community's relatively unblinking support of drug enforcement operations suddenly came under wide scrutiny. The incident occurring in March 2000 quickly became an issue in the racially polarized Senate race between the mayor and the First Lady before Giuliani's abrupt departure from the contest, for health and complex personal reasons.

The Dorismond case had been preceded by another notorious tragedy involving aggressive antidrug operations, the Amadou Diallo shooting, in which four white cops fired forty-one times, striking a citizen—armed only with his wallet—nineteen times, killing him.

In the meantime, a weary, angry and frustrated citizenry looked on and suffered the fallout of thefts, violence, prostitution, and other crimes and demanded ever tougher answers. They got more and better drug enforcement, yet the drugs marched in virtually uninterrupted.

A daring few suggested the prospect of legalizing hard drugs (amphetamines, cocaine, heroin, and the like). By then most police departments were defanging the effort by de-emphasizing enforcement of laws centering on the one drug that had a literate constituency—marijuana. Although some marijuana possessors were serving long stretches and the de facto decriminalization came too late for them, their numbers—and their voices—dwindled as the enforcement effort de-escalated. Sure, cops would still lock you up if they found a marijuana cigarette on you, but they'd ceased really looking for such contraband over the waning days of the twentieth century, except in New York City.

In other jurisdictions learned scientists studied the medical possibilities of marijuana.

Hard drugs were another matter. The buy-and-bust, undercover interceptions, and similar operations continued and intensified.

A Washington, D.C., think tank[4] became the key advocate for legalizing hard drugs but was able to recruit only a couple of former police executives in the effort. Its ostensible aim was to explore alternate strategies. Almost without a single exception police chiefs oppose legalizing hard drugs. The governor of New Mexico called for partial legalization of hard drugs in 2000, citing the futility and cost of a lost drug war.

Would there be benefits in legalizing hard drugs? Indisputably.

We tend to frame these debates in either/or terms, refusing to acknowledge the benefits existing in even the most bankrupt proposals. This is a mistake because it prevents us from weighing the real options.

The violence, profits for the criminals, suspect quality, and the myriad problems created by illicit industries would very likely dry up if hard drugs were available through prescription. England has had what is generally regarded as a failed experience with this approach. Amsterdam has cafes that allow and sell marijuana, and this has worked so far. The addict's economic dilemma—which forces him or her into committing crimes— would be sharply reduced. The government might even reap some taxes with which to subsidize treatment, education, and prevention efforts.

There are undeniable benefits to legalization.

Why then, do I and the near unanimous majority of practitioners and students in the field, oppose legalization?

Simply put, any legalization—of anything—places the imprimatur of the state upon its use. This is a more powerful message than commonly realized. When a government that inspects our food and warns us of risks tells us its okay to do something, the implications of such approval have the psychic weight of mom telling Junior, "It's okay to take the car tonight—just don't destroy it." Our moral fabric is neither sturdy nor secure enough to withstand such frayings.

There is no debate about alcohol, but people drank a lot less from 1920 to 1932, during Prohibition.[5] Legalizing it has produced millions and millions of alcoholics, tons of abusers, endless carnage on our roads, less productivity, and countless destroyed families. Alcohol is implicated in innumerable violent crimes. The human suffering has been well-nigh incalculable. Yes, alcohol can be, and usually is, consumed in moderation and hardly anyone would seriously urge its ban, but the absence of discussion shouldn't blind us to the harm it causes. But to those who would argue that legalizing hard drugs would reduce crime, the easy refutation is the enormously high involvement of alcohol, a legal drug, in all crimes of violence.

Tobacco, altogether too familiar a controversy and explored a subject, will simply be mentioned for its generic relationship to the other three and as a way of illustrating the differing decibels of discussion attending these addictions. Its issues have been widely illuminated in the extensive and tortured debate we continue to entertain. In the welter of perjuries and mendacities—as revealed in the truly shocking testimony of tobacco executives before Congress and in internal memos—a perfectly legal drug incurred hundreds of billions of dollars in litigation, simply because the industry's executives couldn't acknowledge or admit some simple, obvious truth.

But there is a much better example of the dangers of legalization—gambling. All three—drugs, alcohol, and gambling—carry the risk of enslavement, which we call addiction. Our country has also had a very agonizing relationship with gambling but, until around 1960, it was mostly illegal or sequestered in inconvenient places like race tracks and Las Vegas.[6]

Following widespread legalization, gambling is now America's fastest-growing industry. People certainly gambled when it was against the law but it is more than clear now that the amounts pale into insignificance when matched against the action of today's high and low rollers.

The ubiquitous temptations flash at us as we proceed to any pay counter, whether at a grocery store or gas station or wherever. We are fast becoming a nation of "whales"—the Las Vegas term for serious players.

What kind of value system offers the enticements of quick, unearned wealth? Why bother to work, scrimp, save, and plan?

Who is to cope with the army of compulsive gamblers governments are rushing to create with wildly expanding gaming opportunities?

The specter of gambling is in strong competition with drug addiction as the shadow haunting America in the twenty-first century.

My own reluctant entry into this world came out of the blue.

I came home for good at age sixty-one, on January 1, 1989. Having served as police chief for nine years, I had no job prospects but really felt the Minneapolis Police Department needed new blood and a fresh approach at the top. After so many years at the helm, I felt stale and repetitious. I had tackled all of the problems, winning many and resigning myself to accepting the ones I couldn't change.

Our home was my wife Erica's kingdom and I couldn't just plop down on the couch and lose myself in the *New York Times*, throwing her realm into confusion and disrepair, and I didn't think I'd get another job. So I had a house built on the land I'd bought in Cape Cod, which would be ready in August. This would enable me to get out of her hair with periodic sojourns there when I felt I was getting on her nerves. There was also the question of my intruding on a privacy she'd enjoyed for the thirty-one years of our marriage.

I'd been lazing around for about five months when the phone awakened me at 8:30 A.M. one June morning. By then most of Minnesota was well into its workday, pursuing the rhythms of the farm.

It was Governor Rudy Perpich.

I was shocked.

Would I serve as gaming commissioner? "Governor, I'll do anything you ask. I believe in duty and service but I object to gambling as immoral, even having written extensively on the issue. I don't think I'd be a good choice."

"That's fine, just what I need. Could you come over in a couple of hours?"

And that's how I became Minnesota's first and only gaming commissioner, serving for seventeen months.

My objections were an eerie reprise of my attempts, in 1972, to dissuade Commissioner Murphy from appointing me the NYPD's inspector general, with identical results.

Since the people had spoken, I set about creating the most effective, efficient, honest gambling operation possible, starting a lottery and presiding over an industry that went from over a billion dollars of illegal gambling a year to four times that total legal tender a few years later. I felt awful about participating in the creation of a growing army of compulsive gamblers. Still, I enjoyed working for Perpich. He was a Democrat and a genuine populist, emerging from the union-militant area of ore miners called the Iron Range. He was Croatian and a dentist and all his brothers went on to become professionals—one even marrying into Sulzberger branch of the *New York Times* family.

Governor Perpich lost the 1990 election and once again I'd soon be out of a job. My revenge on the gods was to recommend the abolition of the post.

After a year and a half of watching a disconsolate army of farmers pull-tab and pull-arm their way into a deeper misery than the vagaries their tough and dangerous vocation delivered, I concluded that I'd been more than right.

The government's creation of addictions—whether alcohol, tobacco, or gambling—is one of the evils I had to accept if I was to participate in public life. Cops—except in cases where their consciences were violated beyond redemption—had to bow before the people's will.

Gambling was sinful—simply wrong. It was fraying our moral fabric. Gambling—in all forms—in Minnesota and elsewhere, had quadrupled or quintupled since legalization in the early sixties.

While it was criminalized a lot of folks gambled; there was police corruption and the Mob profited. We were better off then than now.

As nutty as it sounds, I'd criminalize gambling and take my chances with the fallout the abolitionists of criminalizing hard drugs and other substances and practices point to with such alarm.

Lessons, to be sure, but painful and costly ones.

But, unlike such police tactics as infiltrations, stakeouts, stings, and decoys—which had to be abandoned because of public pressure, sometimes from the overclass and sometimes from the underclass—the war on drugs could continue to be waged, as mindlessly as ever, because of the rough consensus of approval surrounding its approaches.

WHAT'S TO BE DONE?

Such exercises as these require an answer, even a grotesquely framed one offered as the palliative.

Alas, I don't know one and can't offer a facile response.

I do believe the war must be fought; that the mandatory sentences are nonsense and self-defeating, even as they allow posturing politicians to show us how tough they are; that jailing the street junkies fills the cells with mostly nonviolent offenders; that education, treatment, and prevention are starved of funds and resources; and that joint efforts, between the federal Drug Enforcement Administration and local police agencies, offer the best hope of effective interdiction. In short, the war must continue to be waged, but the absence of public health figures and concerns from this debate is both shameful and tragic.

The crack epidemic in the ghetto has, since 1985, clearly subsided and heroin has shifted its appeal to the mostly white and suburban middle class, but the drug is the variable, and the search for escape is the constant.

Trends in drug use are easier to detect in retrospect than in real time. Criminologists only awakened to the peaking of the crack cocaine epidemic years after its 1985 apex.

The recreational drug of choice among trendy and affluent New Yorkers is powdered cocaine—which is snorted in bars. Daytop Village, the city's largest drug rehabilitation program, reported a dramatic increase in powder cocaine use by its white- and blue-collar outpatients in 2000.

Whether cocaine, heroin, amphetamines, ecstasy, or whatever, the certainty is that illegal drugs—in whatever form—will continue to entice those seeking a mode of flight from the awful realities of everyday life. The hedonistic overclass will continue to pursue its pleasures with relative impunity—at least from arrest, not from the consequences of their actions. Nature is a more severe judge than society.

The public health aspects of crime deserve a little consideration. Americans love easy answers and simple solutions—perhaps all humans do, to be fair.

The most important public health initiatives possible—ones that would secure by far the most dramatic achievable results—would be to diet and control our weight, stop smoking, exercise, avoid addictions—whether drugs, alcohol, gambling, or other physically or psychically debilitating practices—drive carefully, and exercise prudence in our daily lives.

Instead we pop pills, enrich skilled surgeons, and rely on emergency services that deal with the consequences of our excesses. Prevention is tiresome—in personal health and in crime. Reducing the number of guns and addressing the issues of homelessness, poverty, racism, and other crippling social problems cause the collective glance to glaze over with indifference. We prefer more cops, bigger prisons, tougher laws.

People embrace the quick, easy answers and, in public life, we've managed to discredit, as socialism or worse, any notion that seeks to ease the plight of the underclass. We lavish treasure on external protections (the defense budget) and internal controls (the criminal justice system) but balk at any scheme that addresses the true dangers to our society—the rot within.

Buy-and-bust street operations should be leveraged to get the addict into treatment and to force him to give up his supplier as the organizational ladder of traffickers is climbed.

The use of the military in this effort is unwise on several fronts. They have little knowledge of, or real interest in, law enforcement operations that require expertise and it constitutes a dangerous expansion of their role. It should be noted that the military were forbidden from undertaking what are called *posse comitatus* (domestic law enforcement) operations by an act passed in the nineteenth century.[7] Our Founding Fathers had quite enough of armed military intrusions, by the redcoats, in their homes.

Border controls need to be tightened and such anticorruption measures as salting drug sites with money to test the integrity of the enforcers must be pursued. We need rigorous, honest enforcement—but those address only the latter half of the supply-and-demand equation.

In the war on drugs, prevention is discredited—witness the derision at the "Just Say No to Drugs" campaign. Treatment is starved for funds as the resources are aimed at enforcement. Education is only beginning to surface as an approach as the Office of National Drug Control Policy was given $1 billion to spend on movie, TV, and print advertising in 2000.

Foreign involvements, for which some wisely read "entanglements," need to be pursued with extreme caution, lest we be sucked into internal insurrections as we were during the Cold War days in Vietnam and in our interferences in overthrowing "hostile" governments—or attempts to overthrow them. We can't, though, ignore either the growers, such as Colombia, or the transit points such as Haiti. Both are good examples of nations needing carefully measured assistance that doesn't suck us into intractable internal problems or result in only deepening corruption.

The war on drugs waxes and wanes, more as a consequence of attitudes and experiences in the ghetto—where the violence and real social dissolution center—than anywhere else, but no one in power seems to want to confront the American people with anything as dull, prolonged, and discredited (at least in the minds of those who hold that we've fought the war, and lost it) as a refighting of another war, the one on poverty.

Deeply implicated in the drug issue in America is the question of race.

5
RACE[1]

The greyhound and mechanical rabbit chase between criminals and cops has been characterized by evolving innovations, with often excellent results and backlash. We have crammed 2 million, mostly men, in jails in America in recent years, an alpine rise over recent decades and a lot of them during a time of actually declining crime figures. About half of these are black males in an overall population in which they measure around 5 percent.

The black community is systematically stripped of its males by a criminal justice system that refuses to discuss the issue of race. Those males that remain are in such a hopeless fix—in terms of jobs, schooling, or prospects—that some are unable to function as fathers and brothers, notwithstanding the highly publicized televised devotions of world-class athletes. Almost one in three adult black males in the prime of life is under such forms of control as parole, probation, jail, or other supervision. The statistics compiled by the Department of Justice also reflect that the number of adults under the supervision of federal, state, and local correctional authorities rose 3 percent in 1999 to a record total of 6,288,600.

Our American dilemma is that we won't admit that we continue to foster conditions of oppression such as to make the lives of blacks virtually intolerable. They have been made our underclass, in the main. Protest, as we've seen in the form of riots and crime, becomes a tempting mode of expression. Escape, in the form of booze and drugs, may, for some, be the only way out. Even those who have climbed from the slough of economic despondency have not escaped racism.

Arthur Ashe, the noble tennis star, was stricken with heart disease and contracted AIDS through a medically flawed transfusion. When someone commiserated with him over his plight he shook his head and said, "The toughest thing is to wake up black in this country every day."

RACE—ANALOGY FOR SLAVERY

In 1997, I cohosted a TV talk show called *Face to Face*, which aired on two Public Broadcasting System stations in Minnesota, with a conservative radio host serving as my foil. Nothing much came of the effort and I drifted off after a dozen or so shows.

My cohost would sometimes ask me to fill in on his three-hour radio program, broadcast via the local ABC/Disney affiliate. I'd done this sort of thing before and came up with a stack of issues to provoke listeners in cars or at home, enlivening a discussion.

When I arrived, one of the producers casually mentioned that the previous host had intended to raise the question of whether President Clinton should apologize for slavery, but hadn't gotten to the subject.

I was intrigued.

I off-handedly said the president should, as a way of confronting the race issue and generating a much-needed debate, and thought I'd go on to my little stack of topics.

The switchboard lit up. I spent the next forty-five minutes coping with a visceral anger that was truly shocking. The callers loudly disclaimed responsibility for slavery, catalogued how "those people" were getting every break, and reflected a bellicosity that argued both for the need of a discussion as well as the depth of the racism still floating out there.

The only two other topics I'd ever seen provoke this sort of vitriol were gun control and abortion.

I was finally able to segue into other subjects but not before a lot of sulfurous comments were unleashed on the listening audience. It proved an object lesson as to the extent of the racism just beneath the surface.

And has white America ever stopped to wonder at the universal and spontaneous jubilation that exploded from the black community—everywhere—over the jury's verdict of not guilty in O. J. Simpson's murder trial?

The investigation was, in the way of these things, characteristically sloppy. This is a key reason why the rich hire high-priced lawyers—to strike at the vulnerable points in most prosecutions.

It's easy to believe blacks thought him innocent, but the reality is probably that most onlookers, white and black, were pretty convinced of his guilt. One has only to evaluate the nearly universal reaction to the man since to understand his status as a pariah in the "respectable" community, white or black—O. J. is not exactly a *presence* in America's living rooms. As late as 2000, networks were canceling Simpson's appearance because of his status.

That trial did turn on jury selection and on having enough minorities on it to overcome resistance—to what?

What the black community—jurors and onlookers—uttered was a cri de coeur over the foot firmly planted on their necks and of their support for anyone, in any guise—even a likely murderer—who struck out at it in whatever, even heinous, form. The black community was expressing elation over a rare victory over what they perceived as an oppressive white system that rounded up their brothers and sons, as well as, perhaps, a bit of awful, secret glee that the victims, for once, weren't black. A civil court jury partly redressed the balance by finding him civilly responsible for the deaths.

But if whites can't or won't confront the ugly truth of racism, how do the blacks contribute to the perpetuation of the dilemma?

The tortured answer is that blacks, recognizing that the whites won't see the insidious depth and extent of the racism that makes the behavior of some black males inevitable, can't or won't admit that the street crime and urban disorder problems involve too high a percentage of black males. Instead they engage in twisted evasions and seize on ersatz statistics and hope. This is not to avoid the fact that the criminal justice system comes down heavier on black males than their white counterparts, which exacerbates the problem.

Many police operations wind up targeting black youths. Since many of these are "at-risk males" there is a sort of logic to the approach, but it rapidly slides into the creation of stereotypes and into the unconscious development of tactics that wind up becoming blatantly racist. In this social petri dish, the white teenager swims free.

Even a cursory glance at the annual statistics of the FBI will reveal the disproportionate involvement of black males in all aspects of "street crimes." Still, American society is locked in this dance of death in which neither partner is willing to recognize the truisms that might serve as the path to a mutually enjoyed waltz. How do we get whites to acknowledge that racism breeds violence? How do we get blacks to recognize that racism produces crime by some blacks?

RACIAL PROFILING[2]

Why do border patrols question a family of Aztecs in Texas and ignore a similar but obviously very white and suburban group in the same place? The offense, many of the aggrieved would say, is "driving while Mexican."

What makes frontier authorities closely question and search swarthy, Arabic accented males and wave goofily clad tourists rapidly through? The very same instincts that have cops spotting as "wrong" young black males behind the wheels of cars that appear to be, in their eyes, anomalous to the occupant.

However logical this may appear to its practitioners, it comes down to the crime of "driving while black." And doesn't the adoption of a policy that rarely targets whites insure that fewer white criminals will be intercepted?

Cops stereotype and make split-second decisions on the basis of the statistical probabilities taught them through hearsay, data, and experience. The problem with racial profiling, though, is that even when police intercept the occasional criminal they don't have the right to stop vehicles to verify the driver's bona fides or that of the passengers, based simply on race.

Unquestionably, racism is endemic in the ranks.

The wide acceptability of racial profiling was illustrated by a photo of New Jersey Governor Christine Todd Whitman, released in a lawsuit in 2000, showing her frisking a black male stopped by state troopers. The man, innocent, was released.

The event occurred in the Northeast, not the South, in 1996, not so long ago in years, but light years removed from our current understanding of the practice. The governor had been set up, but her willing compliance spoke volumes about what constituted acceptable enforcement conduct only a short time ago.

A cop's everyday initiation and experience lead to the conclusion that black males are "wrong." Period. Cops sneer at such politically correct niceties as references to dangerous predators as "at-risk males." Cops put a face and a color on that abstraction and simply act on it. The result is to make the lives of black males—rich or poor—hell.

The white society, through its oppressions, creates a climate of existence in which poor, uneducated blacks lose and in which the losers strike back or escape into the oblivion of drugs or alcohol.

The dominant society doesn't see itself as racist or oppressive and will even point to the highly visible successes as proof of racial justice. No issue better illustrates the subliminal racial rivalry than attempts to equalize things through affirmative action.

These programs, intended to level the field of action by favoring equally qualified black candidates over white ones, became the center of a firestorm and were abandoned by 1999. Thus, an attempt to redress 380 years of slavery, Jim Crow, and its subtler aftermath was scuttled by cries of unfairness by whites. It is, of course, palpably unfair to favor one candidate over another automatically when they are equally qualified. But doesn't it make some logical sense to suspend the rules of fairness briefly, at least until some measure of justice is achieved? That is the logical conundrum that we've resolved by abandoning affirmative action.

The black leaders, faced with this stonewalling, are left with the choice of futilely decrying the conditions that manufacture misery and crime or denying that too many street crimes are committed by black males. What gets forgotten is that black males are the principal victims of violent crimes, which tends to be swept under our social rug.

Desperate to establish their manhood in a society that strips them of it, black males often respond unpolitically in police contacts. The results are almost always harmful to blacks, and largely unnecessarily so.

In my experience, where a white male is more likely to succumb to obsequiousness when stopped, a black male will more likely turn defiant.

This is perfectly legal, but since the cops have thick tomes crammed with laws to use against him, it proves a mistake. Cops like citizens to show them what they consider to be proper respect, and if the don't get it, they often retaliate one way or another—which, of course, is a corruption of the legal process the officers are sworn to uphold.

Whites have a lot of trouble understanding this need for self-assertion. A possible answer came to me when, while angrily being kept waiting for a restaurant table with my wife and two sons, I suddenly wondered what I'd think if I'd been black. I could see the scene as involving rudeness or stupidity or incompetence—qualities in large supply in any human enterprise—but what if, being black, I had to factor in the question of racism? I concluded that any human who could not discern, with any certainty, between human frailties and racism was bound to feel some confusion and resentment.

An off-duty black police officer dining in a restaurant responds to a dangerous, noisy confrontation developing outside. He emerges, gun drawn, to control a situation in which one of the participants had brandished a gun. When uniformed cops respond—the black officer's colleagues in a department of about 450, with, as ever, very few blacks—they shoot their associate dead. This happened in the enlightened year of 2000.[3]

The usual recriminations and defenses follow, about whether he identified himself, and so on. It would be really hard to imagine he'd just emerged willy-nilly from the restaurant and into the fray, with gun drawn, without announcing his being a cop. But was anyone listening? Had he been white, wouldn't the cops have hesitated that crucial split-second before firing? And what would any black citizen reflecting on this case think?

The shooters were entirely exonerated.

In the now-famous Diallo case of February 1999, the charge was murder. Since this came from a system notoriously protective of such cops, it seemed a bizarre exception. Black leaders demonstrated repeatedly and were, for a change, joined by many equally concerned white activists.

The cops who were charged locally in the Rodney King case in Los Angeles were—to no insider's surprise—wrongly acquitted, setting off the LA riots of 1991.[4] It was a classic example of the high regard in which most cops are held, by most juries—especially white ones—and how very difficult it is to convict cops of anything, not withstanding overwhelming evidence.

There's an instructive lesson there. The burning, looting, and violence dramatically displayed on the evening news moved the Feds to prosecute, quite successfully. Federal prosecutions tend to be much more meticulous and persuasive, and the Feds know they have to prepare airtight cases.

Riots have terrified municipal leaders since towns such as Newark and Detroit were virtually razed following what was usually a police event in which white cops abused black citizens, setting off a rampage of outrage. The disorder greatly expedited the entrance of blacks into positions of local leadership, as mayors and police chiefs. The extraordinarily pacific reaction to a palpably unjust verdict of not guilty—of anything—in the Diallo case illustrates the tortured, cynical, yet effective logic of such a development. In the Diallo case, black leaders called for peace—and got it.

Since the pressures of potential violence abated, the Feds were free to let the case slip through the cracks and, so far, avoid the unpleasantness of a federal prosecution.

In contrast to this case, the 1997 brutalizing of Haitian immigrant Abner Louima by the same NYPD was successfully prosecuted by the Justice Department.[5] Louima was taken to a station house and had a plunger handle shoved into his rectum and then thrust into his mouth, chipping some teeth and causing severe internal injuries. Louima's offense was supposedly having punched a cop during a sidewalk melee outside a club earlier that night.

In both the Diallo and Louima cases, the officers were all white. The victims were black. But the cases were starkly different.

In the Diallo case the cops made a terrible, and very likely good-faith, mistake that resulted in a tragic death. In the Louima case the cops were not only acting in palpable bad faith but, in the way of these things when street justice is being dispensed, they even had the wrong man. It developed that it had not been Louima who had punched the officer. In addition to its more obvious disabilities, it is useful to consider the hideous imperfections attending all forms of street justice. Its foremost problem may well be its fallibility.

But the astonishing thing about the Louima case was the sense of impunity with which the cops acted. The officers felt utterly secure in taking him to their headquarters to alter his attitude. It was this assurance—that they could do as they pleased with a prisoner, in a building housing and hosting supervisors of all ranks—that ought to highlight the systemic nature of the problem to the high officials reviewing this case.

The chief has to ask himself how he came to preside over a system in which such an atrocity was possible. Yes, he might point to the convictions of the cops to date and possibly more to come, as well as to the vigorously coerced testimony of other cops (it would be a dangerous conceit to label this, as they did, a crack in the Blue Wall of Silence)—but it was the certainty of their impunity that ought to chill the contemplations of any executive looking at this tragedy.

It has to be remembered that the successful prosecutions in the Abner Louima case came only after the FBI intervened. Yes, the Feds have the powerful ability to prosecute cops who lie to their agents and they used it effectively here to convict even a tangential player. But it is their skill, determination, and professionalism that ultimately carried the day. The cost of such atrocities is a reinforcement of distrust and hatred of law enforcement officers. Another often ignored cost of these atrocities is the whopping sums won in litigation or settlements. These submerged penalties on the body politic ultimately come back to haunt, in the form of taxes.

BRONX THUMPING

Managing cops has always been a humbling experience. They normally do as they please unless they have a chastening example in their imaginations to inhibit their actions.[6]

I once had a case remarkably similar to Louima's. It was 1975 in the Bronx. Cops were summoned to a "burglary in progress" call. As they arrived, a clutch of Hispanics ran from a building, threw something under a car, and fled. A cop captured one of them and they retrieved a brown bag from under a car. Inside it were a stack of bills with a revolver. Pay dirt.

The aggressive cop who collared the suspect, now trying to figure out where in the tenement they'd been, questioned him. All of the building's apartment doors were secure, none showing signs of forced entry. The suspect lied and said he'd come from an apartment on the second floor because he knew the occupant.

Inside that apartment lived a Puerto Rican man with his wife and infant daughter. Now the tough cop stood silently at the door, clutching the suspect and insisting he gain admission. Inside, the resident was doing his daily task of bagging heroin for his many clients. When he heard a knock, he asked who it was in Spanish. The suspect answered but the response clearly was not satisfactory. Very soon a bullet came from within, penetrating the door, sending cop and suspect scurrying for cover.

The cop cuffed the prisoner to a railing and heroically burst through the door, tackling the resident and sending him flying backwards, smashing furniture in the tumble. The suspect was quickly subdued, the gun recovered and the drugs confiscated, as the baby bawled and the wife screamed hysterically. The cop administered some cruel additional blows, assuming that no one examining the incident would hold it against him. All were taken to the station house.

Over the course of the next six or so hours, the cop, frustrated and angry over the complex mystery, slugged and kicked the heroin dealer repeatedly. The other cops and detectives drifted away and the violence escalated. As the drug dealer faded into spewing blood and agonizing spasms, he was removed to an ancient fortress of a hospital, Morrisania, where he was placed on a gurney and left in a corridor.

By the time a doctor got around to him, the only service he could render was the cause of death—a "green-tree splintering of a rib that punctured the spleen, causing the man to bleed to death internally."

When prisoners die in custody there is always the strong possibility of brutality and I took a direct, immediate interest in the case, responding to the scene and questioning supervisors. I grew up with one of them and, pulling him aside, said, "Think hard before you answer, because I'll have you indicted for perjury if you lie. Is the cop a hero or a bum?" He solemnly assured me the cop was a hero.

The district attorney in the Bronx was a case-hardened politico of the practical and, as far as I knew, rough-hewn, honest variety. I liked him because he gave me what I wanted and he liked me because I didn't embarrass him. I called DA Mario Merola and alerted him to the problem and assigned detectives to work on the case. He assigned a tough assistant.

In no time we indicted a number of the precinct personnel, including my friend, for lying to the grand jury and the tough cop for manslaughter. I knew how hard it would be to convict any of them—on anything—and we quickly lost our perjury cases. I was not even able to press administrative charges against those acquitted.

Merola and I concentrated all our energies on the brutal cop, and the jury miraculously found him guilty of manslaughter. We had a lot of evidence, but even so, half an hour after the verdict, one juror attempted to change her verdict to not guilty, threatening to throw the case into a mistrial and almost certain dissipation and defeat. The verdict held. The cop went to prison.

He'd been a classic thumper—so much so that he was widely feared by other cops, even as they expressed admiration for his heroism and toughness. He'd been a very prominent figure in cases in which cops were wounded and assaulted, being among the first to donate blood, organize searches for evidence or suspects, and follow up investigations and tirelessly chase leads.

But what had initiated the course of events that led to this tragedy?

As so often is the case, it was romance. The brown-bag suspect who'd been captured and led the cops to the wrong apartment had been the lover of a bodega owner's naive niece. She lived with her uncle in a top-floor apartment of that building. In the course of their passions, she'd confided that she and her uncle were going on a vacation to Puerto Rico.

Earlier, she'd unthinkingly described how her uncle secreted cash receipts in the oven. Her boyfriend and two friends climbed down from the roof and into the apartment through a window. The burglars were observed by a neighbor who called 911 to report a burglary in progress— the sort of run cops speed to, adrenaline racing. Inside the intruders found the cash with a gun, in a brown paper bag, and exited through the front door, making sure it locked behind them. As they hit the street, the cops arrived and they scattered. All were eventually caught, but the one collared at the scene managed to come up with a devilish twist because he'd dealt with the drug dealer before.

I pushed very hard to get to the bottom of the incident while my staff worked, with delicious subtlety, to cover up the event. My handling of the case certainly must have inhibited further such abuses by cops, but the fact that I hadn't deterred such an act clearly reflected my lack of impact on the troops' psyches, even two years after taking over the command. It proved an object lesson.

In 1975, in the Bronx, racism was almost as often aimed at Hispanics, as it was in this case, as it was at blacks. Each group represented one-third of the borough's 1.5 million residents.

In the process, I learned the difference between an insurer and a steward. The former must know of, and respond to, each and every incident. The latter must, like a manager, be generally aware of trends, major events, and serious needs. A police chief cannot know of or prevent every single incident but he or she should know about, learn of, and act on those of profound importance. This was the real thrust of Senator Howard Baker's query about President Richard Nixon and Watergate, when he asked: "What did he know and when did he know it?" In other words, how did he exercise his stewardship of his office? Had I failed to personally intervene in this case I'd have been a poor steward.

SMOOTH OPERATOR

I was publicly denounced as a racist in Minnesota in 1990 by the Urban Coalition, as a result of a speech none of its members had heard. An investigation cleared me, although I was helpless in the heated debate that preceded my being cleared.

I was also publicly termed an anti-Semite. I'd been invited to speak to a club of Jewish women at a synagogue and fumed as they conducted an endless series of transactions that included awards, acknowledgments, little speeches, and endless bits of business.

I had warned them that I could only stay ninety minutes—doing lunch with them, and the like—but I had an appointment at 2:00 P.M. and I tried to be punctilious about punctuality.

Finally, they got to me. I gave a twenty-minute talk, concluding by saying that I could only take a few questions. I said the fourth would be the last. A lady raised her hand and insisted she had a question.

"Well," I responded, "you may well have a question but I don't have to furnish an answer," and stormed out.

The ladies gasped at my rudeness, and as I left, they saw me get stopped by a TV reporter, who asked a brief question about gangs—a hot topic I consistently mishandled. I answered quickly and sped off.

The ladies, thinking I had denounced them to the press, told the reporter I was an anti-Semite and called several stations to reiterate the charge. I came to think they were engaged in a preemptive strike, anticipating that I was criticizing them.

The business occasioned a brief press flurry, stopped swiftly by the statement of the director of the Jewish Community Relations Council, who said I may be many things, but I was no anti-Semite.

That killed it in its tracks.

It's tough to answer such charges, but I was saving my response in the hope that the ladies would embellish the accusation and, after a couple of days, I'd say, "Of course I'm an anti-Semite. I've been married to a Jew for over thirty years and if that doesn't make one an anti-Semite, what will?"

I never got to deliver my little gibe.

Humor is risky and powerful.

When demonstrators were arrested, en masse, in Minneapolis in the mideighties, and the press asked me what we were going to do with them, I said, "We're taking them downtown and shooting them."

My wife was among those sent to jail. I reacted with, "At our age, conjugal visiting rights aren't really needed."

I took a lot of chances with humor and found it almost as powerful a tool as ridicule—a truly fearful weapon.

BLACK POWER AND POLICE TACTICS

The black leadership in Detroit, appalled by the carnage wrought on black males—albeit robbers—moved to eliminate the aggressive but legal stakeouts that caused the mayhem. Since many recent shootings and killings of black males by white cops involved the tolerated aggressiveness of police tactics, isn't it fair to suspect that black leaders may soon change their minds about supporting such approaches, even in drug cases?

Blacks' patience with aggressive police tactics has worn thin—except in the socially devastating area of drug use; but even here, police abuses are making the black community restive.

Race lies at the very core of the issue of police abuse in America.

Apologists will hold that an unprecedented feast of prosperity has fed all comers, but that view requires a more egalitarian view of our economy than is the case. Ours is not an economic tide, but a series of locks in which the privileged, upstream compartments—the top 1 percent—get a disproportionately large share of the water. The nineties created large numbers of mostly white millionaires, mirroring the distortion that can also be found in our educational, housing, health, and even recreational worlds.

A cursory glance at our economic data will reflect the disparities.

In 1990, over 14 percent of black households had incomes of less than $15,000, while only just over 5 percent of whites shared that fate. The shift in the figures occurs as we reach the higher levels, where the white percentages swell and the black shrink. In 1997, household income of $15,000 to $24,999 in black households stood at 20.9 percent, compared to 14.6 percent in white households.[7]

Of the 11.5 million arrests for all offenses in 1997, 7.6 million were white and 3.6 million were black. Of the 3,335 inmates on death row in 1997, 1,876 were white and 1,459 black.

Children under eighteen were almost three times as likely to be in poverty if they were black than if they were white—42.0 percent versus 13.4 percent in 1980; 44.2 percent versus 15.1 percent in 1990; and 36.8 percent versus 15.4 percent in 1997.

Our passion for such tough measures as mandated sentences insures the warehousing of hundreds of thousands of young black males who have no history of violence, but are caught with drugs. Moving upstream, our "law and order" champions are increasingly treating kids as adults—and incarcerating them with hardened criminals—because of our perception that they are evil. The disproportionate number of these unformed tots—who may have made serious mistakes, but who need to be understood and treated—are, of course, black.

Presence in college predictably echoes the disparities, only there—because of the enormous rate of criminal justice's incapacitation of males—black women greatly outnumber black men.

Unemployment has certainly declined—across the board—in our burgeoning economy, but black males are more than three times more likely to be out of work than white males, and also more likely to be in lower-level, lower-paying jobs.

The statistics are daunting: high in the areas we'd seek to shrink and low in the places we'd seek to swell. The actual financial chasm between the top 1 percent and the bottom 20 percent of the population has greatly widened over the century's last decade, with the gains at the bottom—such as they are—dwarfed by the enormous capital accretions at the top. The economic boom has the masked inequities and injustices that will come back to haunt us.

The statistics prove the case but it is in the anecdotes that we discover deeper truths. Virgil said, "From a single crime know the nation." Columbine High school taught us the folly of our approach to guns and the costs of neglecting our youngsters.

When a young black man's life ends on the street, look into his life for evidence of the hundreds of racial blows that rained down on his head over his brief life. When that young man revolts into crime, the equation is complicated by economic, racial, and political factors our society refuses to confront.

The current decline of crime—across the board—has proved a temporary respite in the heated debate about urban violence.

6
CRIME
FIGHTING
AS
MYTH

No sane person would say it, but, the reality of urban policing in the last third of the twentieth century—and very likely for some years ahead—has been trying to control the urban underclass, which is mainly black. Riots and street crime—at appalling and ever-increasing levels through the seventies, eighties, and half of the nineties—terrified the overclass and left it shaken. The booming economy probably eased some of the pressures by reducing the number of homeless and employing many of the formerly excluded, but the maldistribution of prosperity's bounty has kept a significant portion of the population at poverty levels.

Is it a surprise that the overclass knows how to get what it wants? It hires and fires, pays and withholds, rewards and punishes. And America, as the centuries segue, is still run by white men. How else to explain their absence from the ramparts of mass protest movements anywhere? With rare exceptions (as when they were to be shipped out to fight an unpopular war in Vietnam) white American males have seen little need to storm the barricades.

In this environment the overclass, nervous about disorders and personal attacks, pressured the police to act. The cops, under a rapidly unfolding series of Supreme Court restrictions, often inspired by Justice

William O. Douglas (if, rightly in a way, credited to the redoubtable Chief Justice Earl Warren), had to adjust—and they did.

CONSTITUTIONAL ISSUES[1]

The police can't just crash in and take the evidence, secure in the knowledge that, as before *Mapp* v. *Ohio* in 1961, the terms of its recovery would not be questioned in state courts (and, when it was questioned in federal court for the previous forty years, the evidence was blithely shifted into a state prosecution, under something hallowed as the "Silver Platter Doctrine"). It is a remarkable testament to the unblinking hypocrisy and moral corruption of the pre-Warren court years that tainted evidence, which federal judges threw out as inadmissible, could be handed over by the Feds to local police agencies for use in state courts, where the illegally obtained evidence was not only accepted, but even welcomed.

The reason wags hold that bad cases make bad law is that the issues that wind their way up to the Supreme Court often involve society's less savory elements. It is the Larry Flynts who define free speech issues at the Supreme Court level, not the local bishops.

A case that illustrated a number of key principles involved a sex shop operator who sought my legal services in the late nineties. His place featured nude dancers and booths where guys could feed coin machines to keep a sexy video going while they masturbated. The dancing and videos were legal and it was impossible, given the privacy of the booths, to catch the patrons in the act. The odors, in these confined spaces, were putrid.

Cops would inspect the place and, being libidinous in the extreme, very likely experienced secret titillation in the process. I base this view on the fact that whenever we confiscated pornographic videos, I'd have to limit their viewing to evidentiary purposes or the cops would get goggle-eyed as they became riveted to the images on the screen. I became an early believer in the addictive properties of porn.

The owner took to filming the inspecting crews of cops as they made their rounds in his premises, a legal but dangerous practice. Cops rarely do well when their authority is questioned.

Mostly these encounters proceeded without incident, but the owner inevitably came across a thumper who roughed him up pushed him out and brought him, face first, down onto the sidewalk, hard, as he twisted his arms to handcuff him. He was charged with interfering with officers, assault (the cop claimed to have been grazed by the owner's video camera as they maneuvered in the tight quarters), and resisting arrest. The real charge should have been failing the attitude test, but this hasn't been included in the codes yet.

The charges in this blatantly false arrest were immediately thrown out by the first judge reviewing the incident. So the owner sued.

I saw it as a classic First Amendment free speech issue and took the case. I had, by then, become inured to giving expert testimony in such issues on behalf of other than prime clients.

After reviewing all of the material I did something I'd never done before, and haven't since—I asked his lawyer if I could meet with the man to discuss settling. The lawyer was happy to agree.

The city had offered about a quarter million dollars and we all thought they could be jacked a bit higher. I told the guy I thought the case was winnable and that he had right on his side. But I warned him that the cops' versions would be very different from his, that his robust appearance belied the injuries he was claiming, and that white juries loved cops, especially in uniform and testifying as to the risks they ran, every day, on behalf of folks just like the jurors. The jury might very easily accept their version of events, notwithstanding the fact that all the charges had been summarily dismissed. Given his employment, the cops' likely testimony, the city's offer, and his appearance, I urged him to settle.

He surprised me with his vehemence. He said he only came to listen because he respected me so much, but he wouldn't settle at that level, or near it, if they put a machine gun to his head.

We went to trial.

I was very tough on the stand but, as I addressed the jury and sought eye contact, their averted bodies conveyed a troubling message of rejection.

We lost.

I was bitterly disappointed because I felt the cops had been testilying, the jury had been taken in, and, most importantly, a great chance to underline the First Amendment right of free speech had been lost.

The sex operator suffered the additional indignity of his lawyer's, and my, fees.

PUBLIC MORALS

Many in the police would believe that enforcing moral values is a key element of fighting crime. The most slippery slope in law enforcement is what is delicately referred to as vice. Laws are generally pretty malleable: Think of the Supreme Court's tortured locutions over the meaning of this or that section in our codes. But it gets positively labyrinthine when sex enters the picture. Wisely, the Supreme Court has mostly avoided the question, being content to set such guidelines as defining pornography (tricky question) in such phrases as "lacking any artistic merit," "appealing exclusively to prurient interests," "lacking any social value," and being beneath "community standards."

What this approach has accomplished is to lend enormous flexibility to our sex laws, enabling enforcement to shift with prevailing social winds. It has also had the effect of encouraging questionable enforcement actions that injure segments of our population in their rights.

Citizens tend to think of the law as rigid and immutable, but in reality it is not only plastic but amenable to priority scaling that enables the enforcers to pretty much pick and choose in accord with personal philosophy. This is why the police chief's outlook is so critical.

In secretly favoring the existence of gay bathhouses in Minneapolis, I was at 180 degrees from the agency and my predecessors, who had waged merciless warfare against these enclaves. My experience had taught me that, were it possible to eliminate these dens, the activities that took place in them would pop up in men's rooms all over the city. Uninterested citizens and their children would be forced to witness sex acts or be otherwise disturbed. Sequestration and privacy removed the activities from public view or access.

And therein lay the key—protecting the larger public from offensive behavior. No one wants to be subjected to intrusions into their privacy.

I frequently received complaints from neighbors that cruising motorists were propositioning them. Tied to this was my sense that prostitutes bore the brunt of punishments in a system sustained and driven by johns. If women were importuned by passing motorists trolling for fellatio, I'd act and send undercover female officers to dress and saunter the streets saucily and arrest the johns for "soliciting for prostitution." These johns often turned out to be respectable blue-collar types—even civil servants—and, in one notable case, a police sergeant. When I was awakened with the news, there was an expectant silence. Would I extend professional courtesies? was the unstated question.

"Well, what would you do if he was a civilian?" I asked.

"Book him."

"You have your answer."

He was, of course, acquitted by a gullible jury of sympathetic whites. The public morals/vice/sex/pornography questions centered, for me, on the first word of the equation—public. I'd strike at street conditions involving the importuning of women, but tolerate off-street behaviors in bathhouses.

I wouldn't allow a billboard showing coitus, defining that as "lewdness" despite the amorphous nature of the term. I was seeing scenes of pretty explicit sex on the screen, but Hollywood had adopted an admission code that protected the public from innocent exposures to something not so innocent. And, besides, the sex occurred in the artistic context of a story that could easily be described as socially or artistically meaningful.

If something wasn't egregiously offensive and public I was always inclined to tolerate it. I believed flag burners were exercising a constitutional right, even as I found the practice very distasteful. It wasn't *my* tastes that were at stake. I thought the Brooklyn Museum "Sensation" exhibit in 1999 depicting the Virgin Mary defiled by elephant dung a legitimate expression of artistic freedom, as was a photograph of the immersion of a crucifix in urine.

America wisely allows traffic in Nazi artifacts and explicitly describes the socially harmful and dangerous incitement of hate messages it forbids. I would have prosecuted—and did—the presentation and sale of clearly pornographic matter whose only object was an appeal to sexual urges, and which was, after all, against the law. I could see the point of setting limits but felt we ought to allow whatever wasn't clearly and generally accepted as dangerously wrong.

Would I have allowed a museum to display a male figure with an erection? A painting of a couple in an explicit sex act? Where does censorship begin and end? No right is without limits. We limit freedoms for the sake of order and civilization. Freedom of religion cannot encompass human sacrifice.

A Supreme Court justice once said he couldn't define pornography but he knew it when he saw it, and a writer once allowed she wouldn't object to any sex act unless "it frightened the horses."

If artistic meaning can be found, if the exhibit is sequestered such that an innocent wouldn't stumble onto it, and if the surrounding society seems generally accepting, I'd conclude yes, allow it and defend the rights of all by protecting the rights of the artist.

It isn't always understood that such freedoms, in every case, have limits.

Incitement to riot, threats, noisy disturbances, and the hoary shouting of "fire" in a crowded theater are all forbidden by law—as is pornography. The meanings shift—James Joyce's great work *Ulysses* was once banned as pornography—but the constant is that there are limits. The protection of children is widely accepted as legitimate grounds for legislatively limiting adult behavior toward them.

In the NYPD, we even convicted a black militant of anarchy in the sixties, for advocating the killing of judges in a speech we tape recorded. He might have found more mercy if his advocacy had focused on another profession, such as bankers.

Still, the activism of the Warren Supreme Court in the sixties created slow changes in police actions and in defining rights and limits that had been mostly honored in their breaches rather than in their observances.

After *Miranda* v. *Arizona*[2] in 1966, the police were compelled to demonstrate the voluntariness of confessions and admissions (acknowledgments of guilt without rising to the level of a full-blown and detailed mea culpa). Grillings and third degrees were out. Deception and manipulation were not.

Other decisions circumscribed police powers, but they had (we can see this in retrospect, decades after their issuance) the surprising effect of making cops more skilled, more professional, and more effective. Evidence now had to be meticulously gathered. Suspects were more skillfully, professionally questioned. Search warrants had to be secured. Lawyers had to be brought into the process. All of these requirements obliged the police to refine their responses and train their members, or suffer humiliating defeats in court.

Training and innovative techniques were adopted and a tremendous national competitiveness arose as to who could develop the most cunning—and legally permissible—crime countermeasures. The courts became the filters through which police actions had to pass.

The decisions also coincided with President Lyndon Johnson's appointment of a President's Commission on Crime that, with its 1967 report, changed policing's national landscape while introducing such startling innovations as 911. It was the last such national undertaking and there haven't been any similar presidential initiatives since.

Innovations abounded.

In 1973, Detroit cops analyzed stick-ups to the point where they could predict, with almost the regularity of a monthly mortgage payment, the appearance of usually two "worthies" at the liquor store or chocolate shop, with guns, threats, and worse. These robbers would not only terrorize the hapless workers, but sometimes pistol-whip or shoot them.

Could the human imagination conceive of a worthier target for police aggressiveness? In the ironies of history, it came to pass that the answer, surprisingly, was yes.

The Detroit Police Department inaugurated a program with a catchy acronym—STRESS.[3] The use of sexy titles became one of the more baleful features of police ingenuity in combating street crime. The phrase stood for "Stop the Robberies, Enjoy Safe Streets." And it worked—but, alas, too well.

This stakeout unit, staffed with sharpshooters, would simply post several of these cops in the back room of the soon-to-be-robbed location.

With a dependability they might profitably have brought to more quotidian enterprises, the pistoleros would arrive and announce a hold-up. The victim would transmit the signal and fall to the floor as the cops emerged with shotguns, shouting "Freeze—Police!" The stunning surprise often paralyzed or galvanized the criminals into flight, noncompliance, or shooting at the armor-protected cops, resulting in a very unequal gun battle the criminals invariably lost.

The body count soared. The black community charged the cops with being judge, jury, and executioner. Controversy flared as a mayoral campaign loomed.

A black candidate—in this now mostly black city that whites had fled in unprecedented numbers—ran on the promise of eliminating STRESS, narrowly won over a white former police commissioner, and kept his pledge. He was reelected repeatedly.

In other cities black mayors and black police chiefs were under similar but less direct pressures, and whites frequently had more behind-the-scenes influence. The innovations being adopted—like the aforementioned stakeouts—impinged disproportionately on black male suspects.

People were getting mugged, so the cops decided to replicate the experience and disguised themselves in the fashion of likely victims. They profiled the victimization patterns and sent out cops dressed as little old ladies, drunken white businessmen, and other likely targets—and they were regularly mugged. The muggers were arrested and a disproportionate number were black males. In Minneapolis, a city with a population of less than 5 percent adult black males in the eighties, produced arrest rates of 85 percent black males. The operations leading to mugging arrests were called *decoy units*.

All of this was going on simultaneously with the relative impunity of white-collar criminals, feeding into the black community's resentment over becoming the cynosure of police operations.

DECOYS AND STRANGERS

Two incidents illustrate the fears inspired by stranger to stranger crimes of violence as well as the challenges—sometimes met and sometimes avoided—that they represent for the police.

In the first, a young woman is walking from church to the subway on a Sunday morning in July 2000, when a stranger carrying a three- or four-pound concrete block, comes up behind her, smashes her on the head—cracking her skull—and flees. She survives the attack and the police, quite properly, go with a full-court press.

The second case is a slasher who emerges from the bushes in a secluded area of Prospect Park in Brooklyn, after midnight, and attacks four males, individually, over the course of four months in early 2000. The victims suffer nonfatal but serious wounds inflicted with clubs and knives. In an area known to attract gays, the assailant may have been a "gay basher"—a familiar criminal type most likely driven by homophobia to attack homosexuals.

These cases, similar to the livery cab drivers, cry out for decoy operations that replicate the victimization patterns—setting out police under-cover liveries, with back-up team and protection, to deflect the attack from helpless civilians to armed-and-ready cops. The cases involve repeated acts of violence by recidivists on strangers, the ideal setting for decoys.

There was no talk of decoys in the latter case as everyone lapsed into the convenient bromides of more police coverage.

In avoiding the risks and complexities of decoy tactics, police exec-utives throw blue at the problem and hope it'll go away. And what are the risks of using such aggressive tactics as sending cops out dressed as victims, to get mugged, anyway? I found out as I implemented the prac-tice in Minneapolis in the eighties.

Every six months or so a group of black ministers, civil rights leaders, politicos, and other activists would ask to meet with the mayor and me. They complained bitterly that 85 percent of the muggers we arrested in decoy operations were black males, in a city where they constituted about 5 percent of the population. They demanded the operation be closed down.

The mayor looked to me to respond and I said they were mugging us, we weren't mugging them, and I wouldn't stop.

The mayor added, "I let the chief run the department and I'll look into any specific complaint of abuse if you have one." They didn't.

That would conclude the matter for another six months or so.

These were good, decent, caring people who, in my view, exerted unwise influence to eliminate a sound program. They succeeded with my successors.

In urban America, homes were burglarized and televisions and such cleaned out. The cops hit upon the notion of opening stores and get the word out that they'd buy stolen goods. A steady parade of burglars would tender their pelf, be secretly photographed and identified, and weeks later—after a large enough haul of suspects had been identified—rounded up. These were called *sting operations*.[4]

And, of course, undercover cops posing as addicts infiltrated drug operations and made large seizures and lots of arrests. This became—and is mainly alone in continuing to be—a genuine war on drugs.

The elimination of stakeouts, decoys, and stings across the police land-scape has been accomplished in stealth and silence; it is one of the gritty little pills chiefs have had to swallow, and silently. One invariable response, when the question arises, is, "Oh, yes, we certainly are still doing those," and they may even be able to produce front organizations that appear to fit the bill. The reality is that no one in American policing is pursuing really aggressive anti-street-crime tactics as the new century begins.

In trying to fight crime, police chiefs have always had to contend with the resistance of police unions and the rigidities of civil service. To these, in recent years, has been added the resistance of black leaders who resent the disproportionate appearance of black males among those swept up by decoy, sting, and stakeout units.

Of tangential interest, yet critical in establishing the importance of politics in policing, is the fact that this period, mainly the sixties and seventies, was also the high-water mark of police and federal infiltration of subversive—and sometimes only activist or unpopular—groups. The decline of aggressive anticrime operations was mirrored in the abandonment of what were called intelligence-gathering missions.

7
INTELLIGENCE OPERATIONS[1]

The NYPD had agents within the ranks of black militant organizations, fascist groups, and, to their ultimate acute discomfort, some merely energetic protest organizations that mounted large demonstrations in the fifties and sixties. It is worth noting that the aide standing closest to Malcolm X when he was gunned down was an undercover NYPD cop. The people convicted of this murder were sometime members of the Nation of Islam, which had expelled Malcolm for the charges he made about its leader fathering illegitimate children by his secretaries.[2] This hideously complex reality has still to be confronted by the black community, with the notable exception of Spike Lee's film *Malcolm X*, which faced the delicate issues courageously.

Unfortunately for the cops, some of the groups infiltrated were composed of highly literate, influential, mostly white, and vociferous protesters against such totally legitimate targets as the Vietnam War. Infiltrating criminal conspiracies was fine. Penetrating some unpopular black organizations, such as the Black Panthers or Nation of Islam, was tacitly tolerated. Surveillance over articulate, powerful, resourceful groups ultimately killed all infiltrations.

The cops had overplayed their hand and had the whole deck taken away. Infiltration, as we have seen in such disparate cases as Waco, where the FBI had an informer it didn't much trust, but not an agent; the World Trade Organization's meeting in Seattle and the mini-riots produced by a small, determined cell; and even such events as the World Trade Center bombing and other terrorist acts, is neither fashionable nor practiced.

INFILTRATIONS

The salient point here, as in the clue involving the dog that didn't bark, is that no recent prominent investigations of conspiracies were interrupted by the sort of preemptive interdictions that marked the unmasking of a number of plots, by infiltrating cops, in the halcyon days of such penetrations.

We do not awaken to stories of how cops interdicted plots through carefully placed agents among the conspirators, with the notable exception of FBI agents in the Mafia.[3]

BOSSI

I spent altogether a too long and too comfortable—i.e., nonlearning, nongrowing—a period in the Bureau of Special Services and Investigations (BOSSI), the department's spy unit: eight years, from 1957 to 1965, with one brief five-month break.

Critics called it the Red Squad.

I trooped regularly to 125th and 7th Avenue to listen to Nation of Islam (NOI) minister Malcolm X declaim against the crimes of "Goldberg."

The NOI[4] seemed a growing threat—the other side of a frightening coin that also featured George C. Wallace[5] striding onto a New York stage to the full-throated animal roar of a crowd being fed red meat.

NOI's leader, Elijah Muhammad, came to New York from his Chicago office, and his visit unsettled me. His security—the Fruit of Islam—took over an airport terminal and whisked the wispy, mystical figure off in the roar of a speeding motorcade of about twenty cars.

At the National Guard Armory, thousands of sober, suited, family-supporting, clean-cut figures patiently submitted to searches before being admitted.

Inside, the leaders breathed fire about "a white man's heaven is a black man's hell" and poured scorn on the "blue-eyed devils." In a piece of grotesque irony they called for a creation of a separate nation—of blacks—carved out of a large segment of the Confederacy. It felt a lot like the scene in *Gunga Din* when the thugee leader exhorts his minions to "kill, kill, kill."[6]

Shaken by the menace and knowing that we had a lot of information on Malcolm X—who was a campus lecture star and who might have been having affairs with the coeds—I made a proposal. I proposed sending an anonymous letter to Elijah Muhammad containing some facts about Malcolm and laced with charges calculated to drive a wedge between these two leaders.

At that time, wiretaps flowed freely. In one wiretapped conversation between Malcolm and his wife, Betty Shabbaz, she'd begun with an unrepeatable expletive and launched a tirade of accusations that melded with our suspicions. We compiled endless lists of information and gossip that wasn't being used.

BOSSI's commander, Inspector John L. Kinsella, promptly nixed the idea, and I was later grateful as hell to him for doing so. Meanwhile, it was learned that J. Edgar Hoover, unrestrained by such wholesome constraints as had been applied to me, was waging his personal vendettas with just such dirty tricks, and worse.

The whole business showed what could be discovered through outside monitoring as well as my own and others' corruptibility. In the end I was even grateful for the ceaseless supervision over me by seven hundred employees in the Minneapolis Police Department, who monitored my every action—public or private.

Years later, while serving as the chief inspector's aide, an old colleague from BOSSI came to see me. It was early 1968. He'd been transferred out to a homicide squad and needed a favor.

"I met this guy and I think he's gonna be a key player in Nixon's administration, if he gets nominated and elected, and I think he will. If I can get back to BOSSI I can be assigned to Nixon's security and work my way into their good graces."

I knew that Jack Caulfield[7] knew how to do this.

"What's the guy's name?"

The answer is as vivid in my memory today as if it happened yesterday, and I'd never heard the name. "John Ehrlichman," he said.

I arranged Caulfield's transfer back to BOSSI, and he went to Washington with Nixon. Caulfield had worked the Cuban desk in BOSSI, and was involved with the plumbers in Watergate. He brought another detective, Tony Ulasewicz—a colorful character who drank Coke for breakfast—to the capital with him and broke up the Watergate hearings with his daring and effective humor.

Tony wrote a book about his experiences.[8] He died in his upstate New York retreat in 1999 but failed to escape Watergate unscathed. Both he and Caulfield were convicted of charges that, while not major, basically changed their lives, and not for the better.

I never sought, or received, any benefit from transferring Caulfield to BOSSI but my ego was such as to derive satisfaction from the mere wielding of such behind-the-scenes influence. It was another lesson in the need to keep that monster under control. Had I resisted the temptation to wield power and perhaps reap some unspecified—and unknown—future benefit from having friends in high places, it is likely these two members of the NYPD would have been spared the tragedy of being a part—albeit a small one—of the country's biggest political scandal.

So it all looks a lot like ancient history, right? Only history has its own ways of updating itself in surprising ways.

In this case, it lay on the words of Leonard Garment, one of the few unscathed Nixon insiders, who surmised in his book *In Search of Deep Throat* that the identity of that mysterious source was Anthony John Sears, who had been a close Nixon associate.

Mr. Sears declined the honor and denied he was Deep Throat. Mr. Garment's charge was an informed guess—much in the style of the guessing surrounding *Primary Colors*, a roman à clef on the Clinton race for president. In the latter case, the author was finally unmasked as *Newsweek* writer Joel Klein.

The *New York Times*, in passing, reported that Mr. Sears had talked to only one of the Watergate reporters, Carl Bernstein, because he had "a client." It turned out this client was Jack Caulfield, which deepened the suspicion for me since I knew how Caulfield loved intrigue.

I had come to the post as key aide to the department's highest-ranking uniformed officer, the chief inspector, through a circuitous route. When John V. Lindsay was elected New York's mayor in 1965, he appointed Howard R. Leary of Philadelphia as police commissioner and Sanford D. Garelik of the NYPD as the four-star chief inspector. Garelik was the second Jew to hold the post in a very Irish Catholic agency.

Chief Garelik and I had worked together for several years, 1960 to 1963, in the notorious Red Squad—BOSSI—spy unit. We had shared many strange moments, including sitting in a car for an entire night near a plane loaded with members of the Cuban Revolutionary Council who were to be flown in to take over as Fidel Castro was overthrown following the Bay of Pigs invasion.

All I knew then was that a lot of secretive guys were scattering crisp $100 bills like confetti, whispering secrets, and moving rapidly. I didn't know they were CIA monitoring the landing. I guessed parts of it because the Spanish equivalent of "Inc." (as in incorporated) is *Cia.* (as in *compania*), and the Cubans referred to the hats as *la compania*.

Every new president was to stumble early—JFK had his Bay of Pigs and Clinton his Waco, although the latter was pretty slick in fobbing off the blame to his attorney general. Chief Garelik and I stumbled late, and incrementally.

Chief Garelik found me useful. In December 1965, I had been promoted to captain and assigned to command street cops. As I looked into their hard faces—which seemed to accuse me of descending on them from outer space—I realized I had a lot to learn about "field work." I had, by then, thirteen years in the NYPD but only two and one half months in uniform as a cop, and five months as a sergeant and none as a lieutenant, for a total experience of less than eight months in "the bag."

So, when the chief inspector came to my home in early 1966 for the first and only time, I was both impressed and honored. He wanted me to be his aide—a choice assignment of great power.

I begged to remain in uniform, citing my desperate need for field experience. The fact was that I had been sheltered from police work and urgently needed the exposure, however grim and unprestigious. We parted on the understanding I'd get some seasoning on the streets, but three days later saw my name on orders transferring me to the Office of the Chief Inspector. It was, to an outsider, high-handed, but to us it was a routine reminder of the realities of the job. I thought I'd been high-minded to forgo a shot at serious power for the sake of languishing in a thoroughly unglamorous street assignment, but the order left me no choice but to go to headquarters to serve as the key aide to the highest-ranking member of the uniformed force.

It was this assignment, which lasted over two years, that gave me the insight and experience that Police Commissioner Leary's successor, Patrick Murphy, would find useful as he took over the reins. In 1966 the chief inspector felt he needed me because of our association in BOSSI.

BOSSI prevented the bombing of the Statue of Liberty in 1964, and recovered a large cache of explosives, through the efforts of an heroic officer who had infiltrated the group. And one of Lincoln Rockwell's closest associates in the American Nazi Party at that time was another New York cop who had penetrated that organization.

No assessment of the practice of infiltration could conclude without a reference to J. Edgar Hoover. His malevolent influence over the infiltration of organizations he didn't like during his near half century at the very epicenter of American policing (1924–1972),[9] discredited many police intelligence operations. Hoover's passion for monitoring persons, developing dossiers, "black bag jobs" (where agents would break in, illegally, to plant a bug or gather evidence or materials), and infiltrating generally ultimately led to across-the-board attacks on all practices—legal or illegal, useful or not. His use of the country's premier police agency—which, in the fashion of Hitler's awakening of Germany's economic energies, must be acknowledged—for the pursuit of personal agendas and vendettas is one of the bleakest chapters in America's history. Hoover wound up being the unwitting ally of policing's most bitter and unregenerate critics. His policies lent credence to the most outlandish charges of police abuse of power, many of which—to my own shock and dismay—turned out to be true. As the new century dawns, a steady stream of revelations flow that illustrate the paranoia guiding police actions at the highest levels.

Before Hoover's actions helped lead to the dismantling of intelligence operations, the NYPD had refined the process to a high gloss of efficiency.

The process of acclimating to the suffocatingly close police environment is tacit, pervasive, evolutionary, and powerful. Not only is nothing ever said, but even those most heavily invested in acculturating the acolytes would be at a loss to lend the process a voice. Still, the bending to form continues inexorably.

The entering recruit is bombarded with messages that lead him or her to adapt and conform. Enough options exist within the matrix to allow a wide variety of directions. Straight arrows are easily accommodated, as long as they buy into the self-protective arrangements encompassed in the Code of Silence.

But molding a neophyte into the desired shape is nowhere as fascinating as in the creation of an undercover officer intended for infiltration of a subversive (i.e., engaged in criminal acts) organization.[10] The agent must have no connections to the agency whatsoever. Lists of candidates for the force who are still employed in their "civilian" jobs are culled for the features needed. For the American Nazi Party, for example, it has to be a white, preferably Nordic-looking male who has not advised those close to him of his intention to become a cop or who is alone and single in the city, and has no tendrils into the department.

The agent is approached and recruited. He is given a name similar to his real one and an apartment or other suitable residence, and either keeps his old job or, more likely, takes another that is more in keeping with his drifting into the target group. He is secretly inducted into the police department on his appointment date and his personnel file is kept by his controllers.

No one ever tells the recruit that he may wind up hauling a load of dynamite with armed and desperate plotters. The process is keyed to drift, it is a seduction. He is asked to wander over to the organization's headquarters and ask questions and get literature. He is given a cover story and whatever bona fides are needed. His penetration of the target group has to be casual, gradual, and natural.

The spy joins demonstrations and picketings and makes himself useful. There is always a need for those willing to undertake the donkey work of activism. He attends meetings and assumes a sort of generic fungibility that, after some months, gets those around him thinking he's always been there. He becomes a stalwart.

His monitors meet with him, secretly, as often as necessary and he is debriefed and coached. "Are some of the members of the organization expressing impatience over the lack of action and threatening violence? Get closer to this element, which is likely to splinter off in more violent directions."

In the event that an organization is worth several agents, none are told of the others' true identities and, indeed, the defection of one agent in the NYPD to a militant group was detected when his reports didn't jibe with those of the others commenting on the same factors. He was fired, quietly.

The agent, never having spent a day in the police ranks, cannot betray himself with jargon or similar slips. In fact, one reported to us that a "police colonel inspected our office today." He'd seen an eagle on the officer's uniform and deduced the obvious, only the NYPD didn't have colonels. This was an inspector.

The agent is coaxed to drift off with the more militant members, being careful not to take initiatives. This would constitute becoming the bête noire of undercover operations—the agent provocateur. He may even get arrested for minor violations, as members of the Bureau of Special Services were in the 1950s and 1960s.

Gradually, the undercover cop becomes a key member, and the danger lies in being given a policy-making role. One had to modestly decline being named head of the Nazi Party's New York office. It isn't hard to imagine the public reaction to the unmasking of a leader as an undercover cop.

It may not be altogether fanciful for criminal organizations to suspect that the members most faithfully participating may be the likeliest to be police agents, at least in the fifties and sixties. These were, after all, the only ones specifically and exclusively devoted to the group's efforts. Everybody else, presumably, had a day job.

The question of when to surface is rooted in the seriousness of the crime being solved. The Statue of Liberty plot was unmasked totally as our agent transported a large quantity of explosives. The identity of Malcolm X's bodyguard as a plant was revealed years after the leader was assassinated in 1965. His role actually enhanced his standing among black militants.

By the time the agent reaches such lofty eminences he has been "around forever" and woven himself deeply into the organizational fabric.

Under surveillance of organizations, some, of course, came a cropper involving such innocents as the Women's Strike for Peace. By monitoring this activist but decidedly noncriminal group of middle-class women, the police tactic of infiltration was ultimately discredited.

Had intelligence operations been guided by such principles as being aimed at articulated and documented criminal acts, not ruining the lives of leftist sympathizers, and just as promptly abandoned when legitimate leads fizzled, our nation might still have the protection of the essential investigative tool of infiltration in terrorist or political-criminal acts. Real intelligence would continue to exist as a weapon against our criminal enemies. With the increase of the terrorist risks involving biochemical, nuclear, and other mass-killing weapons, the absence of the will to infiltrate leaves us largely naked before our enemies.

If any evidence were needed to bolster the arguments supporting infiltration as an effective law enforcement tactic, we'd have to look no further than to the example of the FBI's investigation into *la Cosa Nostra*.

MAFIA[11]

Over the course of the twentieth century, organized crime grew like a cancer across the nation's landscape. Whether it was the teamsters in Detroit, booze in Chicago, gambling in Las Vegas, prostitution anywhere, or construction in New York, the Mafia was dipping its fingers into the cash registers.

Drugs, loan-sharking, traffic in stolen goods, protections, and extortions all helped to bring verisimilitude to the famous gangster's boast, "We're bigger than U.S. Steel"—at a time when that firm was the reigning colossus of American industry.

The pernicious influence of the mob was not only felt in logical and expected places—where a prudent person might tiptoe around them—but even an innocent, unfortunate encounter might produce horrendous results. The neighbor who tragically killed a mobster's son in an auto accident was made to disappear. Sammy "The Bull" Gravano's book *The Underboss* graphically describes his gruesome fate.

Organized crime became, by midcentury, a shadow government over the landscape. Hoover, anxious to keep his FBI free of possible corruption, denied the existence of what would later be routinely and frequently described by his agency as LCN (*la Cosa Nostra*) and ignored the problem. He also sedulously avoided one other potential tainter—drugs.

So the Mafia problem had to await the director's death in 1972 and still in a harness—through a series of presidential extensions of the age limit, very likely reluctantly granted—for the needed assault.

By then, the man who was to become attorney general, Robert F. Kennedy, had already crossed swords with Teamster Union president Jimmy Hoffa and been appalled and shaken by the extent of the Mafia's power over that huge union.

Freed of Hoover's constraints and impelled by Kennedy's activist initiatives, the FBI went on to score what I would call law enforcement's brightest and most important triumphs over organized crime. Plots were unearthed, murders solved, key figures turned, and a steady stream of fabled leaders led off to prison.

Most Americans think themselves safe from the Mafia's menace, since they don't encounter its members in their daily rounds. The fact is that the cost of a house, the charges in waste collection, or even the price of fish may be impacted by the mob's activities. The effect is pervasive.

The FBI's assault was marked by the most extensive, long-lasting, costly, and aggressive—yet legal—tactics ever employed. Phones were tapped, premises searched, and bugs planted. But the cutting edge of the effort centered on the FBI's infiltration of the Mob with such courageous agents as came to be the models for the TV series *Falcone* in 2000.

As the new century emerged, organized crime was the one area still the target of innovative and aggressive techniques by the police. Although the Mafia had been battered, there was growing evidence of its revitalization.[12]

Of more than passing interest is the fact that infiltration—as well as stakeouts, decoys, and stings—is not prohibited by the U.S. Constitution. Lord Acton, as well as the police's critics, had, however, been proved correct—the police, given the power to infiltrate, abused it. And thereby lost it.

The cops, to some degree, adjusted.

Since it was OK to go after druggies, they filled the prisons with addicts. "Three strikes and out" laws, where a third felony conviction automatically leads to a life or otherwise very long term, focused attention on recidivists and helped shift the system's interests onto more dangerous predators. This is acknowledged even though the overwhelming majority of mandated sentences, where the judge has no sentencing option and must decree the stated length the law requires, are judicial iron maidens that confine true judgment and fill the jails with nonviolent, less dangerous addicts. The more serious predators and menaces skate free; they are placed on probation or given suspended sentences because the cells are filled and their crimes frequently don't involve mandated sentences. We consistently read of the atrocity committed by the "just released" suspect who'd been let out to make room for hapless druggies.

And, in the war on crime, another important distinction has to be made—the difference between crimes between strangers and those between familiars.[13]

Most murders occur between people who know each other, and some lives matter more than others in our society—a sad truth no one in the system will acknowledge, but which is confirmed in every courtroom in the land every day of the year. A black murdering a white faces a much tougher future than if he'd killed another black. Check your newspaper to see which murders get the most coverage.

A great many assaults occur between related people, somehow, and even date rape involves those who know one another. Crimes between familiars don't provoke the public fear that stranger-to-stranger violence inspires.

The public reads of an awful stranger-to-stranger crime (or, more likely, gets the graphic details over the nightly TV news), gets a fright, and tries to calculate its exposure to a similar danger. If the crime involves a drunken brawl or a drug deal gone sour, or any of the other actions that suggest avoidance strategies, a sigh of relief emerges. After all, no one cares what happens to drug dealers or prostitutes.

If a way of averting or avoiding the crime is not clear—e.g., a serial rapist striking randomly, a burglar hitting the neighborhood (especially a cat burglar, the daring predator who invades your home while you sleep), or muggers striking at innocent passersby—then the public can't figure out how to be safe. That's when the police chief has a problem. That fear is going to be expressed, in pressure or in public displeasure over the failure to intercept the danger.

Americans will focus their rage on any convenient target. Failure to inform the community that there's a serial rapist out there is bound to result in a media/public frenzy when he strikes next, escalating with each event. And yet chiefs often claim they don't want to provoke a public panic when, in fact, they're really trying to avoid the pressures a disclosure is sure to bring. In such cover-ups it is the public that is deprived of the intelligence information they might use to avoid victimization.

What used to be called "intelligence" has gone the way of stakeouts, decoys, and stings—although for different reasons and under dramatically differing circumstances. Intelligence succumbed to articulate and legal assaults from the overclass and aggressive attacks on street crime (except for drug enforcement, which continues to receive everybody's blessing and support) to subtler pressures applied by a black political community that must still pay its obeisances to what is often called the "white power structure" and take its victories where, and how, it can. The civil rights struggle of the sixties lent momentum and muscle to the effort to ease the pressure on and singling out black males, as well as promoting the modest rise of black political power in some cities.

No discussion of aggressive police tactics and their decline, in both use and popularity, can ignore the contribution that police abuses—by both Feds and locals—made to the public's antipathy to many of the practices. It is the police's tendency to overplay its hand, and lapse into criminal abuses of power, that leads society to impose sometimes crippling restraints.

It is also true that many legal concepts roll trippingly off our tongues, revealing the public's ignorance. This becomes another area where public perception is at odds with reality.

8
LEGAL ISSUES

ENTRAPMENT[1]

S ome argue that sending decoy drunks, with money sticking out of
their pockets, trolling for muggers, constitutes an irresistible temptation for otherwise honest folks to reach out and take the money. They
might also believe that phony "fences" buying stolen merchandise entice
otherwise law-abiding citizens to become burglars.

Infiltrators, sullied in the public's imagination as agents provocateur,
were mostly sent packing as cops overplayed their hand in intelligence
operations.

Opposition to these practices centered on the defense of entrapment—one of the least understood and most commonly mangled notions
in all jurisprudence. The unknowing confuse facilitation with instiga-
tion, yet the hubris surrounding the public's certainty that it understands
the concept fully dies hard, if it dies at all.

The law on entrapment, however, is clear, whatever the fog attending the public's perception of its outlines. It is not entrapment to facilitate, or make possible, the commission of a crime the perpetrator intended committing. Those who make the actual perpetration of a crime
possible—by aiding those whose intent it is to do the crime—are merely

95

facilitating the accomplishment of an aim already formed in the mind of the suspect.

Those who lead an innocent, who does not intend to commit a crime, into such an offense are engaged in entrapment.

Tempting someone is not entrapment. If it were, every bank teller who pocketed the bank's cash would have a defense, as well as the rapist who blamed the victim for being provocatively clad or irresistibly attractive.

Mens rea—criminal intent—is the key element and here, as in so many other areas of criminal law, the state of the perpetrator's (the word is, unfortunately, unavoidable) mind is crucial.

An example would be if a bank robber asks a friend to accompany him to conduct some legitimate business and, in the middle of it, unexpectedly pulls a gun, announces a stick-up, picks up the money, and flees, taking his confused friend with him.

In a far subtler and much more complicated case, Patty Hearst very likely had her will overborne by weeks of captivity and emotional pressures that turned her into a sort of compliant zombie. A better defense might well have argued a form of Stockholm syndrome, where hostages come, over time, to identify with their captors and have their normal antipathies to criminals overcome by the emotional propinquity in their shared fate and danger.

This has to be distinguished from the conditioning to criminal reactions that years of blows produce. In the Stockholm syndrome there is a brief, intense period of manipulation—often involving terror—and in the production of a criminal we have hundreds of blows—racial or physical—that, over the years, produce reactive violence.

In other circumstances we label it brainwashing. It has been demonstrated that cults can effectively shape acolytes' minds with sleep deprivation, repeated messages, and sensory manipulation. The approach has launched an industry of deprogrammers, hired by a cultist's parents to counteract the effects of the brainwashing with which their child was, in a sense, mentally kidnapped.

Another example might be if a cop were to solicit an old-looking teen to buy cigarettes or liquor. An objective look at the purchaser might lead a neutral observer to conclude that it would be silly to ask such a clearly qualified buyer for identification and that the sale should just be made, rather than risk insult. In such a case the seller would be breaking the law, but it would be just as clear that he'd been entrapped since it would likely be proved that, in more logical circumstances, he had punctiliously insisted on identification before making such sales in borderline cases and had refused to sell to the unqualified.

Of a piece with the wrongheaded thinking attending notions of entrapment is the tendency to partially blame the rape victim for being sexy or scantily attired or to assign some responsibility to greedy—but innocent—victims of scams.

It would be very difficult to convince some ardent feminists that date rape does not pose the same level of threat to the public's safety that stranger-to-stranger rape does. The serial rapist endangers everyone, the date rapist endangers someone he knows and he is usually easy to identify and prosecute.

The date rapist represents a serious threat and must be severely punished. And he may well be a serial date rapist. We have to recognize that some threats are even more dangerous than others and we have been slow to recognize this important truth. The law defines both as serious felonies but punishes the serial stranger rapist more severely.

INSANITY[2]

Like entrapment, insanity is actually very rarely raised as a defense in court, despite its frequent appearances in pulp commentaries and the cherished notions of uninformed citizens.

The insanity defense requires medical proof that the defendant is incapable of understanding the nature of his actions, that he cannot distinguish between right and wrong or assess the consequences of his actions, and that he is unable to participate meaningfully in his own defense.

Serial and Rampage Killers

Serial killers[3] strike repeatedly over months or years, usually wreaking some sick vengeance against a discreet target, like prostitutes, dark-haired women who represent some hated figure from the past, or gays. Women are frequent victims.

Rampage killers[4] go berserk and kill a bunch of people in a single explosion.

The latter group constitute about one-tenth of 1 percent of killings, but the number is increasing. Rampage killers were found to be better educated, more likely to have military experience, and much more likely to commit suicide.

The outstanding features of these mass killers is the tragic lack of prevention when the air is full of warnings. Serious mental illness is the most common factor, with little or no treatment, no monitoring of medication, and no response—by authorities or families—to clear indications of danger. There have usually been threats, violent behavior, and years of rage. Unhappy job experiences sometimes trigger reactions.

There can be little doubt but that the virtual emptying and closing of secure mental treatment facilities was motivated by misguided notions. Drugs had been developed to control dangerous urges and we supposedly entered a new, enlightened age. The problem, twenty or more years later, is that too many won't take the medication and act out. It is widely estimated that one-fourth to one-third of the homeless are mentally disturbed—and these frequently have serious criminal histories.

The tragic result has been to deal with the mentally disturbed through the criminal justice system. Corrections officials estimate that there are twenty-five thousand mentally disturbed persons in city jails each year. Their presence in the prison system is wide and pervasive.

The scandalous accessibility of guns lends efficacy to murderous urges that would be a lot more difficult to satisfy in practically any other country.

If the Son of Sam, who took his orders to kill from a neighbor's dog, could be held to be fit to be tried and convicted of murder, who could not be?

The "a-ha factor" can sometimes be accompanied by a bitter aftertaste. A flash of recognition, in a key case, came to me only years after an event I hadn't understood at the time of its occurrence.

My invariable practice in the mornings, while commanding Bronx forces, was to "parooze" (in the word of one of my malaproping colleagues) the "unusuals"—narrative reports of the previous twenty-four hours' events that I should know about.

(Malapropisms abounded. One guy established a "rappaport" with his monsignor—to get his kid into Catholic school. Another spoke of the "certain aurora" about this guy. My most serious regret was not to have catalogued a larger list of these conversational jewels, which often even made their way into reports.)

One of these "unusuals" was a strange incident of the shooting murder of a young woman and the wounding of her boyfriend as they sat in a car in a lover's lane.

I summoned the detectives assigned, as I did in three or four such cases a year, usually involving something I couldn't understand or an event likely to spook the public. These sessions involved my asking questions, making suggestions, and inviting the sleuths back the following week to report on progress. These were never—whether in the Bronx, in transit, or in Minneapolis—popular events. Detectives do not enjoy being grilled.

My tenure, for dramatic reasons to be described later, was coming to an end.

I pressed the inquiry.

Finally, the detective in charge said they had the promising lead of a jealous former boyfriend living in Arizona. At last, something I could understand. I invited them back, but was, myself, gone before the issue could be seriously discussed.

Years later I discovered this had been the Son of Sam's first attack. The detectives, in the parlance of the trade, had been "pissing in my pocket and telling me it was raining."

It was many months, and beyond my power to react, before I stopped looking at the clouds on this one.

Emptying our mental institutions, ignoring the threats posed by the proliferation of guns, choosing not to see the complexities behind a hostage's psychological captivity, and other realities and states of mind all serve to demonstrate the need for legal reforms that would empower society to cope with these problems.

*   *   *

A caveat on the McNaughton Rule on insanity is in order, however.

In a courtroom, just as in every other venue in this nation, the well-heeled fare better than the impoverished.

John Hinckley successfully argued the insanity plea in his shooting of President Ronald Reagan in 1981, through the efforts of very high-priced legal talents. O. J. Simpson, in a different prosecution, was, despite being a black defendant, enormously aided by the great talents available through his considerable financial and celebrity resources.

Perhaps the final irony of the latter case is that the key point of Simpson's trial occurred during F. Lee Bailey's cross-examination of LAPD Detective Mark Fuhrmann and the possibility of his having uttered racist epithets.

The detective's claim that he was as certain of not having used the insulting word "nigger" in recent years as he was that he had secured the crucial piece of evidence in the damning circumstances he had described, inextricably linking Simpson to the murders, now became the linchpin of the entire case. If it could be proved he was lying about the *n*-word, then, by his own admission, he had to be lying about how he had secured the evidence. When Bailey produced a tape recording demonstrating the cop's recent use of the evil word, the premise of the evidence collapsed.

And it was the same Bailey who was part of the team that unsuccessfully defended Patty Hearst. Even Hearst money didn't win that one.

CONFESSIONS AND SEARCHES[5]

No one who has grown up as a Catholic, getting the absolution-induced rush of relief and unburdening that the sacrament procures, needs to be told why people confess. This instinct is strongest closest to the event and tends to be vitiated as the instinct of survival kicks in. Lawyers, like cops, understand this, and a large chunk of their value rests on so advising their clients. They know full well that weeks later, at trial, the defendant will rue his admissions.

Mafiosi don't confess because they understand, first, their interests, and, second, the ephemeral and deceptive nature of the confessional urge. They also understand how mercilessly the code is enforced. Cops understand this even better.

Cops, of course, exploit this self-cleansing tic, and really good detectives will press their questioning across the full spectrum of a suspect's possible interests until they elicit the psychic venue that might lead the target to "spill his guts."

Interrogation techniques also involve such ploys as telling the less heavily involved suspect (e.g., the nonshooter in a holdup) that the other guy had implicated him as the one who shot the victim. The use of deceptions and mendacities are not precluded by law or the Constitution. What is central is that the admissions be voluntary, demonstrably—and the cops have the burden of proof under *Miranda*. That decision, though, merely requires evidence of the voluntariness and the formula of warnings does not have to be slavishly followed if a persuasive alternative can be found. That search has proved so elusive, however, as to force the police to follow the Supreme Court's formula without variation.

Miranda

In a stunning reminder of how jealously the Supreme Court preserves its turf—against legislative or executive incursion—a relatively conservative group of justices reaffirmed the 1966 *Miranda* ruling with a thumping seven-to-two majority on Monday, June 26, 2000. The decision was written by Chief Justice William Rehnquist, a man who has been notably sympathetic to what, in code, are labeled law-and-order issues.

In addition to striking down a congressional effort to legislate *Miranda* out of existence, the court demonstrated the conspicuous difficulty of proving the voluntariness of confessions obtained in an intimidating custodial session. Thus a landmark decision that had passed five to four and launched a roiling debate that lasted for many years—including a vociferous attempt to impeach Chief Justice Earl Warren—came to rest with amazing serenity. No vindication could have been any sweeter.

The bureaucracy's propensity—and talent—for creating grotesque verbal atrocities was never better illustrated than in the verbalization of the approach, as in, "Should we mirandize him, Chief?" which continues to resonate stubbornly in my memory.

Mapp

The issue of searches is much more complex.

Decision after decision had defined and circumscribed the Fourth Amendment's protection against unreasonable searches and seizures.

What is in plain view and actionable?

When is permission to search granted?

Is the door opener who steps aside, as if to allow the police to enter, granting tacit permission to a search?

How far may a cop go to ensure his or her safety and at what point does it become intrusive—and unconstitutional?

The only sensible answer is that, since *Mapp* v. *Ohio*, the cops have had to be mindful of the constitutional restrictions and far more conscious of the limits. Where they once "hit the flat" (a raid on a residence without a warrant or permission) or "tossed" a suspect (searched a target or his vehicle without authority), after *Mapp* they had to be circumspect and correct or watch the evidence get thrown out of court.

Withal, people still confessed, searches were carried out (much more legally, though not always), and the jails swelled with prisoners not only to unprecedented heights, but at per capita rates that dwarfed the efforts of even very repressive societies.

The reality that needs to be faced is that any human institution with great power will be ineluctably driven to protect that power, be tempted to expand its uses and abuses, and work tirelessly to conceal its mistakes or worse.

The police world, prior to the Warren Court, was rife with brutality, corruption, and abuses. The Court's decisions contributed greatly to cleaning up the police act, but, as daily headlines remind us, many abuses still continue. The heightened professionalism of the police can very likely be mainly credited to a Supreme Court that, in the sixties, was reviled and whose chief justice's impeachment was loudly and prominently urged. What an ironic denouement.

If the price of liberty is eternal vigilance, then the cost of clean, effective, responsive police agencies is effective and constant monitoring. Nowhere is the contrast between corruption and cleanliness, or brutality and restraint, more vividly drawn than in the history of the nation's largest police agency.

9

NYPD

T he New York City Police Department I entered on January 1, 1953, was a brutal and corrupt agency run by many unknowing and uncaring City Hall favorites who were basking in the luxurious warmth of a still-benign and undemanding urban clime.

Crime was not a problem. Drugs occasionally surfaced and were memorialized in such movies as *The Man With the Golden Arm*, but they were anything but a pervasive threat to the social fabric. Even killings were occurring at a sedate pace of one or less a day, in a city of 8 million. By the time the number reached more than two thousand a year, in the early 1990s, the population officially numbered about a million fewer (though not actually, as a host of taxi-driving illegal immigrants slipped through the census tracts). By then, of course, the levels of hysteria over urban violence had reached crystal-shattering decibels.

The fifties were, in terms of urban violence, an age of innocence. Mayor Robert F. Wagner's (1954–65) biggest concern was expressed when he said that "every night I pray I don't awaken to a police scandal."

In the 1950s cops in plainclothes raked in monthly payments (called "pads"[1]) from illegal gambling operations while making perfunctory "stand-in" arrests of sacrificial goats. These were street people paid by numbers operators and bookies to "take the collars" the plainclothesmen needed to keep up the farce of enforcement.

103

It was generally possible to stay clean—even while participating in the cult of silence—but an assignment to plainclothes, which enforced liquor, gambling, and what were called "morals" violations, had to be avoided. There you could not stay clean, as Frank Serpico learned and made clear.

The other civilian-clad segment, detectives (never to be called "plainclothesmen," under pain of serious umbrage), were the more prestigious body. They were the sleuths who worked much in the manner of the model, Sherlock Holmes. In contrast, plainclothesmen looked in on bars to check compliance with licensing requirements, arrested bookies and numbers runners (or at least pretended to) and enforced vice laws.

Under the rubric of vice came prostitutes—those working the street and even the higher-echelon hookers working brothels or hotels (it should be remembered that District Attorney Thomas E. Dewey was catapulted into the governorship and, according to the *Chicago Tribune*, the presidency—a small error born in the wish being father to the thought— largely by his prosecution of Lucky Luciano for running what was quaintly called a White Slave Ring. Dewey, fairness requires it be said, also successfully prosecuted Murder, Inc.) Half a century later, Rudy Giuliani would also distinguish himself in another set of difficult prosecutions, this time against organized crime.

In another reflection of the times, plainclothesmen were regularly assigned to loiter in gay bars or in subway urinals nervously awaiting a sexual overture. The cops found it a highly amusing fantasy to clamp down on a gay guy with his pants down, and close-march him out of the toilet with the immortal "Youw undew awest" as their line. This was their concept of humor.

Enforcement of "public lewdness" violations was generally seen as the price that had to be paid for the monthly payments flowing from the other operations, and, frequently, as a rite of passage into the coveted halls of "the Bureau" (the Detective Division to outsiders). Plainclothesmen gritted their teeth and collared gays, and hoped for a graduation into the much more prestigious realm of the detectives.

The sleuths had their occasional "scores" (one-time gains from favors done in the course of an investigation, if not an outright bribe) and less frequent, modest pads, typically from "bucket of blood bars" that generated a lot of crime and violence. But it was possible, unlike the plainclothes units, to eschew participation and function straightforwardly and honestly. Detectives could spend their time solving crimes, without participating in any form of corruption, but, as with everyone else, they could not betray their brethren.

On one point there was organizational unanimity—the scorn and contempt felt for uniformed assignment. The fact that the police uniform was referred to as "the bag" said it all. Old-time cops who spent their careers in uniform were labeled "hairbags."

Corruption at this lowest level among hairbags was more moochery than bribery, though both wrong and dangerous.

ARGOT

Promoting the sense of having been admitted to an exclusive fraternity, while widening the chasm between insiders and outsiders, the Runyonesque characters in the ranks developed their own argot.

Orders didn't come from headquarters but from "the brass," "downtown." The boss wasn't grumpy; he either "had his tight pants on" or, less delicately, "had the rag on." And if he was really angry at someone, he had a "hard-on" for him. But it was forbidden protocol for you to have a "hard-on" for anyone because of the homoerotic implications. People didn't have a grudge, but a "beef." And reconciliation meant "squaring the beef." The lieutenants sent to catch you in "the coop" were "shooflies" and the hard-working cops "did straight eights."

You didn't work in the Forty-first or Seventy-third Precinct, but in the "four one" or "seven three," and it wasn't a precinct but "the house."

You didn't throw a citizen's crime complaint in the wastebasket; you "canned a squeal" and criminals were "wrong" and "nabbed" or "pinched," and were not acquitted or convicted but "skated" or "went to the can."

The sick and injured were "aided cases" and bodies were always "DOAs."

You very quickly learned how very prickly humans become on the question of notification.[2] A uniformed cop at the door is every parent's nightmare. Cops are the bearers of bad news and, in the handings off of these events, they frequently botched the assignment. You don't want the family to learn of the loved one's tragedy from the media or any other third source. The notification has to be sensitively handled, and sensitivity is no police agency's strong suit.

Notification became one of the most serious sources of grief—not just for the targets, but for the deliverers of such sad messages. Cops frequently flubbed the assignment by delivering the news insensitively; by delaying or failing to deliver it altogether, or by making a mistake.

Language was coded—to exclude outsiders and to develop the sense of being an insider. The point was to develop camaraderie.

Criminals weren't armed, but "packing." You weren't a cop, but "in the job."

Your sister, wife, or mother was a "doll," but a lot of the rest of them were "pros."

The height of naïveté would be to be accused of thinking that "the job is on the level." Ethnic, racial, sexual, or national slurs had to be explicitly forbidden because of their tendency to proliferate and spill out into public scrutiny. Every agency had its model code, which could be trotted out to impress the gullible, but only a determined few actually enforced it.

You weren't temporarily assigned to an event, you "flew." You didn't ride in a radio car; you had "a seat" and you acknowledged messages, and spoke, in such codes as "ten-four." It wasn't a badge but either a "tin" (for cops) or a "gold shield" (for detectives). You didn't get a soft assignment, you were "on the tit." Detectives were "sleuths" and those who had no education but a lot of experience had gone to "soup school." Patrons were "hooks" and "rabbis" and solemn agreements were "contracts." And you didn't respond to a call for help, you were "on a run."

Cops lapsed naturally into a secret language that encompassed all of their activities and views. Though technically English, it was used in unexpected ways to defy outside comprehension. It had the effect of reinforcing exclusiveness and facilitating communication. It was the language of a secret society.

The etymology might remain a mystery, as it did in some cases to me, but the meaning was always unmistakable to all of us, and foggy to the world.

Cops ate and drank "on the arm" (gratis) and performed little favors in return, responding, on a priority basis, to calls in these bars and restaurants and ejecting obstreperous patrons. If yours was the other call, you'd wait. That was the problem with free meals: the bistros granting them received high-priority response treatment and *your* problem wouldn't.

By the time I reached Minneapolis I had learned through hard personal experience how much cheaper it was to pay your way. Often, when my wife and I dined out—which was very frequently—a restaurant owner would recognize me and the waiter would say we were his guests. I'd go over to the owner, thank him for his gracious generosity and tell him or her that my policy was to pay or I would not return. It was good for citizens to see me wait my turn in line and pay my bills—just like everyone else.

This usually worked except when we'd be forced to eat an unwanted dessert some owner insisted on sending us.

By way of illustrating the consequences, a vice squad lieutenant came to see me one day. He'd been enforcing late-service violations in bars and at one of them the owner had said, "But the chief and his wife eat and drink here all the time"—the clear implication being "on the arm." "What did you do?" I asked. He gave the right answer: "I gave him a summons for serving liquor after hours." I never went back to that place.

Drinking often assumed mythic proportions. I remember being on switchboard duty when a citizen called to report a uniformed cop lying, stretched out, on the sidewalk on Tenth Avenue, in what is today's gentrified Chelsea neighborhood. It was then, in the fifties, a series of flats for longshoremen.

Sure enough, "Big Jack" had overimbibed.

We sent a patrol car to pick him up and deliver him to the station house. When he sobered, the understanding captain lectured him sternly and assigned him to the cushy job of precinct "broom." As such, he would attend to such domestic chores as cooking for the crew, serve as warder to the prisoners in the holding cells (a key duty was to prevent suicides since a lot of guys brought in drunk would, on sobering, be overcome with contrition and attempt to hang themselves, even though belts and shoe laces had been removed before they'd been locked in), make sure the desk officer had his "flute" (a pint bottle the local bartender would obligingly fill with whiskey), and sweep the building and keep it clean (hence the sobriquet).

The job was Jack's as long as he remained sober and he knew better than to risk it. The building, though, shook to his thunderous and uncontrollable hacking smoker's cough.

Cops sauntered into theaters "flashing the tin" and extended professional courtesies to their brethren—not ticketing a car that had a police union card in the window or issuing a moving violation, even in egregious cases, to someone on the job.

Surprises abounded. Cops had to try the locks of stores on the beat and sometimes the owners forgot to lock up. A shopkeeper's "open door" often served as an invitation to all the cops working to loot the place. Canny supervisors, anxious to avoid an owner's beef or a "squeal" (a formal complaint of a crime) frequently stationed a uniformed cop outside, while the owner was summoned to lock the place, as a way of preventing a law enforcement run on the merchandise.

Bereaved families complained of missing cash and jewelry after cops were ordered to guard the body of someone who'd died alone, until removal by the medical examiner. Sitting in the room with an outstretched, bloated corpse on the floor, with an eerie purple ribbon of blood and vomit leading from its mouth, was part of my initiation.

Another occurred when a horse-drawn fruit and vegetable peddler on my beat beckoned me into a hallway. There he casually pressed two one-dollar bills into my hand. I stuttered in apology, confusion, and shock as I handed it back. The peddlers never had licenses but I had no interest in outraging the horde of Italian ladies who made a social ritual of patronizing his stall, so I left him alone.

And so, cops rutted about for the pickings and accommodated their own system. They "cooped" (slipping into a favored spot on the beat for a sleep) after the patrol sergeant had provided the required "see" (an exchange of salutes). Popular supervisors drove by early on the midnight to 8 A.M. (late) tour to enable the cops to retire early. Or they paid a couple of bucks to the clerical man, who drew up the daily assignments, for a "seat" in a patrol car that promised some excitement and companionship, especially on the late tour. Cops love to sit in patrol cars, sipping coffee, smoking (more then than now), and bullshitting with their partners. Strong bonds are formed.

Boredom was the real enemy. The great cops suffered through this and eagerly awaited the spikes of excitement that punctuated their lives. The rest of us had long before lost interest. That police work is ultimately boring is just another of the dissonances between myth and reality. It was a world of "fins" and "pounds" ($5, in obeisance to the U.K.'s currency, worth almost that in the postwar era) or "sawbucks" ($10), while detectives earned the occasional "hat" ($10 to $25) through favors and accommodations. More serious breaches were bribes involving larger sums.

The many nonplaying grass eaters kept their heads down and gained acceptance, without trouble. As many of the meat eaters put it, it increased their shares. Such aloofness, however, was not permitted in the systemic corruption of the plainclothes squads and all were required to close ranks behind any brother officer accused, no matter what. The department, in the cyclical way of these things (widespread scandals hit the NYPD with stunning regularity every twenty years or so, as if the practitioners had to lapse into levels of complacency and wretched excess to get caught by a reluctant officialdom) had, in the fifties, just emerged from the twin shocks of Harry Gross and business cards.

In the first, Gross,[3] a big-time bookmaker, was caught and spilled his guts as to police payoffs. A raft of retirements, firings, imprisonments, and the inevitable accompanist—suicides—followed.

In traffic enforcement a mysterious practice came to light. Cops were giving trusted friends signed business cards, which they could give to a cop making a traffic violation stop. The cop would take the card (and of course not issue a summons) and call the cop listed, who either had or would collect a $5 or $10 payment (this was in the late 1940s and early 1950s) from the friend and give it to the cop who made the stop, keeping a small commission.

The department's response once the dust settled (it seems one always has to wait for this process before undertaking change) was to forbid the use of business cards for many years. By the time they were reinstituted, to enable the detectives to furnish complainants with their names and numbers, no one could remember why they'd been banned.

Curiously, the malfeasance even extended to exploits.

Supervisors would often mutter "put me in" when a legitimate act of heroism was being written up, to secure a medal. This meant creating the fiction of the commander's presence during the incident when he very likely was home in bed at the time. This resulted in the laughable vision of this or that "most decorated police hero" being named to higher office or even being elected.

An array of enameled ribbons over a police officer's badge could usually be taken as the sign of an active cop, but the same collection over a commander's inspired only skepticism.

So, corruption was pervasive, yet avoidable. What was not was the requirement of silent acquiescence.[4]

The police commissioners appointed in the years following the shocking disclosures were lawyers and prosecutors—but outsiders in the labyrinth that was then the NYPD. It was tantamount to naming the archbishop of Canterbury pope. However talented he might be, he wouldn't be likely to penetrate the inner workings of an agency whose tendrils and connections make Byzantium look like Disney World. It was a conundrum—on the one hand you had unknowing strangers trying to master the arcane ways of a virtually unfathomably secretive agency and, on the other, knowing up-from-the-ranks insiders who were, at the very least, tainted by silent complicity in a system that demanded that they go along.

How to resolve it?

In my experience, reform had to come through knowledgeable insiders who lay in wait—much in the manner of Cardinal Roncalli's metamorphosis into Pope John XXIII (1958–63).

The police have great power and, like all humans, are tempted to abuse it. The abuses can be broadly described as brutality and corruption.

10

POLICE PROBLEMS

BRUTALITY

Nowhere is the public's ignorance of police reality more pronounced than in the question distinguishing between legitimate, legally applied force and police brutality.[1]

Cops are the only workers authorized to kill and to employ all necessary levels of violence below that crest. The law is logical. You kill to save life, yours or another's, and you use whatever force is needed in the circumstances to overcome resistance. Anything more—an extra blow or shooting when the danger is past—is brutality.

Individual ad hoc incidents of excessive or unnecessary force will probably never be totally erased, but they can be reduced. Systemic abuse, as we learned in the NYPD, can be eliminated.

My first real encounter with systemic brutality came as I was translating in a Hispanic murder investigation. Someone had slit a janitor's throat from ear to ear. When I got to the apartment vestibule, children were playing and sliding in the victim's blood.

The investigation was removed to the local precinct where a clutch of witnesses awaited questioning. All were Spanish speaking. A high-ranking detective led the inquiry, sitting across from the witness, with me discreetly to the side. He'd look right into the eyes of the Puerto Rican witness and bark out his questions.

After three or four witnesses, we came upon one that seemed more promising than the others, either as the perp or as an eyewitness. The official asked and the witness answered.

Without warning the supervisor's leg came up, and in a lightning piston move, struck the witness flush in the face with the bottom of his shoe, sending him half flying across the room.

As the shaken guy bloodily made it back to his seat the official casually, all the while looking at him and never at me (I was merely an annoying instrument), said, "Tell him he's lying."

The questioning continued. Finally, an old lady was called who was gasping for air and clutching her chest. This spared her nothing and, midway through her questioning, an item dropped noisily from inside her dress to the floor. It proved to be the linoleum knife that had done the damage; she was protecting a male relative, not the hapless target of the official's ire. The killing had occurred over a tenant's refusal to pay for a hallway window he'd broken in a drunken stupor, and the victim's vehement insistence that he replace it. They fought and the janitor lost.

Case closed.

I left that place feeling good because I'd helped, however tenuously, to solve the case, but with the added sense of unease that haunted me thereafter. How could we fashion a system in which rookies were not shaped to accept such atrocities?

I found myself evolving in unanticipated says. Always a physical coward, I wondered how I'd respond to danger. I found that the badge and uniform—and the weight of expectation—gradually conditioned me to accept my role of having to go to things other citizens fled. It wasn't even as if there was a choice, and it was never an item of interest or discussion within the ranks.

My squeamishness was tempered by the blood and gore that is part of every cop's life—not to mention the autopsies the department was thoughtful enough to assign me to attend. The sound of a whirring saw cutting into a skull makes more of a psychic impression than the same noise in a lumber yard, with different effects on the appetite, too.

Besides the sights and sounds, there were the smells. I recall even my hardened partner covering his face with a handkerchief and heaving over a very ripe, messy lady lying naked across the sheets.

Gradually, repeated exposures and the weight of expectation inured us to the awfulness, enabling us to do our jobs. It seemed the perfect psychic equivalent of a prostitute's need to emotionally distance herself from her encounters.

By the time I left policing, as chief of the Minneapolis Police Department thrity-six years later, my unspoken assessment of my tenure contained the satisfying thought that members of that agency were not forced into the sort of system I'd entered. I had made it clear that the agency was run for the benefit of those trying to do their jobs in good faith and kept my foot firmly on the necks of the thumpers and moochers that constitute 1 to 2 percent of every police force. The problem is that this tiny faction often sets the tone. I never doubted that had I, as chief, the power to fire only this tiny minority, the rest would perform miracles of devoted and efficient service. The paralyzing strictures of civil service tenure precluded any such weeding out of even the demonstrably unfit— or oftentimes even criminal.

Had I come that great distance—from rookie to chief—unscathed? No.

I had, over the years, not only occasionally benefited from the protective cover-ups of my superiors, but participated in things that made me deeply ashamed and which, this not being the confessional, I have no interest in revealing the details of, even as I am compelled to acknowledge their existence. It is also important to acknowledge the hypocrisy inherent in such actions even as I confess that I saw the need to stop somewhere and risk the moral inconsistency and ambiguity inherent in such choices. The only option I could see—to continue in the downright sinful participation—was worse.

The evolution from clean to tainted to clean was tortured and lengthy, but by the time I reached the threshold of supervisory responsibilities, I had firmly decided to become a totally honest reformer.

It would be tempting but dishonest to blame the system. My introspection led me to discover my own complicity, but I determined that I'd shape or help fashion a system that would be open, predictable, and legal, and one where people were punished for transgression.

Resolving the hypocritical dilemma of punishing people for things

I'd been allowed to get away with required a hard, silent swallow—the existence of which is revealed here for the first time.

As a detective I saw myself and my colleagues refuse to process one particular sergeant's prisoners because of their conditions, actual or prospective. Those that this Jimmy Cagney type brought in were either bloodied and mangled or soon would be. We all found things to busy our-selves with or went out on patrol or to interview witnesses whenever he came in with what would, nevertheless, usually be a scumbag or asshole by anyone's reckoning. He could, however, process and question the pris-oner himself even though it was our job to assist him. Yes, we should have confronted him, but no one ever even came close to doing it.

REFORM

I came to see brutality as far the easier problem to solve and frankly despaired of taking on corruption. My best hope lay in sequestering it to identifiable areas of police operations and effectively quarantining it. Corruption looked too deeply embedded to be uprooted and society, or someone, seemed to want us to go after vice (prostitution and homosex-uality in the parlance of that day), liquor violations, and gambling.

An intrepid police reformer proved me wrong and taught me a lesson I never forgot. Patrick Murphy, over thirty quick months as police com-missioner in the early seventies, showed us all what a determined leader could do to clean up the NYPD. He took on the corruption issue, after we had, earlier, battled brutality.

Systemic brutality—the sort of third-degree grilling, egregious thumpings, and other highly visible, easily detected, and protected excesses—was something I thought we could stop. With a reform mayor elected in 1965 and a brand-new, unstained police administration led by the strange police commissioner from Philadelphia—whose claim to the job was that he'd "learned to live with a civilian review board[2] there"—the issue was joined.

We, the new mayor, police commissioner, and chief inspector—my boss—were, in 1966, ready to implement outside review. In this case, as in so many public controversies, the rhetoric concealed some complex truths.

The public debate centered on the creation of a civilian review board that would shift oversight of brutality from the police to outsiders.

As aide to the man making the key internal decisions at the time, and over whom I then exercised substantial influence—I served as a sort of Svengali to his Trilby—I worked to fashion an approach to brutality. I knew then, and continued to believe for many years thereafter, that no outsider or group of outsiders could really control the inner workings of the NYPD. Even as canny and experienced a cop and police executive as Philadelphia's chief couldn't begin to grasp the New York maze as he became a silent partner in our tortured effort.

The sad fact is that no civilian review board has successfully curbed police abuses, anywhere. Nevertheless, we plowed forward and the police union—then beginning to grow in political power, capturing newly won dues check-off monies and able to hire real public relations and legal talent—pushed for, and got, a referendum. Its scare tactics, featuring a high-powered ad campaign depicting handcuffed cops, carried the day by a three-to two-margin.

It looked like a rout, but I was secretly pleased. Out of the ashes of political defeat we could fashion a really effective internal system of control, and did. We called it the Civilian Complaint Review Board, but it was staffed entirely by cops. The difference now was that careers turned on the results and the body was staffed with a huge group of ambitious young captains whose fate was in my boss's hands.

They got the message, and quick. A few examples soon conveyed the determination of the administration. Police brutality, in terms of the sort widely condoned and covered up—sometimes even joined in by higher-ups—vanished.

If someone got beaten up in a station house, the desk officer was called on the carpet along with those directly involved. Precincts with poor records of compliance lost their commanders—a career-shattering demotion in most cases. Everyone now knew that incidents of police violence—anywhere—would be investigated.

CANNING

Tied to this effort was reforming crime statistics by relabeling categories.

Burglaries had been misclassified as malicious mischiefs and robberies as lost properties. These scalings down kept the crimes off the FBI's crime index, which calibrated, exclusively, murders and manslaughters, rapes, robberies, burglaries, thefts, auto thefts, assaults, and arson. Any crime that could be slipped from these categories brought the index down, reflecting crime-fighting efficiency on the mayor and the police chief. This practice—fudging the figures to look good—was also hallowed by another wonderful label. It was dubbed "canning"—as in crunching the "squeal" and tossing it in the wastebasket. Cooking the books was not the exclusive province of crooked accountants.

The FBI, of course, knew police departments juggled the books and could easily, with a few spot checks, verify their suspicions. But J. Edgar Hoover prized his standing among the chiefs, whom he courted with the same assiduity and skill he displayed in his dealings with the federal government (only probably with more affection; he seemed to genuinely like the chiefs who fawned all over him and who regularly opened their departments to his uses and sent their members, proudly, to his FBI Academy[3]), and tolerated the practice. The only caveat he'd offer would be a pious "we only collect the figures, we don't vouch for them."

Once the precinct commanders saw we meant to get honest crime figures (a few noncompliers lost their commands in highly visible demotions) crime statistics soared, proving the mayor's point that prior figures couldn't be trusted and that we could now proceed with reforms tabula rasa.

Burglaries and robberies more than doubled. Murders and auto thefts remained roughly the same—although even these could be coaxed into accidents, natural causes, "loans," and other misadventures—and rape continues to be underreported, for many societal reasons, to this day. Thefts were easily categorized as other events—when they were counted at all—and arson (it was, after all, the eve of the blazes that would consume the Bronx and parts of Brooklyn and even Manhattan) was still a nonstarter.

The cops, always expert at reading the tea leaves that clearly meant business, readjusted and complied.

With no one punished for higher crime figures and encouraged to report astronomical rises, and with cops being punished for thumping, systemic brutality and "canning" came to an end, even as individual actions continued ad infinitum. Ad hoc and isolated incidents of police brutality continue to exist, in every agency, to this day. The temptation to look good continues to lure ambitious mayors and chiefs, many of whom are not shy about mangling crime statistics.

The connection between honest crime figures and eliminating brutality seemed clear to me. Lying about the precinct incidence of crime made precinct commanders look good—falsely. In such a hypocritical system other abuses would surface.

An enlightening sidelight for me was when someone asked if I'd written the order demanding honest crime figures. I had.

"I knew it," the guy said, "because I couldn't understand a word of it."

Inwardly, I swelled with pride over my sesquipedalian talents, a reaction that makes me wince with embarrassment today as I contemplate how bureaucratese and dead Latinates crippled whatever talents I might have developed as a writer. If brevity was the soul of wit and simplicity and clarity its very sinew, I had furnished the very antithesis of communication in that orotund work.

As we demonstrated our willingness to punish those still "canning," the order was followed to each polysyllabic letter.

In the chief's office I watched and learned such lessons as that it wasn't as easy to secure compliance when policing large-scale problems as it was in getting honest crime figures. Mass brutality, such as occurred in dealing with street riots, the 1968 Columbia University bust, and such, would never be successfully tackled by anyone, anywhere. Most chiefs learn, to their chagrin, that their power extends only to "go" or "no go" decisions and, once loosed, cops become just another mob—albeit an armed one—battling the foe.

By the end of 1966, the NYPD had been, in terms of protected and covered-up acts of brutality and in the fudging of crime figures, reformed.

Plainclothesmen were, to the dismay of some daily communicants high up in the ranks, reassigned and gays were no longer enticed into anonymous sex and arrested. The policy had deep roots in a Catholicism that exercised extraordinary power over the inner workings of the agency. The cardinal's residence was called "the Power House" by NYPD members.

Arresting gays—in New York and Minneapolis—had more to do with reflexive homophobia than crime fighting. One of the casualties of the previous enforcement program was, sadly, the subway toilets that never reopened. They'd been the centers of same-sex trysts and the sense of horror with which such images were greeted led the administrators to consign millions to the discomforts of distended bladders rather than risk such immoralities. Administrative convenience—or perhaps prejudice—won over the people's interests.

The issue would shift from condoned, widely practiced, and covered-up atrocities to such painful, if isolated, incidents as the Abner Louima sodomizing and the more ambiguous Diallo case.

THE DIALLO VERDICT[4]

New York State's onetime chief judge Sol Wachtler contributed one of the memorable phrases to jurisprudence before being hauled off to prison himself for a lurid scandal involving threats against his onetime mistress and her family: "You can indict a ham sandwich."

That's it, and in this scornful assessment is buried the insider's knowledge that grand juries are just a bunch of average citizens engaged in trying to please the prosecutors who do things in what is called an ex parte; in other words, only the prosecution's case is usually heard.

In the Amadou Diallo case four white cops shot at a black male forty-one times, striking him nineteen times and killing him.

It was clear that the cops were suspicious of Diallo's behavior. They were investigating drug trafficking in the area. In the confusion one of them apparently stumbled, another shouted "gun," and one of them fired. This led the others, who thought they were in a gun battle, to start shooting spastically.

In the adrenaline rush of these things, events happen in seconds. There are few police executives in America who can't imagine a gun battle between two guys in a phone booth in which thirty shots are fired and no one is hit.

Prosecutors, especially experienced ones such as those in the Bronx, are only too well aware of how hard it is to convict cops of anything, much less something they didn't do. Petit juries (those at trial) love cops and believe them.

So what happened here?

I waited patiently while the analyses poured forth but nobody got it.

The Diallo case failed because a prosecutor, black himself, succumbed to the black community's demand for a murder charge. It was a case of a community getting what it asked for and a sobering reminder that granted wishes sometimes turn out unexpectedly.

So, as the Reverend Al Sharpton[5] shouted "murder," District Attorney Robert Johnson accommodated and had the cops indicted for a crime they didn't commit. He was a defense attorney's dream: Any murder charge would have required an intent to wrongfully kill from the outset.

Of course the cops were wrong. Of course racism was involved. Of course they should be convicted of something. But does anyone really think the cops set out to deliberately and wrongfully kill Amadou Diallo? This was the threshold.

Manslaughter would have been the appropriate charge. Indicting them for murder enabled the defense to focus on an insupportable charge.

The FBI has the power to investigate these cases as violations of federal law in which the victim is deprived of his right to safety. The Feds may or may not take the case. They're under intense pressure to do so but there's a lot of weight from the other side, too.

The Justice Department's best hope was to hold that the prosecution was fatally flawed from the first because of the DA's indicting the cops for an unprosecutable crime.

On January 31, 2001, in the depths of a long, cold winter—in which riots were unlikely—the Feds decided not to prosecute the cops. A civil suit would now proceed, for a total of $61 million in compensatory and punitive damages.

So, I'll add a postscript to Judge Wachtler's clever observation. Sure, you can indict a ham sandwich—but can you convict it?

Was this a case of brutality? Perhaps not, but it was certainly a criminal misapplication of force.

There were no articulable grounds (which is to say, evidence) justifying the use of any force—much less deadly action. It is not a crime to reach for your wallet, to misunderstand a cop's instructions, or to fail to comply with them, in most cases. This was an example—as was the Patrick Dorismond case—of aggressive antidrug tactics gone haywire.

The cops were much too quick to shoot. They must be forced to wait—however dangerous this becomes—for the evidence on which they can base the use of lethal force. It is not too far-fetched to hold that, had the victims been white, the cops might have waited the essential split second before firing.

This is a tough call—demanding that cops assume the risk inherent in holding their fire until clear and unequivocal evidence of danger is presented—but it must be made.

Too many police executives turn a blind eye to shootings triggered by a "sudden, suspicious, menacing" movement; a "flashing object that looked like a knife or gun"; and similar police boilerplates for the remission of sins.

With the elimination of widespread brutality, such as occurred in the murder investigation cited earlier featuring the kicking incident, the issue of corruption was shifted to the back burner from which it would not be moved for five years, until the advent of the Knapp Commission[6] in 1971.

CORRUPTION

Mayor John Lindsay could be said to have had three distinct phases in his eight years at City Hall, 1966–73. Elected in two fractionalized contests, he never reached 40 percent of the votes cast, yet won both because of the strength of opponents who managed to split the other 60-plus percent of the ballots. A classic limousine liberal (rich, Republican, concerned with social issues) he might be described as patrician if one were confined to a one-word appraisal.

Worried over urban unrest (it was his aide who attempted to dissuade Serpico with the expression of concern over getting the cops riled up "with a long, hot summer ahead" when he tried to get City Hall to address his corruption worries), he spent the first few years listening to brilliant, young, often Ivy League aides who spun off innovations and daring programs with dizzying virtuosity.

Gradually, however, the Sisyphean nature of big-city problems in the 1960s intruded, making the glamor of national office seem more attractive. Lindsay's abortive search for a wider platform came a cropper when a plane flew over Miami beaches with the trailer "Lindsay Spells *Tsouris*" (meaning "trouble" in Yiddish). So concluded the second phase, with a figurative, rather than literal, plane crash.

By the final years of his second—and last—term, Lindsay seemed to have shifted his focus to running the city and seemed to have discovered the secret—appointing outstanding people as his commissioners. Fiorello La Guardia, a much earlier yet revered predecessor, had brought men and women into these key jobs whose names—Robert Moses, Newbold Morris, Anna Kross, and many others—would become synonymous with dazzling achievements.

Now Lindsay moved to get effective executives into commissioners' chairs. Nowhere was this more dramatic than in the NYPD.

The mayor's mysterious Philadelphia choice left on a cruise after almost five years of shifting a power he didn't seem to have the inner-working knowledge to wield himself among key subordinates, leaving a cryptic sort of "I quit" note on his desk as the only notice. This Byzantine act was totally characteristic of a fabled survivor who would exit in a manner that made him totally inaccessible to inquiry, especially from the press. Indeed, it was his invariable practice to mutter, "Well, the country boy's still here," to those who seemed to be asking how long he could survive. By playing off one faction against another, Howard Leary had survived.

Into this void stepped Patrick V. Murphy in the fall of 1970.

Murphy called me before he was sworn in and asked to have lunch. I was then a midlevel executive in charge of the nascent 911 operation.

Rarely did toughness come so innocently wrapped. Murphy was slim, slight, pasty-faced, with a naïf's doe eyes, and spoke in such soft, diffident tones as to invite a genuine effort to catch the words. The impression was of an altar boy who'd just shed his vestments to see the visitor.

Murphy asked a lot of tough questions, mostly about the cast of characters he was about to inherit. He'd grown up in the NYPD but left it to head police agencies in Syracuse, Detroit, and D.C., and briefly to serve as President Johnson's advisor on criminal justice. He'd lost a bit of touch and knew the importance of rediscovering the labyrinths and connections.

I had a really passionate interest in the NYPD, an agency I loved and at whose center I had been for years. My "rabbi" had gone on to political office and I was, in 1970, now on my own again and among foes. I always ardently studied the NYPD's workings and, especially, the people running the machinery. Although far from the centers of power then, I probably knew as much as only three or four others in the department and gave Murphy the full benefit of my views, knowing full well he'd also consult others.

Murphy took over and I returned to my aerie. I would have little to do with him over the next six months as he assembled his inner circle.

The new police commissioner began his reforms and found the political muscle he needed in the breaking maelstrom of Serpico's revelations and the interest of such pillars as the *New York Times*. His target was, specifically, corruption.

With a tough crew of aides, Murphy devised insanely clever schemes to detect dishonest cops. They basically replicated the decoy experience internally. These were called "self-initiated integrity tests" (i.e., they were not predicated on a citizen's complaint but simply randomly selected cops to be tempted into routine misdeeds, with the results widely publicized).

Undercover supervisors were turning "found" wallets, with cash, over to cops. At first, few were turned in by these cops, who kept the proceeds. As they were unmasked and severely punished, the others shaped up with alacrity.

Narcotics sites were salted with cash to see whether the investigators would faithfully inventory the full amounts. Even a cursory glance at such places as Columbia and Mexico will demonstrate that the greatest current danger of corrupting the police comes from drug dealings that involve huge sums in untraceable cash.

Shops' open doors, formerly the sites of police lootings, were monitored and filmed with dramatic footage that led to a steep price paid by errant cops. The videotaped sight of cops carrying a building's contents to their radio cars exposed a problem that everyone knew about, but no one had confronted head on.

Murphy promoted me and put me in charge of planning, where I served for six months. Soon I had the most extraordinary concentration of talent in the department marching up to the police commissioner with great and neglected ideas. Under his predecessors, who were anything but activists, the most certain entombment of troublesome notions was to "send it to planning for analysis," kind of like sending a resume to "human resources."

In planning, a gifted covey of cops laboriously collected by my predecessors had been preparing impressive documents that were left to gather dust: an army of talented sophists. Now we blew the dust off and sent them up for implementation. These buried notions became the catalysts for progress.

A coconspirator of mine, Neil Behan, with whom I studied, in whom I confided, and who was the only associate I plotted with—regularly meeting with him so we could make personnel decisions and decide on programs to support or scuttle—had gathered a formidable array of the department's talent pool in the Planning Division. These greyhounds had been employed in the futile chase of a metal rabbit called "further study." They'd come up with dazzling programs and innovations, only to see them founder on the shoals of downtown's native caution.

Now an existentialist, Murphy, who would embrace new ideas, was occupying Teddy Roosevelt's desk and, ironically, Behan was not to enter the promised land. His having been a favorite of Muphy's predecessor made him suspect to Murphy.

As I chatted with Behan about the organization that I'd be taking over from him he concentrated on the personnel—many of whom would, in later years, rise to the very top of the department and even lead other city agencies.

"Watch out for that kid, though. If you turn around he'll take over your desk."

He pointed to Lawrence W. Sherman, a twenty-two-year-old Quaker who was discharging his conscientious objector duties by working with the police.

I quickly learned Larry was a brilliant guy and devoted myself to using, and ultimately serving, his great talents. Over the next clutch of decades I was to see him develop into America's foremost criminologist, conducting experiments in New York and Minneapolis that changed American policing profoundly.

It is because of Sherman that men who batter women are arrested.[7] It was he who laid the theoretical scientific foundations of community policing and it was he who conducted scores of experiments, on the street, that enabled us to test new approaches and evaluate old ones.

Neil Behan, a gifted executive, will also be remembered as the character who urges Serpico to attend a religious retreat in the memorably eponymous film. Behan's career was only temporarily derailed and he rose to three-star rank under Police Commissioner Codd and served as the longtime chief of the Baltimore County, Maryland, police. It is he who was shocked, years later, when I coaxed him into not taking Daryl Gates on when the LAPD chief criticized an organization whose board Behan chaired. I'll describe this incident in detail later.

I rapidly became a superannuated supernumerary and went to see Murphy to ask for a field assignment. He promptly sent me to Harlem and I happily left for the sort of street experience I'd sorely missed in the mostly cushy jobs I'd held. I was in charge of the three most violent precincts in Manhattan and reveled in the daily challenge of policing what we called "busy shops," the neighborhoods of greatest need of police services—from crimes to the emergencies afflicting the poor and the excluded. The numbers racket was, then, probably the most significant employer.

A boyhood friend was one of the plainclothesmen assigned to my division. He knew me as "Tucho," the nickname I'd carried over from Spain, and comfortably lapsed into its use despite the separation of five ranks between us.

"Billy," I said, "I know you can't give me any details, but would I be making a mistake if I replaced all of the plainclothesmen in the division?"

"No, Tuch, you would not."

Years earlier we'd been playing stickball on Brooklyn's Eleventh Street, now we were obliquely discussing the sort of plainclothes corruption that would soon shock Frank Serpico.

That was the whole conversation, and I swiftly returned all of these enforcers of the gambling laws back to uniform and replaced them with new faces. I was certain I'd only short-circuited the connections for a brief while but I bought a bit of time and hoped.

HARLEM

My brief stint in Harlem in 1971 was intriguing for its exposure to a culture I had only briefly encountered in 1954, when I spent a fair amount of time working on youth gangs there. Now I commanded the Twenty-fifth, Twenty-eighth, and Thirty-second Precincts.

I had a black subordinate, Thomas Mitchelson, who would later skip over me and become my boss. I think he saw me as a sort of unguided missile who desperately needed controlling.

Now he wondered why I ordered the jackhammering of the sidewalks in front of the three precincts, to plant trees. This tree-hugging instinct was to find its reexpression in beginning the cleanup of the Bronx River in 1974, with a program called the Bronx River Restoration Project.[8] He also warned me that a black cop was accusing me of addressing him as "boy." This stunned me, at least until I realized I had lapsed into the habit of some of my friends, to punctuate the conversation with what I hoped were affectionate references to "my boy."

I called up the cop, pointedly went to see him, explained, and apologized. I never again used the phrase. Years later, when a municipal executive in Washington, D.C., was demoted because some black citizens thought his use of the word "niggardly" an insult, I understood better than I might otherwise have.

The discretion available to the police is enormous.

Because I wanted to have the streets cleaned on schedule, I was very tough on cars obstructing the target area, yet tolerated miles of double parking—on the other side—and the cacophony of horns from trapped motorists that followed.

I didn't get along with my boss, but drew comfort from one of the other division commanders who was even more of a maverick—our boss's attentions had to be divided between us.

The Harlem hiatus lasted only five months and Murphy, in the dulcet tones of the confessional, asked me to serve as the one and only inspector general the NYPD has ever had. It is a testament to my approach to these jobs that it was not a rare experience to have my superiors abolish the positions after I'd served in them. Years later I became the one and only gaming commissioner the state of Minnesota has ever had.

INSPECTOR GENERAL

By then, though, I'd had some savings and was eligible for a pension and thus had "fuck you money" to go with the "fuck you attitude" that seemed to intrude irrepressibly into my life in unwanted and unanticipated ways.

Besides being a frantic saver and buyer of real estate, I'd also bought seven acres of forest in Woodstock, New York. I had discovered the miracles of reinvesting dividends and compound interest. These were the secrets of capital accumulation for me. It was this psychic support that afforded me the freedom to act in ways that men like Murphy often found useful and that others dreaded or scorned.

I lasted nine months in the post before my activism got me bounced, but in that brief time the police commissioner had me employ a tactic that struck real terror in the hearts of the entire department.

In his trademark sotto voce, Murphy asked me to create a unit of officers who would clandestinely report wrongdoing in their precincts. "We could," he suggested with ersatz tentativeness, "perhaps call them police officer associates." In a couple of months I'd created—with a lot of help—a mechanism for recruiting three hundred spies. I was now Walsingham to Murphy's Elizabeth I. There was hell to pay.

As wrongdoing got attacked in ways the troops recognized could only come from "a rat" among them, lockers got overturned or filled with glue; threatening calls were made, anonymously, of course; unwanted items were delivered to the homes of suspected cop "stoolies"; police radios crackled with imprecations; and all manner of harassment and fights ensued. The real spies remained unscathed and undetected, but the unpopular in the ranks became frequent targets.

The union was furious but the revelations of the Knapp Commission strengthened Murphy's hand and weakened theirs. It was a reign of pure terror to rival the Thermidor but it performed the miracle of cleansing the department in ways I never—until I saw it—considered possible. I'd learned that police departments could really only be run by terror, even as all the accouterments of modern management theory received lip service, and that it was possible to change police behavior even if the underlying attitudes resisted all attempts at alteration.

My own unceremonious departure—the *Daily News'* headline was "Murphy Tarnishes Brass He'd Polished"—was occasioned more by my inspection reports on the fecklessness of commanders favored by Murphy's close associates than by the hugely unpopular police officer associate program.

I accepted my fate—exile to the Traffic Division as number two— with a soft and yielding voice and served my durance vile. My boss there, in still another delicious piece of irony, was my erstwhile borough commander in Harlem who was now, himself, in exile.

As he was leaving, in the spring of 1973, Murphy shocked me by promoting me and placing me in charge of the Bronx. I always had the sneaky feeling that, although he'd chosen his successor, I was to serve as a sort of farewell "gift"—as in "Greeks bearing . . ."—to the new police commissioner.

The police officer associate program would probably be described as alive even today, well over a quarter century later, and executives might even be trotted out with "proof" of its viability, but it died with Murphy's departure and it remains safely interred. No other department was ever tempted to such extravagant measures but these spies helped to bring the NYPD to unprecedented and never since matched levels of integrity.

In still another illustration of Murphy's simple and direct effectiveness, he changed shooting practices by the cops across the nation.

Prior to 1972, cops nationwide were indiscriminate shooters—period. No accountability, no control, and precious little training. In battling Hispanic rioters in East Harlem in the summer of 1967, I was present as cops fired their guns in the air to disperse the angry mobs. A lady looking out of her second story tenement was struck in the temple and killed. It was a measure of the times that this tragedy occasioned little notice.

Murphy decreed that every shooting would be investigated by a supervisor, who would account for every bullet and its trajectory, and submit a report to a newly created Firearms Discharge Review Board for review and recommendation to the department's chiefs. Cops became, literally overnight, disciplined and restrained shooters. Police shootings were reduced by more than half.

A curious—and serendipitous and unexpected—result was to halve the numbers of police officers shot by criminals. Reducing the violence at one end reduced it at the other. The reform was widely adopted nationally, producing the unexpected result of reducing the number of police deaths dramatically. So great was the animus toward this reformer, however, that the achievements went largely unremarked.

So Patrick V. Murphy became the model I'd been seeking, although I was never able to affect his softness. I saw him transform the NYPD in ways I couldn't have imagined possible and, when he left in 1973, it had reached levels of efficiency and cleanliness it had never previously, or since, achieved. But what a concatenation of events had been needed to perform Murphy's miracle!

MOONLIGHTING

Moonlighting, or off-duty employment, has always been a source of concern to me. It lends itself to wide abuses as employers hire cops at a fraction of the police salary and often use them inappropriately, exploiting their official status to secure what frequently are illegal services.

I was shocked when I arrived in Minneapolis to discover the cops hired themselves out in uniform. This was strictly forbidden in New York, as was functioning as bouncers in bars or in any capacity resembling law enforcement. Conflicts of interest are endemic to moonlighting by any public official—but especially cops.

When I uttered a few tentative objections, the vehemence of the response from the council and the police union were strident enough to cause me to back off. The practice seemed embedded in the culture and I'd have to trim around the edges. I finally managed a modest level of control.

Still, I often had to discipline cops for such peccadilloes as interceding in the arrest of a client (trying to bail a wrestler who needed to be at a match, for example); functioning inside bars as bouncers (I insisted they could not be inside the premises, counting on Minneapolis's savage winters to discourage the practice altogether); or securing classified information for a client.

The worrisome excesses in Minneapolis paled, however, in comparison to what would be going on in Nashville, Tennessee, in 1999. A reporter, Willy Stern, for the *Nashville Scene*[9] asked me to serve as a panelist to pass judgment on the practices of moonlighting local cops.

A study had shown that senior police personnel were extensively involved in outside businesses. It found a pattern of influence within the department. Inevitably, off-duty employment practices get reflected in official relationships. Favors abound. Roles get reversed. Corners get shaved. It becomes easy to shortchange the official role to accommodate off-duty job needs.

In Nashville the study by the investigative reporter, who won a national award in 2000 for the series, found that the moonlighting cops and the private security firm for which they worked abused their powers in a residential complex they'd been hired to protect. The cops had cars towed illegally; pocketed cash from illegal immigrants too cowed to complain; and engaged in physical abuse, racial epithets, and illegal searches. Even internal affairs officers were engaged in these suspect activities.

Among the abuses cited were:

- Official work schedules were molded to suit off-duty work needs.
- Internal cliques formed and favors were dispensed.
- Official work was sacrificed to the off-duty job needs.
- Senior officials were involved.
- Car-towing abuses abounded.
- Parking and traffic laws were used to victimize citizens.
- Illegal weapons were carried and mace was used inappropriately.
- License plate, driver's license, and criminal history checks were illegally run by Nashville officers.
- Automobile accidents were handled in ways that favored friends and punished outsiders.
- At one point more than fifty Nashville cops were on a private security firm's payroll.
- Business conflicts led to retaliatory police action as cops used police powers to enforce economic interests.

The chief resisted the inquiries, pooh-poohing them and attacking the methodology—and then it was revealed that he'd also worked off-duty, while serving as chief, at one of the functions.

Another advisor in this effort complained in a newsletter relating to police ethics that a chief of a southern city that had been the subject of a moonlighting inquiry had forbidden his information officer to talk to the newsletter's staff. It wasn't hard to figure out the city's identity.

Nashville is a good example of the excesses to which moonlighting can lead. In the end, the investigation was turned over to the FBI because no one had any confidence in the willingness of locals to clean up this soiled act.

The police exercise awesome power, mostly out of public view. The temptations to abuse are everywhere, and practically irresistible. Continuous oversight and random checks of many-pronged inquiries must be employed.

The bitterest lesson, for me, was learning that police officer behavior can only be controlled through the use of fear. Robespierre had been right.

Another lesson was the importance of managing the agency truly in the people's interest.

11
MANAGING[1]

I couldn't map out a path to the chief's job, since so much of the final selection is unpredictable and chaotic, but I could delineate the road to being a finalist or to rising to the upper reaches from which a leap into the ranks of the anointed becomes possible.

Hard study was the first requisite, both vocational and general. Shakespeare has as much to teach us about managing organizations or motivating their members as any text. If there is a better motivational speech than Henry V's on Saint Crispin's Day, I've never encountered it. It's hard to imagine any coach giving a better halftime rouser. And can there be a finer analysis of the paralyzing effects of overintellectualizing an issue than Hamlet's "To be or not to be" soliloquy and its view that the "native hue of resolution is sicklied o'er with the pale cast of thought"? How often have we been confused and rendered impotent by the fears and shadows conjured up by overactive imaginations?

Too many executives are defeated by imaginings when the best course of action is just that—action. Most major decisions have to be made when only about a third of the desired information is available. The insecurity becomes palpable, but the effective administrators act and the ineffective wait for events to make the decisions for them—and these rarely work out. Existentialism requires us to take a stand or suffer the consequences of the vacuum being filled by others. Shakespeare, once again, reminds us that tides must be taken at the flood.

I learned from playing softball just how debilitating imagination and trepidation can be; how important it is to confront the need for action with a relaxed and serene mien. At ease and unworried in the practices preceding games, I was a mediocre player, making catches of balls hit to me with fair regularity; in real games, as I camped under these flies and thought about all the awful consequences that would attend my error, I'd botch the play.

I never did learn to relax on the ball field but I did learn to make decisions in my work and not worry too much about the results. Really successful generals have to learn not to agonize over casualties, in the way of Grant or Patton. In order to do this I had to accommodate my need for security.

Poverty leaves an ineradicable memory on the psyche and forever stamps its victims with the fear of its return, like a Hamlet's father's ghost. I was no exception. I needed the security to feed and take care of my family, educate my children, and survive old age with a measure of dignity.

Toward this end I became a furious saver and a daring investor in the stock market. It was easy to see that I was also fated to be in the real estate business. The market rose over the half century following World War II and anyone not in real estate was left out of the vehicle most likely to lift them into the middle class.

I bought several houses in sequence, trading up, and bought some land that greatly appreciated in value. By the time I reached the upper levels where I was closer to the exit than the entrance, I had sufficient capital and income to survive firings such as the one I experienced in 1979 after three years in the transit police. By then I realized that my instinctive and unsought maverick status inevitably brought me into conflict with my superiors and threatened my employment—yet something impelled me to such quixotic exploits as refusing an order to transfer an unqualified candidate into an assignment his "rabbi" had sought for him. Such events dotted my experiences, especially in later years, and I came to accept the inevitability of occasional comeuppances.

A lot of energy has gone into explaining the need for skills and talents in rising through management's ranks, but insufficient attention is paid to the need for psychological comfort that frees us to act effectively and energetically. I had sensed this need in myself and worked to acquire the capital that would afford me the security I needed to act.

The maverick models I admired were frequently brought down. I didn't have their courage; I needed a cushion. It was equally clear that Oscar Wilde had been right—"It is better to have a steady income than to be fascinating."

Louis Comfort Tiffany had been able to create his wondrous glass objects because of the freedom afforded by an independent fortune. I'd seen my wife, a jeweler, forced to mass-produce simple pieces I labeled "cheap costume jewelry"—that sold—rather than the creative, expensive, and artistic pieces that didn't. And I had no appetite to emulate fevered, starving artists of the sort who sacrificed everything to their creativity. I was definitely with Tiffany in that I'd have to have a financial cushion in order to become a serious reformer.

Gertrude Stein said, "Those who say money can't buy happiness don't know where to shop." I agreed.

Yet I would not have described myself as possessing particular investment acumen. Had I had my life to live over, I'd be an even bigger risk taker. I missed the boat on countless opportunities and made some terrible investments such as buying one thousand shares of a stock at twenty-three dollars and having to sell it for six cents two years later. To those who might say I could afford to be straight because of successful investments, I'd answer with the deeply felt view that I had about the same number of breaks and roughly the same amounts of money go through my hands as most. Except for the lucky few who inherited large sums, or the tragic handful who were visited with misfortune, the majority of us in the middle can be distinguished, after many years, by how we used the time and money available to us.

It occurred to me that most financially successful people stumbled but kept on taking chances. And those who didn't remained in the bywaters of genteel poverty. Risk takers lose, too, but they keep on trying and they know they can't win without calculated aims at life's rings. Gamblers, though, are programmed to lose—they are not risk takers.

I'd seen my mother sweat and suffer at a sewing machine, sometimes driving a needle through her nail and finger, for three decades, and emerge with $70,000 in savings, a nickel and dime at a time. Then we coerced her into buying a house and, when it was sold, the profit was twice her life's savings. Therein lies the difference between saving and investing.

Experience in the form of seeking a wide variety of assignments, preferably of the unpopular variety (another counterintuitive reality that must be accommodated—nobody wants to clean the toilets but it is more honorable work than sometimes has taken place in the Oval Office) is essential, but only if the process is studied and the experience seen for the learning it provides: which is to say nothing more than that it is important to bring a high level of consciousness and awareness to these matters.

Within the police force, no rookie ought to imagine him- or herself chief—it is too great a leap, even for the imagination. The process is incremental—think about the next step, sergeant. Then see just how far talent and sweat can take you.

Hard work, yes, even in civil service, has a payoff. Unconnected for all of my early career in the NYPD, I relied on knowledge and hard work to attract the attention of sponsors who would become my "rabbis."

Yes, there is a lot of log rolling and back scratching in the ranks but this is precisely the reason hard work, study, and experience get rewarded. Somebody has to do the heavy lifting to keep the rest above water.

In the febrile bush beatings that become searches for the football coach, the objective is clear and unmistakable—winning. Everybody in the process understands the goal. When corporations look for CEOs the activity is more genteel, at least on the surface, but the mission is equally apparent—profits.

And then there is the search for police chiefs.[2] There the city parents look for . . . what? That is the question.

In answer, I would offer a manager—but my personal experience has taught me how very scorned such rarities become in the civil service.

POLICE CHIEF SELECTION

From the inaction characterizing the majority of America's police agencies an observer would be justified in concluding that the chiefs are just a bunch of feckless caretakers, incompetents, or worse. They'd be wrong.

The chiefs I met, over two decades of close observation and interaction—comprising the top executives of the nation's major cities—were direct replicas of corporate heads of large businesses. The chiefs were capable, experienced, and educated and had risen on the basis of political acumen, ability, and learned skills, precisely as their counterparts in commerce had done.

What set them apart?

What accounts for the utter lack of distinction among America's police leaders?

There is an anti-intellectual tradition and civil service does not reward risk takers. Ultimately, there is a larger dimension—the political leaders (mayors, usually) don't know enough about policing to make informed demands. They react to individual crises, hopscotching from one to the other.

Minneapolis, for instance: in the seventies, the politicization of the cops reached such outrageous excesses as to focus everyone's attention on addressing this problem. In the post-Knapp era of the NYPD, in the early seventies, the issue centered on corruption and the imperative need to combat it. In the early nineties the LAPD faced the Rodney King issue of brutal racism and attacked it only to discover the emergence of another sort of problem altogether, in 2000, in the form of systematic frame-ups.

Political leaders responding to the scandal du jour were simply asking for trouble. Those who appoint chiefs need to establish a sensible scale of priorities on an ad hoc basis—perhaps developed by a blue-ribbon panel—rather than succumb to the next crisis.

Politicos love to mouth tough-on-crime slogans but are loath to bring a systematic management perspective to this critical area of government. As I was rising through the ranks, it occurred to me that if I wasn't careful these people would make me chief, and then what would I do?

I felt altogether unequal to the task and set about figuring out what it might look like and what skills I might acquire to pull it off. Management seemed the answer: by that I meant the ability to prioritize; communicate; assess; decide; deal with the press, public, and personnel matters; draw up budgets; decide on physical plant and equipment issues; and control the troops to the point that their behavior, on the street, was altered to conform to the desired model. Management meant efficiency and effectiveness—doing things better and cheaper.

I first learned of the surprising reactions of my superiors, on a large and obvious scale, while running the Bronx forces.

I was a two-star chief and established priorities and held commanders accountable. Careers were made and broken in my war room, whose walls were festooned with charts measuring how effectively the eleven precinct commanders met the challenges of street crime, response to emergencies, and traffic enforcement. In the way of modern corporations, there were quarterly reviews.

Except for the few whose careers were in my hands—and these gave me only what I demanded—I found the overwhelming majority of supervisors worse than useless. Several were little more than cover-up artists or apologists for wrongdoers.

In an excess of enthusiasm and without being asked, I sent Police Commissioner Michael J. Codd—central casting's vision of chief, but actually very sympathetic to the ranks he'd risen from and with which he continued to identify—a longish list of captains I could spare and who he could send to other commands that were always clamoring for "more" of everything. Codd reacted as if I'd personally and publicly insulted him and ordered me to withdraw the list, with the curt addition of "no captains will be transferred."

Later, when I noticed the distaste with which he greeted my creation of a unit to protect the elderly—which I'd titled the Senior Citizens Robbery Unit (Codd loved acronyms and used them frequently, in the way of a military many cops sought to emulate, but uttering SCRU was offensive to this very upright and religious man)—I decided to tweak his beak a bit. In a mischievous moment, I labeled another organization I created to fill a real need, even if not very diplomatically named, the Firearms, Arson, Robbery Task Force. Codd was so angry he sent a visibly nervous captain to check that the name was scraped off the office door and personally verify the elimination of the unit.

The same police chief had me abolish a towaway program I'd used to declog congested Bronx streets where fire trucks had trouble reaching the endless blazes. Only midtown Manhattan rated a towaway program, even if I did have the general legal authority to remove impediments to free-flowing traffic.

Codd even responded to my attempts to teach thousands of Bronx kids to swim with, "That's not police work." Knowing from personal experience that swimming was an important middle-class skill—at least then—and hoping that these black and Hispanic kids might remember one positive experience with cops, I kept right on doing it until I left.

If Codd didn't formally and explicitly order me to do or discontinue something, I'd just do as I thought best. No one was much interested in the Bronx in the early 1970s, anyhow. His underlying message seemed clear to me—don't spoil a good thing. My interpretation of his stance: Change and innovation constituted terra incognita; management is invariably discomfiting to the troops and is to be avoided. Innovations would be sent to planning "for further study."

In the end Codd, the man I'd recommended to Police Commissioner Murphy to head the uniformed force, drove me out of the NYPD, yet his disgust with my attempts at managing was not the precipitating cause, only the backdrop.

So, by the time I got to Minneapolis I was well aware of the antipathy directed at management and its practitioners, but I was altogether transfixed by the notion.

In nine years in Minneapolis, I returned unspent budget surpluses for eight of those years; hired women and seriously tried—and failed—to hire blacks; experienced no scandals or major lawsuits; attacked wrongdoing in the ranks without mercy; consolidated the six precincts into four new or refurbished buildings; imposed one-person patrols where all cars had formerly been staffed with two cops, an outrageously expensive practice still widely honored in the NYPD and other agencies; computerized and bought the best cars and equipment; helped bring in an advanced version of 911; adopted name tags; asked for not one additional cop and reduced the supervisory levels by much more than half through a nine-year freeze on promotions (we'd frozen promotions in the much larger transit police for the three years I was there); slashed overtime costs to the barest minimum; responded to all real emergencies within six minutes; swelled the arrest figures; quadrupled traffic enforcement and made the department a test bed for such experiments as led to the arrests of batterers of women; performed community analyses that helped develop the policing that, not altogether accurately, bears the name community policing;[3] developed police executives who went on to lead many other departments as well as Minneapolis's; and a host of other innovations and reforms.

In the end, I concluded that no indifference is quite as cold as that of most politicians for management reforms.

TRANSPARENCY

"Rank has its privileges" is one of the most subversive and wrongheaded notions I've ever encountered. The mind-set undermines integrity and promotes the "I'm gonna get mine" thinking that is the very opposite of service. What rank has is responsibilities, benefits, and a damn good salary.

By seeing every visitor I not only spared my secretary the necessity of battling every psycho, hump, drunk, or citizen at the door but ensured myself a steady flow of information on cops' behavior.

The encounters rarely lasted longer than it would take me to slurp a quarter of a container of coffee and, by personally escorting many visitors to the Internal Affairs Division (IAD), I assured follow up of any complaint.

I've always been a diarist and would note the names and expect to get a report back from the IAD in a few weeks. I'd often send these back with questions or demands for more follow-up. No one would risk canning a case with those kinds of controls in place, and the IAD was a catapult to higher assignments.

A lot of folks believe that callers control phone conversations: in short, the "gotcha" factor. However, I've long thought I controlled the calls and kept them mercifully brief.

I was not exhausted or drained by these approaches, which took only a tiny fraction of my time. What I had observed was the penchant of most chiefs for kaffe klatsches in which subordinates were subtly encouraged to kiss ass.

Transactional analysis suggested the terrific impact of hearing the CEO's voice without having first to run a gauntlet of queries and screenings. I well remember having occasion to call the president of Pillsbury Company and hearing "Spoor here" immediately. What an impact. Bill Spoor left an indelible and ineradicable impression through the simple expedient of answering his phone without a phalanx of screeners.

Most of the emoluments of rank added to a seductive sense of self-importance. On taking over the Bronx in 1973, I reassigned my chauffeur to patrol and drove myself, the only borough commander to have done so. I erased all reserved parking spaces and initiated a first-come, first-served policy. The spaces belonged to everyone.

Little things, to be sure, but they convey the egalitarian notions of populism that girded my approach to government.

VALUES

In order to function as an executive, you have to know who you are. Among a lot of other things, this has to include a sense of values; for example, what is your number one value? Mine is family. Number two? I say, this great nation and its people. And three? My job.

A lot of execs are confounded and perplexed by such simple exercises and retreat into clichés and bromides that, upon examination, turn out to be simple-minded: "Men, your safety is my first concern." Really? What an absurdity. Why not send them—men and women—home to their families and TV when danger beckons, then?

Such executives aren't even aware that it is the public's safety that must be their number one concern. Successful generals seek victories, not the elimination of casualties.

The reactive call for more cops whenever a spike in certain crimes occurs, as the public gets spooked by fear, is another tactic that is in need of exposure.

We cannot mean to take a callous attitude to our associates' safety, but the hypocrisy and confusion of those claiming this as their top priority needs to be unmasked.

In New York City, Giuliani kept adding cops at a dizzying pace, with help from the president. The union subtracted them with such ploys as "wash-up time" (preperation for the approaching tour and time, at the end of it, to prepare reports), which ate about twenty-six workdays from the annual schedule; a sick policy so liberal the average cop took about a dozen a year; and frequent resort to four ten-hour tours followed by three days off, which added about forty-plus off days.

In Minneapolis I'd vigorously and successfully resisted four-and-tens on the notion that a twenty-four-hour day divides itself neatly into eight-hour tours; that I wasn't getting anything like seven hours of work out of them now, so how would I get additional productivity by merely extending the workday? And this meant one less workday every week.

Cops envied firefighters—all the free time they had to pursue "real interests" and fought for anything that reduced the number of days working. Immediately upon my departure from Minneapolis, the city parents reduced the citizens' police protection by about 20 percent through the simple expedient of adopting a citywide four-and-ten program. I'd reserved it for a couple of small elite units that had to produce in order to continue to enjoy this perquisite—now they all had it. Like two-person patrols, it was a sovereign remedy for the disease of efficient management.

As cops got added, the coverage eroded. In 2000 it was not an exaggeration to say that cops worked about half the year, or far less than two hundred days. In Minneapolis it was far less after I left. And the cost is horrific, even as protections diminish. In the process of watching the politicians give away about 20 percent of the police coverage citizens were paying for, I learned, again, how unesteemed were the virtues of management in the bureaucracy. The politicians' answer—including former President Clinton's—was to hire still more cops, when the real challenge was to get them to work harder, faster, smarter.

The result was that I left Minneapolis with the bitter enmity of the rank-and-file and as the only department head whose retirement was not accompanied by a City Council Resolution of Gratitude for my service.

My recompense lay in the affection and warmth with which the people greeted me wherever I went and who invariably thanked me for serving them. Still, I'd been made heartily sick by the self-congratulatory valedictories of outgoing chief executives who'd "righted the ship of state and set it on its course."

These very same smug politicos usually went on to discover religion in retirement and argue passionately against the policies they so sedulously clung to in office. I was not going to be the secretary of defense or state, or chief of police, who'd not be out-jingoed in their bellicosity in office, and find the beauties of peace and negotiation in pasture.

I'd tell the truth to the degree possible. Of course I'd lie, but rarely, and—hopefully—to a useful purpose. I'd try to base my actions on the basic question of whether they'd be good for the people and hope to gain, as the supreme encomium, the epitaph, "He was a true servant of the people."

REFORM AND THE PUBLIC'S ATTITUDE

The public welcomes, applauds, and supports efforts at police reform. The quest of this effort is to part the curtain of these bromides and expose the more complex truth behind.

Yes, the public wants the police to be reformed, honest, vigorous, and effective and it welcomes most reforms that it understands—and it is critical to make the stakes and issues clear—as being aimed at these objectives.

But a lot depends on whose ox is being gored.

The public has its own favored myths and resists their exposure. For example, it is clear that the police are much more efficient when in cars, dispatched by computer and radio, and surrounded by useful tools and equipment, yet there is nothing more reassuring to the public than the sight of a uniformed cop, on foot, on their block.[4] Such officers hardly ever make important arrests. They tend to displace crimes, not prevent them, and are, by any measure, hopelessly unproductive—yet the people love them. As they love cops on horseback—an expensive frill—or on motorcycles, a dangerous and costly approach that results in too many disabling injuries. Canine patrols, however, prove productive and aggressive tools.

The public likes to believe civilian review boards[5] ensure effective oversight and control over police wrongdoing but would, after arduous study, be at a loss to point to a successful model anywhere.

The public, subtly and even subliminally, promotes racism by insisting that "those people" be controlled or kept out of sight. Citizens love residence requirements[6] that ensure that the police live in the cities they patrol, but would be surprised to discover these are widely flouted. In the few places they are tried, they're unenforced, probably unenforceable, and a chimera.

And the local precinct stations—how people love them! That they soak up personnel for clerical, administrative, and maintenance tasks is blithely overlooked. That it is virtually a truism that the fewer the police buildings, the larger the proportion of cops on the street on patrol is widely ignored.

The NYPD is rendered significantly less efficient by having too many precincts (as well as far too many cops)—a surfeit of about a third—that are not even geographically consistent with the planning districts that really delineate and define the various communities of the city. That they are physically disgraceful in their decay only prompts debates about the costs of refurbishing them, rather than tempt leaders to eliminate about twenty-five of them altogether. Try closing and realigning these precincts to conform to a clearly more efficient model.

Minneapolis, a fraction of New York's—or even the Bronx's—size, had six precincts when I arrived and four when I left. There were objections and I debated the issues and finally just did it. I melded it with a rebuilding program that had us abandon the decrepit quarters I thought unworthy of our cops.

New precincts—light, airy, welcoming places, with athletic facilities for the cops and community rooms for local residents—went up.

I wanted the black community in North Minneapolis to have a precinct but the African American leaders at first resisted the idea. The sense that a white cop's gifts had to be suspect hung palpably in the air as I attempted to sell the notion.

I selected a site—a city-owned building I could get for one dollar—and a plan, and then proceeded to make my case to the council. There was a late afternoon meeting of the council's safety committee on the proposal. The room was empty, save for three council members and me—or so I thought.

Two of the councillors—both white women—argued vigorously for the precinct in their wards, which were contiguous to the ghetto. The third, a black male, warily represented the area I'd chosen, and remained studiously aloof from the notion. It was clear he warmed to the idea of the precinct as his colleagues vigorously pursued the issue with me.

I listened silently.

Finally, both women, having spoken at length, asked for my view.

I said the event reminded me of an election in Mississippi in the 1940s. A professor from the local black college appeared to cast his ballot. Being black, he was met with a literacy test. He easily passed. A more difficult test was brought forth and this erudite man conquered it. Finally, the officials brought out a Chinese newspaper and asked the professor if he could tell them what it said. "Niggers ain't voting today," he answered.

At this, the two women exploded, one in outrage and the other in tears. It was the most drama that room had seen.

"Are you calling us racists?"

"I'm only citing a simple parable."

That, I later found out, put the black council member over the line. He soon adopted the issue and presided proudly at the ribbon-cutting.

Unbeknownst to me, there was a *Minneapolis Tribune* reporter seated out of sight in the rear. The entire incident was reported in the next day's paper and not a single person remarked upon it. We strain at fleas and swallow elephants. It proved an object illustration of the maxim that if you're not ready to see your words or actions in the next day's headlines, don't utter them or do them.

The Fourth Precinct was built, to specifications, and stands today in the center of the black community in Minneapolis. I elevated a black sergeant to inspector and placed him in command.

However, nowhere in America was management skill in law enforcement particularly prized. This was more than obvious across the national landscape, with fearful consequences for its citizens. The chiefs would bear the brunt of the criticism for the crises produced by mismanagement, but it was the politicians, as stewards of the cities, who were truly responsible. And despite the crowings of police chiefs over the decline in crime in the late nineties, it is just as true as the twenty-first century began as it was in the mid-twentieth.

In the dawn of the computer age and the explosion in communication technology, though, the chiefs faced management problems of unprecedented complexity. I discovered that there was a deceptively simple solution to what had been a mystery.

12
MANAGING TECHNOLOGY

Although I'd helped adopt 911[1] in New York in 1968, somehow the Minneapolis cops and citizens in 1980 appeared never to have heard of it. Their absorption with a union-driven political spoils system relegated such innovations to the back burner.

911

Exposed to 911 in 1968, I marveled at its impact as a response tool and slowly awakened to its psychological value in inviting the public to call the cops.

I had taken no interest in police technology until the day Chief Inspector George P. McManus called me into his office.

I was deputy inspector—one rank over captain—and in the NYPD's Narcotics Division following my boss' departure for the presidency of the city council. He had been McManus's predecessor.

Not wanting to be taken aback by any surprises I reviewed all the possible reasons for his summons.

"Tony, I want you to take over the Communications Division."

I concealed my genuine shock, I hope, and said: "Chief, I don't know anything about technology. That job has always been held by an engineer. I'll do whatever I'm asked to do, of course, but I can hardly dial a phone."

The author as a rookie cop in 1953.

The author as sergeant in the NYPD in
October 1960.

The author in 1960 with Jack Caulfield, who went on to involvement with the Watergate scandal.

President Kennedy visits Mr. and Mrs. Arthur Krim in New York City in 1961. Shaking his hand is Anna Rosenberg. The author is in the background.

Gov. Ross Barnett of Mississippi visits City College in 1964 and is pelted with tomatoes and eggs shortly after this photo is taken. The author is at left.

The author (right) with Vice President Lyndon Johnson in New York City in 1962.

The author and his wife, Erica, and son Tony at the Christmas promotions to captain in December 1965.

Police Commissioner Howard Leary shakes the author's hand upon promoting him in May 1968, as Chief Inspector Sanford Garelik looks on.

Young Exeutives of the NYPD attending a planning conference. Seated at left is James Meehan, who became chief of the transit police after Garelik. Right of him is Neil Behan, who became chief of police in Baltimore. Joe McNamara, at the end of the first row, headed the Kansas City and San Jose police departments. The author, standing, is fifth from the right.

Commissioner Pat Murphy with promotees in March 1971. The author, standing, is third from the right. Seated are the higher ranking, with Chief Sydney Cooper third from left.

Congratulating a winner of the August 22, 1975, track meet in McCombs Park in the Bronx.

The author with fire department officials and Mayor John Lindsay in the Bronx in 1975.

The author with Police Commissioner Michael J. Codd in the Bronx's "Fort Apache" in July 1976.

The author, around 1980, dishing out hot dogs to seniors with son Dominick and Minneapolis Police Inspector Arthur Maxwell, at left.

The author in his new office in 1980, with his wife, Erica.

In March 1980, Minneapolis's grateful Chinese community presents the chief with a plaque containing a badge made of solid gold. It is immediately inventoried into the city treasury, lest it "disappear."

The author with Mayor Don Fraser, "School's Open—Drive Safely" campaign, August 1980.

Speaking at one of many hundreds of community events in 1980.

Minneapolis School Superintendent
Richard Green presenting school patrol
officer Art Morris with a certificate of
appreciation. Green later went on to head
the New York City school system and died
tragically of a sudden asthma attack after
only about two years of service.

The author in the early eighties with K-
Police Officer Bill Jones, who the autho
put in charge of the 4th Precinct some yea
later and who was later appointed deput
chief of the Minneapolis police departmen

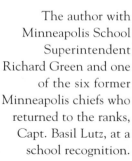

The author with
Minneapolis School
Superintendent
Richard Green and one
of the six former
Minneapolis chiefs who
returned to the ranks,
Capt. Basil Lutz, at a
school recognition.

group of Minneapolis leaders gather to make an antiprejudice public service announce-
ent for the Twin Cities Area Human Rights Coalition in 1982. In the last row is the
linnesota Viking great and future State Supreme Court judge Alan Page, second from
he right. In the penultimate row are Minneapolis School Superintendent Richard Green,
r left; St. Paul Police Chief William McCutcheon, center; and Minneapolis Mayor Don
raser, far right, standing next to St. Paul Mayor George Latimer. NAACP head Hobart
litchell is in the light suit, center of the second row.

The author with St. Paul Police Chief William McCutcheon (left), his aide, Barbara Andrus, and St. Paul Police Department Deputy Chief James Griffin in February 1983—right around the time of the statewide adoption of the 911 system.

The author with the U.S. delegation at an international police conference in Madrid in October 1984. Professor Gordon Meisner of the University of Illinois is at left.

Minneapolis officials kick off October 1984 as Crime Prevention Month with a proclamation by the mayor and introduction of the Crime Prevention postage stamp featuring McGruff. The author is third from the left, seated next to Minneapolis Mayor Don Fraser.

Taking a bite out of McGruff.

Attending the police chiefs conference in Clearwater, Florida, in March 1985. Pictured with the author are Miami, Florida, Chief Clarence Dickson (left) and Charlotte, North Carolina, Chief Reuben Greenberg, who represented a measure of racial progress in America's cities.

The author with Raleigh, North Carolina, Chief Fred Heineman; Atlanta, Georgia, Chief George Napper; and Dave Jennings of California's Community Crime Prevention Program.

The author with Raleigh, North Carolina, Chief Fred Heineman, who won a congressional seat in 1992 and who the author put in charge of barricades at Yankee Stadium on September 28, 1976; and Baltimore County, Maryland, Chief Neil Behan, the author's closest confidante rising through the ranks of the NYPD and the legendary figure who advised Frank Serpico to attend a Catholic retreat house in the eponymous movie.

The author and Mayor Donald M. Fraser (left) flanking a typical class of new recruits into the Minneapolis Police Department in February 1985. There were five women among the fifteen entrants but, sadly and frustratingly, no African Americans.

A mideighties class of new Minneapolis cops flanked by City Council President Alice Rainville and Mayor Don Fraser. Of these twenty recruits, eight are women and three are black, reflecting the mayor's and the author's pursuit of affirmative action programs.

Ground breaking for the hugely controversial new 4th Precinct building, to be built in the center of the black community in Minneapolis, in 1987. Present is Councilmember Van White, second from the left, who took some time to decide whether if was a blessing or a curse. He ultimately decided, firmly, on the former.

The three deputy chiefs of the Minneapolis Police Department—Bob Lutz, John Laux, and David Dobrotka—circa 1987. All were plucked from minor ranks to high offices and all went on to head other departments—Lutz to Bloomington, Minnesota; Laux succeeding the author as chief of police in Minneapolis; and Dobrotka to Glendale, Arizona.

The author speaking with fellow immigrant and U.S. Senator Rudy Boschwitz at a Police Executive Research Forum conference in Washington in 1989.

The author with his wife, Erica, in the midst of an ill-fated run for governor of Minnesota in 1994.

"That's okay. We need a manager."

Sanford D. Garelik had overplayed his hand as chief inspector, garnering so much publicity with his dazzling innovations that an insecure outsider, Police Chief Howard R. Leary, had finally thrown his weight to First Deputy Commissioner John Walsh, the most dreaded Savonarola-like figure in the agency. I had been complicit in the blunders and learned from it. Our two and a half years of innovations and pyrotechnics were now heaped upon a latter-day bonfire of vanities.

With Garelik's departure, Walsh reigned supreme. The Irish Catholics were back in firm and total control. Walsh despised Garelik and I inherited a smidgen of that resentment, being a much smaller fish. The real losers—as usual, historically, in the NYPD—were the actually more numerous Italians, who were systematically excluded from the upper reaches.

Now Chief Inspector McManus had been picked by Walsh to head the uniformed forces and I remembered my first sighting. It was 1953 and I was a recruit. McManus was a lieutenant teaching us at the Police Academy. He had a master's degree and seemed the very embodiment of knowledge to me.

Over the years, I became very disillusioned with McManus, an engaging and articulate man I felt did not do justice to his talents. He was the antithesis of the executive models I'd chosen—risk takers who were committed to the mission.

For McManus this was a no-lose situation. The Communications Division was a headache. If I failed he could punish me and show a toughness that was really alien to his character, but which would, if used, enhance his stature in a job that needed occasional displays of steel. If I succeeded he wouldn't have to reward me.

The Communication Division was an empire of almost a thousand employees—phone and radio operators, technicians of all sorts, and a really mysterious band of guys working on computers. It was out of control to the point of near mutiny. Every day there were incidents of refusals to work, kicking furniture, defying supervisors, inadequate or downright rude service, utter lack of radio discipline, and a general sense that it was the NYPD's biggest can of worms.

That, at least, I knew how to approach.

I established a rigid organizational structure, filled the air with formal charges of harsh discipline, and pretty quickly brought the agency under tight control. A few dramatic examples and everyone got the message.

Technology was something else.

I approached 911 and computerization warily but gradually discovered, to my pure delight, that the issues were managerial, not technical. I needed to find the technicians who could do what I wanted done and then I had to prod them to get it done on time—sometimes simply ordering that a new system be adopted, in toto, as of 12:01 A.M. on a fixed date.

The one event I recall vividly from my three years at the Communications Division occurred when I was told, in genuinely shaken terms, that First Deputy Walsh was "on the floor." The Communications Division was an isolated fifth-floor aerie and no one of any note ever stepped foot in it.

There had been a bomb explosion in that doge's palace of a headquarters and I'd been given responsibility for security following the blast. Ours was the only large unit in the building working around the clock and, hence, always present to check visitors and parcels. I set up a system of visitor checks, admission of regulars, and searches of everything, although I never cared much for the trappings of a garrison state.

Walsh, a daily communicant, was genuinely dreaded as corruption's nemesis in the agency. I thought that reputation ill-deserved since the evidence for it was lacking. He was a tough, canny, and stubborn bureaucratic infighter of the first rank.

Ironically, Walsh was the man Frank Serpico[2] would be referred to as he attempted to report widespread corruption in the plainclothes units, and he sloughed him off. Serpico got the same treatment at City Hall. By the time the Knapp Commission began in 1971, others in the NYPD saw Walsh as I had—as lacking substance.

Now Walsh sat at my desk.

"Tony, your staff is going through some very confidential papers of mine every day and potentially compromising the integrity of some very sensitive investigations. That type of search is not necessary."

The security staff had been ordered to check every package and briefcase, to preclude another bomb explosion.

Ever wary of Garelik's—and my—dreaded nemesis, yet determined not to give in to his bullying, an answer leapt to mind. "Certainly, Commissioner. Quite right. We'll cease those searches immediately. Please send me a memo to that effect and I'll implement it at once."

His face darkened. He mumbled something about getting back to me, rose to his feet, turned, and stomped angrily out.

I never heard from him on this matter again and the searches continued.

We implemented 911, computer-assisted dispatch, and an automated center, and I could still just manage to make a phone call unaided.

So when I got to Minneapolis, twelve years after we adopted 911 in New York, I was amazed by the ignorance of the system I encountered, but also saw it as a heaven-sent opportunity to do some good. Thirteen years after its inaugural, 911 was still terra incognita in Minnesota.

There were folks working on it, but in a desultory and unpromising fashion. I became a fiery advocate and was surprised to discover pockets of resistance. The main one centered in the other twin of the Twin Cities—St. Paul. There, Chief William McCutcheon spoke out on the cost and lack of need for 911. Since he was also a state senator—in a state with a farmer/legislator tradition—his voice carried weight.

I went to see him.

"Bill, I respect and admire you. You run a very professional operation. I want you to know I've had a lot of experience with 911 and love it. I am going to work as hard as I can to bring it about statewide. I'd hate to get into a public row with you over it."

He thanked me for coming over and we parted without commitment. He is a proud man and I didn't think I needed one.

As far as I could tell, he never again voiced an objection or gave the slightest evidence of working against it.

By 1983, Minnesota adopted a statewide 911 system, only fifteen years after New York's, but I was grateful. No one, thereafter, ever asked what 911 was. By 1988, we computerized the entire department even though I had not once sat at a terminal. The issue, I came to see, was not to become a techno-nerd, but to manage them.

But reforms involved changing behaviors much more often than modernizing the equipment or better buildings. My coming to Minnesota was only one piece of a national puzzle that revealed problems everywhere.

13
THE NATIONAL SCENE

Wh... hat is it that qualifies me to speak about policing nationally? My career included three police departments: the NYPD for twenty-four years, number two in the transit police (then a separate agency, today a part of the NYPD) for three years, and the Minneapolis Police Department for nine years.

I interacted with colleagues from all over the country, did a lot of discussing and writing about problems and programs, attended several international conferences of police executives from all over the world, and, as chief, met with the fifty or so other major city chiefs at least twice a year. I took a lively interest in my profession and would have described myself as a loving critic who was willing to pay the price of making policing better. I published seven books as well as countless articles. There was nothing particularly noble in this since the country had fed, educated, and enriched me as it brought me to heights undreamed of in my immigrant's imagination. It was a simple matter of making a partial repayment.

A number of leitmotifs wound through my experiences. The surprising lack of interest in management skills—or the willingness to measure results with the same baleful realism that attends the private sector—was one. Next was the gross conceit of politicians that they could select the best chiefs, unaided, when they had only to look at the tortured meanderings in choosing the local football coaches to see what they should have been doing; and finally, the anti-intellectualism in police ranks that has left the field abandoned to sociologists and criminologists who really drive thinking and progress in policing. Think of any book, article, or innovation and you'll be considering a scholar's—not a cop's—perspective.

In my lectures to police executives I often dare them to report to their colleagues that they've spent the weekend writing poetry, if they don't accept my assertion of the antiintellectualism endemic to policing. That usually settles the issue.

The utter predictability, sameness, and lack of imagination that attends policing across the nation—albeit allowing for internal differences that reflect the individual proclivities of the various chiefs—proves eloquent testimony to the paucity of wit in the industry. I marveled at how, by closing my eyes, I couldn't tell what police department I was hearing. The internal discussions precisely mirrored the concerns and myths across the board.

By serving as an expert witness—mostly, but not always, in forty or so cases across the country in which police wrongdoing was charged—I was afforded a view into the inner workings of large and small departments. I very rarely, if ever, encountered what I'd call an unfamiliar culture.

While police departments tend to be remarkably similar in their attitudes, internal workings, accepted myths, and driving philosophies, being dictatorships rather than democratic bodies, they also tend to reflect the characters of their chiefs. This is particularly true in the cases of long-serving executives and those following long-entrenched, similarly minded predecessors.

Daryl Gates, the long-serving chief of the Los Angeles Police Department, followed long-tenured, powerful, and like-minded police chiefs.

William Parker, Ed Davis, and Gates led the LAPD[1] for about forty of the last fifty years of the twentieth century. They shared a contempt for corruption and ran an agency that managed to avoid the sorts of bribery and payoff scandals that terrified New York mayors. Of course, in the FBI,[2] J. Edgar Hoover had managed it by avoiding the tainting possibilities of going after drugs or the Mafia, while concentrating on shooting public enemies in the street, hounding "Reds," and compiling dossiers on just about everyone of interest to him—salacious, political, personal, or otherwise.

This notable trio embraced modernity in all its technological and equipment guises; shared an open scorn for political figures and politics, while playing the game with extraordinary deftness; and worked to enhance their autonomy and freedom from outside interference. That this could seem, in my opinion, to also mean freedom from the democratic controls of representative government did not trouble them excessively, even though one of them, Davis, went on to elected office—the California State Senate. The chiefs managed to create a firewall, in the form of an independent police commission, between themselves and the city's elected officials. This act did not rid the agency of politics—and it ignored the larger question of freeing police agencies of partisan politics, a bane of many departments.

This shelter enabled Gates, in later years, to treat the city's mayor, Tom Bradley—himself a former lieutenant in the LAPD—as if he were still just that.

Parker, Davis, and Gates were openly contemptuous of the byzantine excesses of eastern agencies (mostly meaning the NYPD and, especially, Patrick V. Murphy) and shared uncompromising views on efficiency, military bearing, and total integrity and a distinct tolerance for police aggressiveness. This reached its public apotheosis in the March 1991 videotaped beating of a black motorist, Rodney King, by a large number of LAPD officers who either participated or watched, in tacit complicity, and in which case—despite the persuasive evidence of the video—none was moved to testify against his fellow officers. The Brotherhood in Blue held fast, on both the east and west coasts and everywhere in between.

The message the LAPD had received from its leaders was, "We're the good guys; they're the bad guys. Whatever we do is okay and whatever they suffer they deserve."[3] It was a message that had resonated eloquently with the dominant white society that enshrined the agency in the glowingly flattering images of the earlier television serial *Dragnet*. The overclass was ultimately horrified by the extremes such policies produced when confronted with the King video.[4]

Mindlessly tough policies invite the cops to indulge their instincts without necessarily producing the desired results. Those who boast of being tough on crime still eschew such really tough strategies as decoys, stings, and stakeouts. Zero tolerance for crime becomes a form of intolerance for behaviors that might be either tolerated or skillfully manipulated. The ballyhooed assault on street crime in NYC in the 1990s and after was little more than harassment of street people, dotted with such tragic spikes as the brutalities, shootings, and even handling of street rallies we've examined elsewhere.

Toughness on crime results in politicians outbidding each other in a rush for bigger and better mandatory sentences in drug crimes, and in asset forfeiture practices that are confiscatory and probably violate the Fourth Amendment's protection against unreasonable seizures. Humans invariably discover that, if they don't protect the rights of pariahs, there will be no one to protect theirs.

In an eerie echo of Gates's tough approach, New York Mayor Rudolph Guiliani also tactically urged the cops to "go get 'em." The result mirrored the LAPD's unhappy experiences—across the board—as illustrated by such dramatic cases as Louima's, Diallo's, and Dorismond's.

I got to know Gates very well and, in the complex nature of these things, we became friends despite holding polar opposite views on most central questions—such as Warren Court decisions, affirmative action, the need for civilian control and oversight by inspectors general, and the primacy of elected figures over government departments.

Physically very fit, neither a drinker nor a smoker and a determined exerciser, Gates was tough, smart, and confident. He exuded authority and loved his agency and the men loved him.

I had served as a public law firm's principal expert witness against the LAPD in an attempt to force them to hire Hispanics, blacks, and women. I was not happy to undertake the assignment, having had to do it against an old friend in the New York State Police and in several other highly unpopular cases, and doing it pro bono, at that. This, and a series of other similar trials, placed me in the ranks of pariahs who were disloyal to the profession. Invariably, there was a price to be paid.

It was not a time hospitable to the notion that police departments needed to hire minorities and women in large numbers. Since I was the rare high-ranking police executive willing to take on these issues, I was regularly called to testify.

At the time of the trial, Ed Davis was the chief of the LAPD and he famously said, "When the Los Angeles Rams [then the local National Football League franchise] hires women as linebackers, I'll hire them as cops." Davis had also made headlines by calling for the transportation of portable gallows to sites of plane hijackings, so that the criminals could be hanged on the spot. Hyperbole, to be sure, but everyone got the message.

I hated testifying in these cases. In the New York State case I'd had to oppose a dear friend's insistence that his troopers be tall—in order to be able to shoot over autos—and demonstrate an upper body strength that excluded most women. Sitting on the stand and testifying against a man I'd studied for lieutenant with when we were both in the NYPD, and whose home I'd visited many times, was not my idea of how best to retain his friendship. He was heading the New York State Police and I had joined a suit to attack their height requirements, and arm and shoulder power. Neither the federal government, then anxious to press forward on recently enacted civil rights laws, nor the shoestring-financed, mostly volunteer law firms that fought these cases seemed able to find sufficiently senior, credible, and knowledgeable—and willing—witnesses, so I was impressed, reluctantly, into the breach. I achieved a near monopoly in the field.

WOMEN IN POLICING

I'd become, by default and certainly not because of any forensic or other skills, a champion of women in policing.

The army and my first fifteen years in the NYPD had taught me that the mindless physicality of all-male societies contained savage elements desperately in need of soothing. Women were a stabilizing, civilizing influence.

It was clear that women didn't usually possess—before physical equality became more than an aberration—the upper body strength of men. The opposition to their entrance into the macho police world was visceral and nearly universal. The passage of civil rights legislation, however, served as the wedge available to willing administrators. I became one of them.

Women would fail, of course, but men failed, too. It occurred to me that, in any given ten cases, men might fail in numbers five, six, and seven because their bellicosity heightened the violence. Women might succeed in mediating or conflict-resolving numbers five, six, and seven— effectively defusing a volatile circumstance—but fail in numbers eight, nine, and ten because of their inability to physically dominate a situation. The success rate would still be 70 percent.

I was also influenced by the female models around me, but in a curious way.

There weren't many "policewomen" then, in the 1950s and 1960s, but they belonged to two distinct camps—the collaborators, which were the overwhelming majority, who took clerical jobs, sought male protectiveness, conformed, and kept quiet; and a tiny handful of what many saw as pain-in-the-ass mavericks who fought, sued, lobbied, and took an awful lot of crap.

To my surprise, I found myself gradually siding with the feminists and ultimately emerging as an ally.

In September 1975 an article I wrote, "Women in Policing: An Idea Whose Time Has Come," appeared in the *FBI Bulletin*—but only after I seriously lobbied an influential agent I knew.

Cops in the Bronx refused to ride with women When I ordered them to give me their objections in writing so I could investigate the charges, they grumpily rode. I never saw a single written document outlining such objections—but heard an awful lot of persiflage. I did the same when objections to blacks arose.

GAYS

I knew President Clinton was wrong to temporize over gays in the military, as a result of these experiences with women and blacks. I simply ordered the white cops to comply, answered their arguments, demanded documented objections, and forced the policy on them. It was not a question I'd have put to a vote. Mayor Fraser and I did the same thing for gay cops in Minneapolis in the 1980s, without a single whimper of official protest—although there was plenty of bitching, moaning, and bullshit.

UNIFORMS

I testified all over the nation as to the need to employ women as cops but I really became a hero to them in a very unlikely way.

In the 1970s, the Bronx female police officer's uniform consisted of a navy blue tunic and a matching miniskirt. When these leggy gendarmes emerged from their radio cars, the tough street guys whooped, hollered, whistled, and made gestures. The females objected and came to see me. I agreed and sent a memo to Police Commissioner Mike Codd asking for permission to have them wear trousers.

The police commissioner's answer dismayed me. He was not a man to say yes or no, but seemed addicted to circumlocutions. In this case, he'd sent my proposal to the uniform committee for evaluation. This was not a group noted for its activism. The police commissioner's action spelled entombment for the notion. But he hadn't said no to me directly.

I couldn't issue an order in writing since this would be seen as mutiny, or at least as an intolerable affront, so I had my staff phone all the Bronx commands saying that, in that borough, it would henceforth be optional to wear pants or miniskirts. A pixie in my brain almost tempted me to add that "this goes for the men as well as the women," but I didn't.

Overnight every female in the Bronx—about one hundred then—was in pants.

Then, of course, came the problem—what about the rest of the department? Miraculously, and without anyone's official action, they were suddenly all in pants. Another idea whose time had come.

I was disappointed that no one—not even the delegation that petitioned me—ever came to thank me for this. I gradually came to realize that this was what leadership was about, and that it carried its own rewards and responsibilities—and gratitude was not included.

It is likely that the uniform committee is still grappling with the issue.

On the issue of LAPD's hiring of women and minorities, I begged Davis—and later, Gates—to settle, offering to pressure the law firm to accept a reasonable compromise, which I could manage because of the leverage my testimony gave me with them.

The LAPD fought the case tooth and nail. I'd warned them that the reed that does not bend to the prevailing wind breaks, but they were having none of it. The LAPD wound up with a court mandate and consent decree that forced hiring quotas of women, blacks, and other minorities on them well into the twenty-first century.

RECRUITING CHIEFS TO CAUSES

It was many years and a lot of wooing on my part before Gates forgave me.

As a result of this suit, Gates and I had engaged in bitter debates, across the panoply of police issues of the day. Titters of excitement would attend these exchanges, as chiefs awaited the combat. My ego swelled in the encounters.

One day I had an epiphany.

It was in the early 1980s, in Salt Lake City, and Daryl Gates was at the rostrum, denouncing an organization I was a member of—the Police Executive Research Forum (PERF). As my buddy Neil Behan, standing next to me, said, "I'm sick of Daryl's outbursts. I'm gonna take him on." He was the chair of PERF's board and felt compelled to defend his organization.

I suddenly realized neither of us ever got Daryl to go along with any of our proposals—and he took a lot of sympathizers with him. This was particularly true of our efforts to thwart a National Rifle Association (NRA) that was cozily in bed with the nation's police chiefs.

The NRA ran schools and training programs for the chiefs and hosted all manner of events and showered goodies on these influential, if largely backstage, officials. Now we were trying to effect a divorce and get the International Association of Chiefs of Police to take the first tentative steps to this break by adopting some fairly tepid resolutions about gun safety. Gates had refused to join in with, "You kooks and lefty weirdos," offered half-jokingly.

I determined right there to change my whole approach to Daryl and urged my friend, Behan, to ignore this diatribe. He was stunned, certain that I'd be the first to goad him to go after the LAPD chief, but I said we ought to try to win him over to whatever we could and my way wasn't working. He slowly came around.

I would, thereafter, sometimes have to disagree publicly with some of

Daryl's more outrageous positions—I hadn't abandoned my principles—but I was, thereafter, always careful to be deferential, flattering, and obviously reluctant to disagree. I excised ego from the process. The substance hadn't changed much, but the form had been radically transformed.

The new approach would have warmed Dale Carnegie's heart. Daryl and I became friends. A friend of mine was doing a film on street crime and asked if I could get Daryl. He was glad to do it and I got him, and me, $10,000 for one day's filming. The flick died.

Later, in 1987, I got Daryl to appear in a Public Broadcasting System documentary—*The Police Chiefs*—that analyzed different chiefs' styles. The other CEO I persuaded to join in this effort, became, thereafter—though not as a result of this epic—the police commissioner of the NYPD, one of President Clinton's drug czars, and, later, mayor of Houston—Lee Brown, a preeminent scholar and accomplished black chief. I even got Daryl to share a stage with a nemesis, Ramona Ripson, director of the American Civil Liberties Union, who regularly pilloried him, for another of my ill-fated projects.

In what I considered a miraculous turnaround, Gates was dubbed one of the "Ten Biggest Gun Grabbers" by the NRA only a few years later, when he very reasonably called for a ban on semiautomatic weapons that had taken the lives of his colleagues. Gates had been shocked by the NRA's characteristic overreaction and was, kicking and screaming, thrust into our camp of weirdos whether he liked it or not. Ironically, I was never thought worthy of the attention of being listed among the notorious "Gun Grabbers."

Police chiefs are hugely influential when they speak ex cathedra—or from perspectives flowing from their expertness.

POLICE CULTURE

Separated by a continent the LAPD and the NYPD could not have been more sharply contrasted, yet, internally, they remain alike in their worldviews. The inner cultures were tempered by attitudes toward brutality and corruption, and even such approaches as physical fitness—the LAPD prided itself on looking trim, military, and smart while the kindest thing that could be said of the NYPD is that its remained, in its appearance, socially relevant to its environment. But both agencies understood, in their very bones, that they were there to keep the underclass under control.

In the Bronx, the cops had dubbed the Forty-first Precinct "Fort Apache" before I arrived there and I had to force them to remove a sign reading "The Alamo" over the Forty-fourth Precinct. The cops saw the surrounding ghetto as a sea of hostiles they were there to put down and control. The notion of "protecting and serving" did not translate to the ghetto very faithfully.

The gigantic scandals involving the LAPD, uncovered in 1999 and 2000, had their roots in the cops' styling of themselves as the "biggest, toughest, baddest gang" in a culture of gang violence. The cops defined it as a primitive struggle for control and acted on that premise. Law and the Constitution became irrelevant in this savage contest.

In tortured and distant relationship to the LAPD's festering problems was the situation in Philadelphia, where in 1985 a black mayor allowed his white police chief to fire-bomb a radical back-to-Africa enclave called MOVE. The resulting fire razed sixty-one homes and took eleven lives, five of whom were children.

A task force was appointed that catalogued a raft of problems, none of which were significantly addressed before the city and its police lapsed back into their routine. By 2000 the city had spent $16.3 million to rebuild and repair the block but failed to satisfy the occupants who complained of shoddy construction.

I pointedly asked Philadelphia's then commissioner about the accuracy of his famously low 1980s crime rates. He offered a two-word appraisal that confirmed my view and said it all: "They're suspect." An astonishing admission, and one he'd have certainly denied if I referred to it in any setting. As for those who'd cavil over the faded, historical references to statistical fudgings, we need only point to the disclosures in 2000 that the Philadelphia Police Department for years mislabeled rapes as lesser offenses or shelved the cases altogether.

Added to this was the new commissioner's assertion that the city's crime statistics were unreliable because, for years, they'd been canning. He, however, had to confront his own crisis with a videotaped display of his cops punching, kicking, and stomping a wounded black suspect in mid-July 2000. The suspect had been shot four times after shooting a cop in the hand and fleeing.

The more things changed . . .

In the late eighties, Philadelphia appointed a black police chief who failed to enact the needed reforms. Los Angeles, pressured to repudiate the shocking practices of the LAPD under Gates and impelled by the Warren Christopher Commission's findings, undertook a search for a new and different chief.

The Warren Christopher Commission's principal recommendation had been for tough, independent outside review and audits of the LAPD, so the city parents decided to search for a black police chief instead—and settled on Philadelphia's. They chose Willie Williams. Had the searchers spent any little time examining his tenure in Philadelphia, they might have thought twice. Five years later, the city bought out his contract and sacked him. Los Angeles replaced Daryl Gates—the embodiment of what some might call mindless police aggressiveness, often focusing on blacks —with a black police chief, Willie Williams, who never conquered the culture even while enervating—rather than redirecting—police energies.

By 1999 a new black police chief, up from the ranks, was coping with the legacy of the LAPD's tangled history, from the activism of Parker, Davis, and Gates to the socially significant passivism of Williams.

By late 1999 and through 2000 the new chief faced a horrifying and rapidly widening scandal, in which scores of officers were accused of framing, planting evidence, perjuring themselves, and even shooting totally innocent citizens they suspected of wrongdoing—mostly involving drug dealings.

By the spring of 2000, Los Angeles officials were estimating the civil liability potential (the King case had resulted in a settlement of several million dollars) in the hundreds of millions. As many as forty convictions were quickly discovered to have been falsely obtained, with the number increasing daily. A bitter dispute arose between the police chief and the district attorney, who promptly lost his bid for reelection in November 2000.

Amazingly, in many of these cases the very attorneys assigned to defend the accused had strongly counseled pleas of guilty, and totally innocent persons were persuaded, under the threat of very long mandated sentences, to reach out for deals. Facing enormously long mandatory sentences in drug cases, and what looked like airtight cases—which were frame-ups—skeptical attorneys advised their clients to accept the plea bargains offered. It was one of the most grotesque twistings of American justice ever revealed. It discredited—deservedly—mandatory sentences, and undermined a plea-bargaining system essential to the continued functioning of the process. And yet, in its outlines, it was of a piece with the department's history, involving, as it did, aggressive police tactics that mercilessly went after what they deemed to be "bad guys." It proved another colorful—and expensive—illustration of the fallibility of street justice. It also served as a cautionary tale to those, like me, who insisted on employing aggressive operations on the street that inevitably produced pressures to perform. Such demands could result in terrible abuses.

The case had been cracked not because of a conscience-stricken breach in the Blue Wall of Silence, but because, in the style of many recent Mafia prosecutions, an accused cop was coerced into talking because he needed a deal in order to mitigate his own punishment. To his credit, the newly appointed chief, Bernard Parks, moved swiftly and energetically to expand the inquiry but, choosing to work closely with the Feds, he sacrificed his relationship to the Los Angeles district attorney, resulting in an unnecessary public brouhaha. There was no need to allow internal squabbles to spill over into such important public issues.

The legacy of a culture shaped almost half a century earlier threatened to turn the LAPD into a virtual ward of Washington as revelations of a Justice Department study pointed to systematic abuses involving false arrests, unlawful shootings, and illegal searches. All of the cases emerging from this incident were unrelated to the horrific scandal involving a widening series of frame-ups.

The Los Angeles Police Department was faced with the prospect of a Justice Department suit that would place it under the virtual control of the capital or force it to agree to a consent decree—thirty years after the one on minority hirings—that created an elaborate monitoring system.

In one of the LAPD's recent scandals, the police not only shot and paralyzed a supposed drug suspect, they also planted a gun and evidence to secure his imprisonment. This is a piece of their "good guys/bad guys" approach that had characterized that agency's philosophy and served as the inevitable denouement to such legacies.

In 2000, this widening scandal has exposed every citizen to a steep monetary liability, a price that might do more for reform than countless exhortations.

OTHER CITIES—SAME CULTURE

Los Angeles faced the fate shared by Pittsburgh, which in 1997 was the first and largest city to be placed under such an order, as the result of a classic racial profiling incident involving a black motorist shot to death by white officers and a series of related incidents.

Also in the 1980s and 1990s, the New Orleans police agency was, to put it bluntly, out of control.

The reality behind this abstract assessment was the beating death of a suspect who'd killed a cop. The case never came to trial, since the city settled with the family. I was in agony over championing the cause of a cop killer—even one who'd been himself murdered by furious cops. My agreeing to serve as an expert for the family of the deceased would be sure to ignite a fury among cops.

Nothing creates as hot a frenzy in the ranks as a cop killing. I knew it, but it seemed imperative that the rule of law be extended even to— probably especially to—such outcasts.

The killing of a policeman in New Jersey in 2000 sparked a frenzied hunt for the killer. A black suspect was picked up three days later and brutally beaten by the cops. He died in custody.

It was the sort of case—like Diallo's—that normally results in acquittals for the accused police officers.

In this case the prosecution was by the Federals, for violation of the twenty-seven-year-old victim's civil rights. Four cops and one supervisor were convicted on December 19, 2000.

The case illustrated two rarely grasped yet critically important issues, namely, the fallibility of street justice (the deceased was not implicated in the officer's death; another man pleaded guilty to the officer's murder and was sentenced to a life term) and the importance of federal intervention in such cases. It is not too grand a statement to say that this— together with civil suits, the media, or the presence of a determined chief—is one of the very few tools for ensuring the accountability of police in America.

I remembered the results of a Bronx investigation into a cop killing. The cops, to a soul, were hyper and conducted endless dragnets for days. It was inconceivable that the case wouldn't be solved—all cop killings were—and so it was.

The detectives assigned worked tirelessly and pressured their sources mercilessly for leads. Finally they hit pay dirt. As the cops closed in, they captured the killer on a rooftop and very nearly killed him in "overcoming his resistance."

I watched in helpless fury as the prisoner was hospitalized. It seemed so idiotically counterproductive. The cops had very nearly blown the case with their excesses. A better-heeled defendant might well have mounted a vigorous and effective defense. We managed to convict him.

Years later, as chief in Minneapolis, I had an identical case, on August 25, 1981.

The killer was not immediately identified and a massive search went underway for the murderer of Officer Richard P. Miller. As the killer's identity became known, the search focused and intensified. I very explicitly and carefully warned the cops that they'd answer for any hair out of place when the suspect was captured. He was arrested and brought to the station house in mint condition and promptly convicted, in a state without a death penalty, and given life.

In New Orleans, police brazenness escalated to the arrangement of a police killing of a witness over the police radio and the casual slaying of a boy in a drug inquiry, which led to a settlement in a case that became a cause célèbre in the mayoral campaign, resulting in the settlement's overturn. Compounding the tragedy, the dead boy's mother went from a million dollars to nothing. I felt she had been wronged. I acted as an expert witness in two of these cases, but was both frustrated and relieved that I never had to take the stand.

In the late '70s and early '80s, New Orleans was probably, in terms of illegal force and dishonesty, the most criminal police agency in the country.

In such cities as Detroit, as we've seen, the debates took the form of not-too-subtly addressing the black community's concerns over the criminal justice system's treatment of its young men. Where other cities engaged in avoiding blatantly disturbing white sensibilities, as black chiefs or mayors deemphasized some of the more aggressive approaches, Detroit's mayor tended to make it a much more clear-cut issue, probably banking on the advantage of an overwhelmingly black electorate. Nevertheless, even in Detroit, the mayor managed to convince the business community into such glittering downtown projects as the Renaissance Center. Mayor Coleman Young, despite the adoring support of the city's black voters, still had to woo the white establishment if he was to generate such downtown projects.

The Chicago police riot of 1968, where the force went after protesters at the Democratic Convention, was a solid example of that city's approach to dissent. The city's all-powerful Mayor Richard Daley viewed the agency as a personal political instrument. Opponents of the Vietnam War took to the streets and the cops responded with such ferocity as to earn their handling of the demonstrators the title of "police riot."

Society's reactions to these events differs markedly if the protesters are white. Then, there is likely to be articulate and resourceful opposition to police overreactions.

The Chicago event was also wonderfully revealing in that, when this mayor opted for reform, earlier in his tenure and after a bad spell of disclosures and articles, he chose a modernizer and technocrat rather than a corruption/brutality fighter as his chief.

O. W. Wilson, whose *Police Administration* became our bible, was the rare exception to the nonwriting cops, although he was more professor than cop. He brought modern management techniques to an outmoded department and equipped it with the most advanced bells and whistles then available to police agencies. The more intractable problems were left more or less to fester, unseen and untouched behind the more cosmetic reforms being vigorously undertaken.

Thirty years later, the mayor was still Richard Daley—only this time it was the former mayor's more enlightened son.

BLACKS AND POLITICAL POWER

While the advent, nationally, of black police chiefs and mayors has blunted the weapons used to keep the underclass in line in the ghetto—

such as decoys, stings, and stakeouts—there has been the gain of defusing a lot of ardor for rioting following each crushing disclosure of racism by the police. Such appointments and elections may serve to deflect anger and mask egregious acts of police wrongdoing if black executives don't resist becoming apologists for these outrages. The pressure is on them to avoid riots and thereby prove their value to the city's rulers. The calm with which the Diallo verdict was greeted in the black community is the first available evidence for the value of the approach.

SEATTLE AND D.C.

Central to the questions of dealing with corruption and brutality is the character, ability, and determination of the chief. But management issues come into play, also, in a police agency's everyday life and how it copes with more quotidian concerns, such as large demonstrations.

In late 1999, protesters objecting to the globalization of markets and the exploitation of underdeveloped countries and their peoples attempted to interrupt a meeting of the World Trade Organization in Seattle. As these protests often do, this one included a large mass—thousands—of peaceful pickets and marchers and a small band of aggressive militants. In Seattle, the aggressive militants paralyzed the city, blocked traffic, smashed windows and destroyed other property, and managed to shut down parts of the World Trade Organization's agenda.

International publicity followed, little of it crediting the city administration's handling of the event.

In mid-April, an almost exact replica occurred in the nation's capital, at least in terms of the play, the players, and the objectives. The result differed markedly.

In preparation for the World Bank and International Monetary Fund meetings in Washington, D.C., the police closed the protesters' headquarters as a fire hazard; trained, prepared, and mobilized the troops with crisp efficiency; gathered comprehensive intelligence on the demonstrations; and made effective plans to cope. They made six hundred arrests the first day and only twenty the second.

Participants in the meetings were whisked to and fro smoothly. The agenda was met and, while the protesters numbered in the thousands and interrupted traffic, there was none of the chaos surrounding the Seattle event.

It must be said that the cops' foremost ally—heavy rain—played a significant role in the D.C. event (ironically, it didn't rain in Seattle, a city famous for its wetness) but the contrast in planning, preparation, and tactics could not have been more stark. In Seattle, the chief quit in a storm of criticism. In the capital, the chief basked in the glory of victory. It proved a welcome irrelevance that the chief in Seattle was white and the one in D.C. black.

I might not have agreed with all of it—especially closing the protesters' headquarters—but it proved a textbook case in the handling of such events, and for its positive aspects, I was sure it would serve as a future model to other chiefs.

Adding to Seattle's burdens, a lawsuit began in August 2000 in which alleged victims of racial profilings sought hundreds of millions in damages.

Elsewhere, the slippery slope of policing major cities took an unexpected international twist.

ELSEWHERE

In 2000, the mayor of Miami, angry over his police department's cooperation with the Feds in taking six-year-old Elian Gonzalez out of his uncle's home and restoring him to his natural father in Cuba, fired the city manager—himself a former police chief—for refusing to fire the police chief for failing to advise the mayor that his department was extending assistance. The drama centered on anti-Castro politics among Miami's exile community, and the return of the child to a perfectly fit parent was seen as impermissible surrender to Fidel Castro's antics in the case. The police chief, spared, quit anyway. The second in command—the officer who rendered the aid to the Feds—also quit.

It was an ugly example of rabid partisanship intruding into a family drama that, absent Fidel's shadow, would've been resolved—by all concerned—by returning the child to his father and thereby preserving the family values they all cherished.

And the presidential election in 2000 dramatically displayed the importance of the anti-Castro vote in Florida.

Notwithstanding the grotesque positions of the principals, the underlying principle of control of the police by elected representatives was widely ignored, indeed, if it was seen at all. The elected officials had been excluded from the operation. The cops had believed their bosses couldn't be trusted—a fatal flaw in democracy—whatever the merits of the suspicions.

The little boy needed to be removed and restored to his father. Even when the political leaders are wrong, democracy requires the subordination of the military (in this case, the police) to the will of the people's elected representatives—another tricky lesson.

The national landscape is heavily dotted with police problems that reflect a serious need to attack and resolve them. A determined, able, and energetic chief is critical to this process and appointing officials should be held responsible for the failures.

We've seen the critical importance of intervention by the Department of Justice, yet a presidential candidate promised to end these inquiries. We have seen the critical importance of FBI intervention in cases of police wrongdoing across the nation. Eliminating this oversight would leave citizens at the mercy of some brutal cops, with little or no recourse.

The centrality of the press is inherent in each of the crises.

In addition to racial profiling, individual acts of brutality, and incidents of corruption, cops have sometimes lapsed into massive violations of citizens' rights in order to achieve a twisted sense of order that would be more familiar to people living in dictatorships.

The awesome power of the police—and its discretionary use—created the temptation to abuse it, and the desperate need to guide and control its employments.

14

SWEEPS, ROUNDUPS, AND OTHER ABUSES

In the late sixties, a perfectly sane and even progressive police chief was spooked by a shaken, paranoid President Nixon and his compliant attorney general, John Mitchell, into herding thousands of Vietnam War protesters and arresting them in the nation's capital.

This would have been fine if the cops had been able to articulate some specific criminal act by each and every prisoner—one of the more modest requirements of our system of jurisprudence—but they didn't bother. They just swept the thousands away and carted them off to a stadium, held them for a while, and released them. It would have been worthy of a Latin American junta's actions—and certainly of a piece with Nixon's baleful view of democratic processes—but clearly out of place in America.

These were, to put it baldly, classic examples of false arrests, and on a massive scale. Those arrested sued and, many years and at least one administration later, won. By then the principal architects of this constitutional violation had long since left the stage to lucrative retirements, prison, or disgrace. Such a time gap between the outrage and its redress evil is one of the deficiencies of a democratic system—the villains have usually left by the time a just outcome arrives.

It has been my experience, particularly in cases involving blatant miscarriages of justice, that the Feds often simply temporize, delay, seek adjournments and leave it to their successors to take the inevitable hit. By then all can claim clean hands in the specific controversy. No one wants to be saddled with a lost trial on his or her watch.

One such case, the false arrest of a radical in San Francisco, was postponed beyond the young woman's sad demise from cancer and today remains—many years after the abuse—untried. My testimony, in a long deposition, clearly failed to whet the federal attorney's appetite for speedy justice.

The case illustrated the importance of lawsuits as perhaps the principal way of inhibiting the police from blatant miscarriages of justice. The woman, an environmental activist "tree hugger,"—literally and figuratively, in the jargon of the day (she was trying to preserve the giant redwood from logging)—was on her way with a friend to an Earth First demonstration. As she got into her car and drove off, a bomb exploded under her seat, injuring her pelvis severely and injuring her passenger less seriously.

The FBI, familiar with the activism of these militants, some of whom had dangerously spiked trees to be logged with metal objects that caused chain saws to shatter and injure loggers, jumped to the conclusion that the explosive device belonged to the occupants.

The FBI pressured the Oakland cops, who arrested the pair as they lay in hospital beds. That any evidence linking the victims to the explosive was lacking troubled no one. In the way I'd seen my own detectives repeatedly perform, they'd flown from conjecture to conjecture and acted on the suspicion. I'd developed a ready antidote to such speculation by saying, "Great. I agree, they're wrong. Where's the evidence?" No evidence, no arrest.

To compound the miscarriage of justice—blatantly false arrests—the Oakland cops stretched the truth to the breaking point in preparing an affidavit to secure a search warrant. It took a measure of chutzpah to confront a judge with the tortuous affidavit. The warrant was granted and the search turned up nothing.

The charges were quickly dropped but the harm, in terms of a flurry of publicity surrounding the arrests, the deprivation of freedom of the person, and the security of their property and effects from unreasonable search and seizures—had been done.

So, did the FBI and Oakland police move speedily to redress the injustice? As of 2000, many years after the event and the death of the main victim, the temporizing and appeals continue. Justice delayed . . .

In the same area, a knowledgeable, politically savvy, and even enlightened police chief also directed his department to sweep up and corral hundreds of demonstrators. They were bused to remote locations, detained over most of a weekend and released without charges. The demonstrations in that city usually focused on gay rights, the Vietnam War, or police brutality.

This was another colorful example of what could be considered false arrests.

I was retained as an expert witness on this one but the city settled for a large sum rather than risk a trial.

Just to prove how politically tone deaf he'd become, this same police chief actually had his cops confiscate copies of a free newspaper that had printed an unflattering photo of him, holding his baton in a sexually suggestive manner. He was fired as a consequence of this outrage. The mayor, in this case, was the former police chief against whom I'd testified in earlier abuses, and in which the plaintiffs I helped won. He was defeated in a reelection bid.[1]

The events served to illustrate just how far we can wander from our principles when sycophants insulate us from the realities we need to confront every day if we are to keep our bearings. In these cases the losers also include taxpayers, who increasingly and invariably have to pony up long after the details have slipped into the fog of memory.

MEANS AND ENDS

The simple lesson is not that you have to prove a person guilty, but that you do have to have sufficient evidence to establish that a crime has been committed, and that there is good reason to believe that the person arrested committed it. Articulable grounds. The temptation to evade this simple standard sometimes proves irresistible, but if our democracy is to have real meaning, resist it we must.

But, as a practical matter, mustn't a chief sometimes resort to tactics such as sweeps and roundups to preclude a greater harm?

The answer must be an emphatic no. If Homo sapiens has learned nothing at all he has learned that you cannot achieve noble ends through ignoble means. The methods employed ultimately shape the outcomes obtained.

The idealists behind the effort to rid the Teamsters Union of James Hoffa's influence were so convinced of the rightness of their cause that they bent the law in order to finance the candidacy of an insurgent. The end sought, eliminating gangster influence over America's largest union, could not have been more high-minded. The idealists sought no personal gain in this; they were motivated by clearly altruistic motives—which is why this case is a classic—yet they became criminals, soiled the process, and subverted democracy in their attempts to clean up the union.

The genius of our democracy lies in the primacy of the law.

MASS DEMONSTRATIONS

During my tenure in Minneapolis I was faced with many large-scale demonstrations—often in the form of sit-ins, trespasses, or blocking traffic—involving many hundreds. They involved protests against the manufacture of armaments; against aid to Central American rightists; against a president's policies when Reagan visited; and related issues of racial, economic, or social justice. I would first establish that they were violating the law, inviting those that wished to avoid arrest to leave, and order the officers to arrest the violators individually, charging them specifically with whatever act led to their arrests.

This laborious process took hours and hours but the wheels continued to grind and the accused—including my wife, who protested six times—were taken to court and almost always convicted. My wife served two ten-day stints in the workhouse. And there were no suits for false arrest, although we only narrowly missed one.

When one of my subordinates arrested a large group for protesting when they'd clearly broken no law and he'd been wrong to order their roundup, I petitioned the court to release the group of about forty and apologized to them. There was no doubting our vulnerability to a suit for false arrest, but the demonstrators explicitly eschewed this course. I later demoted the supervisor in charge of this miscarriage of justice.

PUBLIC RELATIONS

I did a number of unpopular things to promote better police-community interaction.

In the Bronx, I'd taught ghetto kids to swim. In Minneapolis I bribed the cops—with a day off—to play an unusual softball game with a gay group. I could not say it helped diminish the palpable homophobia in the agency, but I attended the four or so games I managed to organize.

In another attempt at promoting civility, I bought donuts and coffee both for the arrested protesters at Honeywell, objecting to their manufacture of weapons, and for the cops, using a fund created by my honoraria for speeches.

I asked a demonstrator how she'd enjoyed the treat, she returned, "What coffee? What donuts?"

The cops had been unable to bring themselves to share and had wolfed the goodies down. I had to *order* them to put out the donuts for those arrested. They reluctantly complied.

The event sparked three reactions—the conservative Right scorned and condemned the collation (coffee and donuts) as inappropriate; the supportive Left thought it the least I could do; and the majority in the middle laughed at the gesture as an unexpected and rather nifty bit of bureaucratic humor.

By 1976, I'd had a lot of experience with cops functioning in large formations. My view of such operations was pretty skeptical. However elaborate the planning and preparation, the actual loosing of phalanxes of cops on a mob very quickly became two clashing mobs. I had watched our mistakes in Harlem and East Harlem riots and in such fiascoes as the April 1968 Columbia University bust, in which cops burst in on students sitting in, in protest of the school's cavalier treatment of the surrounding black community.

It also became clear to me that police decisions flowed from the personal perspectives and philosophies of the decision makers. So it was obviously essential to examine the beliefs animating my own responses to these crises.

COLLEGES

When Columbia University students occupied several campus buildings in 1968,[2] by way of demonstrating solidarity with a surrounding black community that bitterly resented the erection of a college gymnasium on a small local park's grounds, it looked to us as the irresponsible actions of militant, pampered, contemptuous, willful darlings. The student sit-ins were, to us, self-indulgent expressions of beliefs the students couldn't possibly understand.

These occupiers of a hallowed institution were ungrateful radicals with no sense of class loyalty, order, or decency—or so we all thought in the NYPD. They were trespassers and interlopers and had to be taught a lesson.

The school's administration was infuriated by the invasion and occupation and cooperated heartily with police planners who were determined to restore order and who would cleverly position highly visible black commanders in key action roles. Finally, late on an April night, the police struck—literally and figuratively—chasing, clubbing, gassing, and arresting—triumphantly clearing the premises. Calm returned to Columbia as it resumed its loftier purposes. I had been an unblinking participant.

Yet something in the event continued to trouble me and the questions bounced in my head inconclusively for years. They would not jell until shaken by events in the mid-1970s in the Bronx.

The city university system announced tuition rises to still very modest levels—a small fraction of the costs of private colleges and way below the Ivy League sums. Still, the students were often poor, black and Hispanic, striving to scale the class ladder. I had been a beneficiary of the opportunity, attending Baruch College from 1957 to 1968 at night and finally emerging with a master's degree.

Now students suddenly sat in at Hostos College and Lehman College to protest the tuition rise.

I was the commander of all Bronx forces—a job I adored, but for which there was little competition at that rank level—and immediately went to see the Lehman president, Leonard Leif, whom I hadn't previously known. By then I'd been in the NYPD over twenty years, risen eight rank levels one rung at a time, and had become persuaded to the charms of conflict resolution, mediation, and the massaging of issues, as opposed to direct assaults. Surgical strikes did not appeal to me, having seen too many fail.

My exchange with the president was troubling.[3] He wanted the buildings cleared. The vandals were inside the gates. There was no equivocation in his tough approach. I had expected a more thoughtful, professorial mien.

It became obvious that my lame temporizings were bothering him. They were to me, after all, students.

He promptly rejoindered with, "Some of them are Vietnam veterans. These aren't kids." He wanted them out now.

The Hostos president never called and we never met or spoke. The student body there was largely black and Puerto Rican.

I returned to my office determined to negotiate. My approach was driven by one simple conclusion—that the students had at least as much a stake in the institutions as their presidents, and possibly more.

I appointed a liaison to meet with the students at both schools and he transmitted my simple message—don't assault anybody or destroy any property and I won't barge in without prior notice. I'd be available to them and would allow anyone to leave peaceably if I had to intervene and clear the building. They were given my number.

The demonstrators, swept by the firestorm of rumors that find easy haven in such settings, did in fact call me several times to complain that they'd learned a raid was imminent, and so on. I gained credibility with assurances that proved accurate.

In the meantime, President Leif was strongly pressuring my superiors to force me to act. My immediate boss, responding to his pressures, called. He wanted to know why I didn't go in and clear the demonstrators out and arrest them. The two colleges were in turmoil and a lot of classes had been suspended.

I pleaded for time and offered that I was negotiating with them and was hopeful, a much more optimistic assessment than I truly felt was warranted by the facts, but I didn't feel it was best to burden him with hard truths.

Lehman's president intensified his efforts and now my boss's boss, the highest-ranking uniformed officer—four stars—who'd also been an erstwhile subordinate of mine, called to communicate his angst over my ditherings. I stalled, hoping that the passage of time would persuade everyone to negotiate a reasonable solution and, perhaps, tire everyone into accepting a compromise. After all, besides the suspension of some college activities, nothing terrible was happening. The chief reluctantly gave me a bit of time. I assumed full responsibility for the outcome.

President Leif then had the Board of Higher Education sue me to force me to act. I was not subpoenaed but very pointedly attended the court hearing. The sit-in had, by then, lasted about seven weeks.

The judge was wonderful. He noted my presence and said he was confident I understood my duty and that he didn't feel the need to coerce me into it. He would not, just then, order me to act but his meaning was crystal clear. I left knowing my time had run its course and now had to do something.

I had my liaison officer visit both groups to tell them all that had occurred and that we would arrive, in force, around 2 A.M. the next day.

When my cops assembled the demonstrators were told all who wanted to leave could go home, the remainder would be arrested for trespass and an additional charge of resisting if we had to carry them to the waiting vans.

About thirty-five or so chose arrest at each site, so calmly that the event was reported in a two-inch blurb around page 37 of the next day's *New York Times*. It was nonevent at both colleges.

A postscript arose when a media guru named Tony Schwartz asked me to visit his studio. Schwartz was an independent radio and TV wizard who'd been involved in major national campaigns. He taped my version of events. Then he had President Leif do the same.

Without identifying the speakers, he'd ask listeners what they thought and the answers were uniform: a routine encounter between a tough, rigid, uncompromising cop and a liberal softie of a college president—only they'd always identify Leif as the cop and me as the president.

HOMOPHOBIA

Police agencies have historically been pretty homophobic: none more virulently than Minneapolis in the seventies. The last raid on a gay bathhouse occurred on February 10, 1980. I was sworn in on the eleventh. The history of police abuses in the late twentieth and early twenty-first centuries centers on the clashes between cops and blacks, or gays, or the underclass.

People are always confusing condition with behavior. Both hetero- and homosexuality are human conditions—how these are expressed is the behavior. One does not inevitably dictate the other. We entrust our daughters to heterosexual male teachers, who might well secretly lust after them but—rightly—focus on their behavior.

When politicos and cops objected to my willingness to hire gays as cops, I'd ask why.

"Well, you know what they do, don't you?"

"Sodomy, you mean?" I'd ask.

"Well," they'd stumble, "yes, and you know . . . "

I responded that if they—or anyone—committed a crime I'd be happy to arrest them and charge them with it.

The kicker would come when I added that I didn't inquire into the practices of heterosexual cops—male or female—in the darkness and privacy of their bedrooms, but I hoped, for everyone's sake, that they were doing something reasonably imaginative.

The law mainly, in its wisdom, focuses on behavior, not condition. President Clinton could have learned that lesson and spared himself, and the nation, a lot of unnecessary grief over gays in the military. In fact, he might have been a lot better off concentrating his energies on inquiring into the sexual harassment of women in the ranks—a far more serious matter.

In both New York City and Minneapolis I worked hard to eliminate police harassment of gays, a widespread and even popular practice.

THE PEOPLE

From the painful stumblings of the riots in Harlem, East Harlem, and elsewhere—inspired by black outrage over a police shooting or such a ghastly tragedy as the Reverend Martin Luther King Jr.'s assassination in 1968; or the official handling of the 1971 Attica Prison uprising, in which many died; or the eighty-plus deaths (the number was never precisely fixed) at Waco—I gradually developed an approach to these problems.

First, in street disorders, take control of the avenues, protect the glass of the shops to prevent looting, and leave the residential side streets to the demonstrators where peer pressures would act to prevent vandalism against their own property.

Second, arrest selectively and only for articulated acts of wrong-doing: no sweeps or roundups.

Third, do as little as possible once the situation is contained and stabilized. Isolate and control the site.

Fourth, in such events as sit-ins, negotiate endlessly and patiently. Ignore the rumors. Who can forget Attorney General Janet Reno's lame defense of storming Waco with the questionable charge that children were being molested there. If true, it had been going on for years, with official tolerance, and no one could frame the problem as an emergency requiring immediate and deadly action.

Fifth, prepare an action plan for attack to be used only if the actions clearly demand it. This means to act in defense of life—not on the basis of dumb speculation.

Sixth, bring the public along with you. One of the really great mysteries of public life is the power of the people in a democracy. Their support is critical to the success of any mass action.

Seventh, remember that once loosed, the police—local or federal—is just another armed and uncontrolled body and you're going to have to live with the consequences. The order to "go" has to be pretty much a last resort. Surgical strikes are possible but rare.

Eighth, don't be afraid to make concessions. The British government appeared to cave in to Pakistani militants in a plane hijacking in 1999 and the Indian government released terrorists to accomplish the peaceful end of the crisis. No additional lives were lost. The hijacking ended in peaceful surrender. Sticking to any policy—such as "We don't negotiate with terrorists"—with rigid consistency can become a dangerous and self-defeating straitjacket. The principal stress in training special weapons attack teams in Minneapolis centered on endless negotiations—even as we taught them the use of explosives and other weapons.

Ninth, violence has its uses and shouldn't be excluded from planning, but it can be seductive in its appeal, especially to macho types, and its limits need to be recognized.

Tenth, don't be afraid to take calculated risks based on logic. The administrator who empties a building over an anonymous phoned threat is at the mercy of any idiot or psycho with a quarter. A credible, detailed threat requires more serious treatment and a scale of precautionary actions—such as searches, locking of doors, restriction of access, and the like—should be included. The point is to distinguish between a plausible danger and the rantings of a drunk or a nut, or the prankishness of kids.

EVENTS

If Governor Nelson Rockefeller had responded to the inmates' demand that he negotiate when they'd taken over Attica Prison in 1971 and captured about fifteen guards, it is very likely that the many deaths could've been prevented and the enormously expensive lawsuits that followed successfully interdicted. The governor's refusal to go to the scene and negotiate was in the most vivid tradition of toughness. A terrible tragedy ensued.

Attorney General Janet Reno's surrender to a discredited FBI director's pleas for action resulted in Waco. All that was needed was to fence off the area, contain the occupants, cut off all services, and negotiate endlessly—preparing for the option of assault if it clearly became necessary. The predictable train of lawsuits rumbles on in 2000 with, perhaps, incalculably high costs to taxpayers.

Events in Central America had American militants of the Left hopping mad in 1988. President Reagan seemed to be siding with every repressive regime there—clandestinely aiding right-wingers and hounding "freedom fighters" in the hills.

A demonstration broke out in the center of Minneapolis one March night. Traffic was stopped as militants took to the streets and burned garbage in the intersection.

I had a large body of cops present, itching for action. I held them back and stood there for hours. It didn't escalate and I repeatedly warned the commander to cool off.

Finally, late at night, the demonstrators began to drift off. They returned the next night and so did I, with my contingent, which remained leashed. The night petered to a desultory dissolution.

On the third night the demonstrators burned the flag—it became a front-page picture nationally—and blocked traffic, marched, and broke the glass at a military recruiting office. I did nothing.

By then the events had received wide publicity. The public was exasperated. Letters to the editor, calls to phone-in shows, man-in-the-street interviews, and other harbingers clearly showed the public patience to be at an end. The people saw the need for, and demanded, action.

There was no demonstration on the fourth day and I exploited the hiatus by pointedly complaining that everyone's patience was exhausted and that we'd make arrests and respond vigorously at the next event, scheduled for the fifth day in front of the federal courthouse. My warnings received wide exposure.

The demonstrators showed up, sat in the roadway blocking traffic, smashed some courthouse doors, and disrupted the downtown area. I ordered the cops in and they relished the task. Using batons, mace, and dogs, they arrested scores, carried them off, and cleared the area over the outraged shrieks of the militants.

The arrests were prosecuted. Everyone was charged with a specific act; the allegations of police brutality—and I'm certain they occurred (I was there)—were investigated and shelved. Press attention—clearly reflecting the people's view—was understanding and tolerant, even as occasional cavils were expressed.

A curious postscript came over the flag burning. This really tested my principles because I publicly supported the right to do so—but it was a felony. We identified the burner and charged him but, in a landmark case, the law was held to be an unconstitutional infringement of the right of free speech.

In the end, I had the feeling that I'd kept the faith and learned from my mistakes at Columbia. There, we'd crashed in, chasing and clubbing and arresting what I later came to see as caring, involved students determined to seek justice. It took me years to realize we should have waited and negotiated with the protestors. The entire outcome was driven by our mistaken view that the students were criminals. Indeed, at the end of thirty-six years I felt that whatever cleverness I brought to my actions emerged from the ashes of the blunders and worse I had committed. Experience is a nice name for it; wisdom is a bigger lie.

In dealing with large-scale demonstrations or disorders there is a need for gathering intelligence, planning the response, distinguishing between peaceful protesters and violent dissidents, and bringing the public along with you.

The critical role played by the media is too frequently ignored by police policy shapers.

15
THE
PRESS

If there is a more important indication of a free society than the press, I've not encountered it.

The media is our public forum for debate and reshaping policy. No one who has spent any time under the press's scrutiny doubts the strength of its power. Public life is public exposure—and the means for conveying revelations is the press.

The American people get their information, have their opinions shaped, and develop their approaches to problems very largely as a consequence of the information they receive from the Fourth Estate.

Public figures often fear and loathe the press and find themselves at war with it. They rarely see it as a simple vehicle for transmitting information to the public—but that's what it is.

Public officials are often surrounded by sycophants and toadies. In this environment it is not hard to believe in your essential wonderfulness. The press's approach is a cold douche thrown on this warm glow.

In order to function in government—at any level—it is essential to view the press as a neutral transmitter of information. Yet the attitude of many officials is hostility, paranoia, or worse.

Public life requires that the press be viewed as the informer of a people perennially hungry for news. Officials must thicken their skins, not take items personally, respond to neither criticisms nor flattery as if the ego were involved, and recognize a free press as the firmest pillar of a democratic society.

I observed many incidents involving the press and came away with genuine gratitude for its services and amazement at some of the reactions of otherwise sensible people.

From 1989 to early 1991 I served as Minnesota's commissioner of gaming and worked for Governor Rudy Perpich. I liked Perpich because he loved the little people and reflected it in his initiatives. He thought big—once inviting Mikhail Gorbachev to Minnesota, and, to the surprise of many, he came; and conceiving America's largest shopping mall, which had the distinction of becoming the Mall of America. He had a few clinkers, but the man was a big thinker and a sure champion of the lunch-pail worker.

Perpich taught me the meaning of uxorious, as he doted on his wife, Lola, whom he took everywhere. It was a treat to watch his affectionate fussing over her. He had a son, who suffered from a disorder that sapped his energy, and a lovely daughter.

Perpich came to my defense when, in delivering a speech on race at the University of Wisconsin, I was asked why I hadn't mentioned Native Americans as having suffered the same deracination as the blacks.

They had, I responded, but they didn't spring to mind because of their small numbers. Then I added, "They are a blasted and defeated people."

The Urban Coalition branded me a racist and demanded my firing. I publicly welcomed an inquiry. Perpich appointed his Human Rights Commission to investigate and his report, and my black host's efforts, cleared me.

But Perpich, ever the devoted family man, was particularly thin-skinned where they were concerned. He'd once hired his ailing son in a consultant capacity and was stung when he was accused of nepotism.

Perpich had been lieutenant governor in 1978 when the sitting governor resigned. Perpich rose to the governorship and appointed him senator, to occupy a seat vacated before the term expired. Perpich served two years but the Democrats, as a direct result of this cynical maneuver, were swept from statewide power in the two senate seats and the governor's chair.

Perpich waited and ran again in 1982 and won, and won again in 1986. By 1990 he'd served a total of ten years—longer than any predecessor.

Minnesota's governors are entitled to a portrait at the capitol, and one was done of him.

In 1990 he was running for reelection against Arne Carlson, a credible but uninspiring opponent that Perpich should have been able to handle.

Now, in the midst of the campaign he demanded a second portrait at the capitol, this time to include his beloved Lola. The press went wild over the image. Perpich pointed out his immediate predecessor's portrait with his horse and cartoonists promptly inked an image of a portrait featuring Perpich standing next to a horse's rear. Somewhere he uttered the word "goofy," objecting to such characterizations, and he was immediately dubbed Governor Goofy. It would not have stuck, except for the vehemence of his objection. Railing at ridicule—public life's most fearsome weapon—is a certain prescription for its enhancement. It invites piling on and reduces the target to ever-increased levels of ridiculousness. As the campaign heated up, I felt I owed it to the man to candidly tell him he was on a Titanic-like course, so I went to see him.

"Governor, the people of Minnesota get their information from the press. War with the press is war with the people. Your campaign is suffering because of your outbursts against the press."

Without uttering the word, his rejection of the message could not have been more eloquent or direct: "I know you wouldn't take it if it were your family, Tony, and I'm not going to sit by and take their lies and libels."

I suddenly remembered being sent an advance copy of a vicious columnist's lie about my family. On that occasion, I calmly called the editor and said, "If you run it, I'll sue." They didn't.

I'd been psychologically thrown out and respectfully departed.

Vindication came in June 2000 when a portrait, including the beloved Lola, was finally hung in the capitol.

I'd been through an identical experience in 1973 when I went to see my old NYPD boss, then the president of New York City's council, to advise him to postpone his race for mayor. It looked like Beame's year, I said. He dismissed me with the pronouncement, "I can be mayor." He was wrong. Fate decreed he'd head the transit police instead and I joined him, for the third and last time, as number two in 1976.

Perpich's problem was that he hadn't thickened his skin sufficiently to function successfully in public life.

Perpich lost in 1990, and a few years later he died of a lingering disease he'd characteristically managed to keep secret from his closest friends. He was a man of great virtue and such trivial flaws as an obsession with secrecy.

An early example had taught me the danger of seemingly innocent announcements to the press.

I'd been assigned to investigate the disappearance of a Columbia University professor who was an exile from Spain's Civil War and who had worked in the government of Rafael Trujillo, dictator of the Dominican Republic. I got the case not because of my sleuthing skills— scant, to be generous—but as a result of speaking the language. I worked on this mystery for years and made little progress, finally concluding a concatenation of events that made their way, because of possible libel, into a roman à clef—as yet unpublished.

In the course of this delicate inquiry—full of international ramifications and generating a fair amount of press interest—officials sometimes stepped on land mines. One such occurred when my supervisor, against my advice, acknowledged the plausibility of a kidnap by boat. After he expressed the view, on television, that the professor had been spirited out in a Dominican ship, Trujillo snapped the trap by proving it couldn't have been so. A classic red herring across the investigative path. Trujillo now held he couldn't be guilty of this crime, and that the charge that he was responsible was a canard. It had been a cleverly set trap.

The NYPD was acutely embarrassed and the supervisor was demoted and driven to retire.

SOUND AND OTHER BITES

Public life is very like Madison Avenue—a place of catchy slogans and arresting phrases. Tedious explanations don't get you far in a thirty-second commercial—arguably the very apotheosis of our creative thinking—or in the lead to newspaper stories.

I learned to distill—to take a reasonably complicated idea and reduce it to a few punchy words. Brevity and clarity were the goals. The point, after all, was to get your view into the headline.

I'd think and think about an issue, try to conjure up a suitably dramatic literary allusion or quote, refine it, and finally produce it. I was obsessed by the punchy, pithy communication skills reflected in marketing efforts.

We—my boss and I—became altogether too good at this and incurred the enmity of an invisible police commissioner, rendered even more opaque by the overshadowings of the chief inspector's announcements and pronouncements. This was the NYPD from 1966 to 1968.

A key test, for us, was to make the Quote of the Day in the *New York Times*. Over the two-and-a-half-year period my boss made it twice.

The man I worked for, before Perpich, was the very antithesis of the prickly, thin-skinned press paranoiacs I had come to expect in public life.

Minneapolis mayor Don Fraser never minded my freewheeling, publicity-harvesting ways and even saw the point of informing, and getting the support of, the public. Although this was useful, it inflated my image into something of a political force but he was never threatened by it, secure as he was in his own skin.

When I questioned one council member's integrity and accused another of being the former union-chief-cum-mayor "in drag," Mayor Fraser called me. I was out of town to give a talk. He asked if I'd said that. I confirmed I had.

It was, to frame an analogy, the attack of appointed staff on elected officialdom and, to Fraser, impermissible. He suspended me, without pay, for three days. It was the one and only time I'd ever been disciplined over a thirty-six-year career.

When the press called, I quipped, "The Lord giveth and the Lord taketh away; blessed be the name of the Lord." The reporter who wrote the original story was grateful I hadn't finked out on him by saying I'd been misquoted.

I was undeniably stung by the humiliation and eagerly sought, and failed to get—after an unsuccessful meeting with Mayor Wilson Goode—the Philadelphia chief's job.

The suspension was very likely an infringement of my free speech rights—there were clear precedents and I was confident I could, by suing, overturn it—but my respect for Fraser kept me from challenging his act in any way.

While chief in Minneapolis, I encountered two examples of what might be labeled the power of nonpress events.

I had never—and wouldn't have—a press information officer to spin, massage, and cosmetize the simple truth. Reporters were urged to speak to the cop assigned for the poop on a case.

Once a reporter called to say the detective on the scene wouldn't talk to him.

We had a serial murderer who was picking up Native American women at bars and driving to secluded places where he'd beat them badly, sexually mutilate them by inserting broomsticks and such into their genital areas, and murder them. This call came from the site of the latest murder and the detective—a talented guy up to his ears in this terrible series—knew he couldn't say much, so he'd refused to talk at all.

I asked that he be put on and asked him about it. "It's a continuing investigation, Chief. The family hasn't even been notified. We don't want to reveal stuff that only the killer and we know. This isn't the time to talk about it."

He was, of course, totally right.

So what I said to him was: "Fine, I agree. Then just say as much or as little to the press as you think wise, including, 'We simply can't comment on the issue at this time on camera and for the record.'" He understood this was not a suggestion and did it.

As it happened, he finally came up with a suspect but the evidence we had was tenuous. An indictment was clearly doable, but a conviction for murder was a decided risk. In the meantime, we were holding the suspect on a welfare fraud charge that was real, but unconnected to the series of murders we thought he'd done.

I was so outraged when the county prosecutor demurred over presenting the case to a grand jury that I went across the street to see him. He felt the case was tenuous, at best.

I bluntly told him he had to submit the case. I was sure that the vision of horrifying headlines, in a public row, was not appetizing.

He surprised me with his answer, but I saw the threat as animating his response. "Okay, I'll submit the case if you'll assign the two detectives to this case, for one month, to secure additional evidence."

"And," I responded, "what if they can't get anything more on the guy?"

"Then we'll go with what we have."

It was a deal.

The cops toiled, came up with some surprisingly weighty additional evidence, and the man was tried, convicted, and imprisoned.

Internally I had, in 1980, inherited a hotbed of political intrigues in Minneapolis.

Exasperated beyond endurance by the subtle subversion of former chiefs in the ranks, I undertook a radical remedy. I ordered that two captains be assigned to report to an office every day from 8 A.M. to 4 P.M., with one hour for lunch, and do nothing at all.

Since I ran a totally open and accessible system, I was very soon confronted with a front-page cartoon, with story, in the *Minneapolis Tribune*. The cartoon depicted two captains, at facing desks, in a bare room with only a phone at each desk. A conspicuous wire led from one phone to the other. The captains could only call each other.

Well, there was a furor.

The city council's public safety committee summoned me. They clearly expected me to engage in tortured evasions and excuses but I said the story was accurate. I couldn't trust the captains to do any task in good faith; they showed up every day, sober, in uniform and on time and went through all the motions faithfully. I couldn't trust them and wouldn't use them. Civil service protected their tenure.

I did though, with a bit of secret glee, offer to detach them to serve the council in any capacity that was consistent with their job titles.

The council dropped the matter cold, the captains remained in exile—until one of them, months later, begged to be given an assignment and he'd carry it out in the best faith. I tested him, found him sincerely chastened, and put him in charge of a precinct. The other guy remained in limbo for the rest of my tenure.

In another example of the importance of truth telling, especially when dealing with the press, I was invited to appear on a national talk show.

When asked, on the *Today* show in April 1991, whether the Rodney King incident was an aberration, I said the only remarkable thing about it was that it had been videotaped. There wasn't a black male in the country who couldn't identify with King, I added. The event seemed a perfect illustration of the yawning and growing chasm between public understanding and police reality.

An unexpected result of my outburst was to be summoned by the chairman of the Center to Prevent Handgun Violence to a board meeting the next day.

I'd only just taken over the presidency of the agency two weeks earlier and had moved to Washington, D.C. Now, they wanted my resignation. Bryant Gumbel had asked me, on the show, if the appointment and election of black chiefs and mayors hadn't made a difference in American policing and I answered, "Colin Powell [then the Army's Chief of Staff and, of course, an African American] may think he's black, but he's doing the bidding of the white power structure."

I apparently, if unwittingly, added insult to injury when, in response to another question on homelessness, I said, "If President Bush would only part the curtains of his residence he could see homeless people camped out in Lafayette Park across the street."

No one beside the chairman had, or has, ever commented on this totally forgettable exchange—not a ripple from anywhere—but they insisted and, over the next few days, I negotiated my departure.

The chairman's first offer was such as to prompt me to tell him that he'd made my task easy because, since I liked and respected him, I'd have taken any reasonable tender. His proposal was so chintzy that I insisted on a year's salary and an exchange of flattering, if mendacious, letters. He blanched and would get back to me.

I decided that, in the event of their refusal, I'd insist on a board meeting (I was a member) and a formal vote: I'd sue for breach of contract, since I had moved to Washington on the understanding that I'd serve a year, and notify the *Today* show that my appearance had cost me my job, even though my comments had no real relation to the center's activities. I would also advise the press and face the center with the sort of ugly public controversy I had, by then, some experience in handling.

Their lawyer asked to meet with me and I told him he had to return to the board with something, so I reduced my demand to six months' wages. He'd get back to me.

They finally acceded to my requests and I left, totally satisfied that I hadn't let them bully me into another defeat. I had, in the parlance of my profession, certainly "stepped on my own schwanz," and I returned to my home in Minneapolis with my wife.

Before I left Georgetown, Minnesota radio stations, having heard of another of my missteps, called to ask about my brief tenure. "They've discovered what a hideous little incompetent cretin I am and unmasked me. I return to Minnesota a whipped dog, with my tail between my legs."

They all thought I was a great card and proceeded to say things like, "You probably tried to make too many changes, too fast." It was a fact that I'd made some much-needed reforms and stubbed a lot of toes, engendering resentments that led to those displaced pressing for my ouster, but I'd totally misread the political climate and consequences. I said nothing about the real cause, made no excuses, and continued making jokes about it. I never, until now, revealed the story behind my departure.

And it all began with a commonplace reference to the behavior of the LAPD in the Rodney King case.

Nevertheless, my faith in the press grew.

It will come as a surprise and disappointment to many of my colleagues when I say that I found reporters intelligent, interested, honest, fair, and objective—in the overwhelming majority.

I never knew one to breach an off-the-record agreement even though I felt I was, and should be, always on the record. They erred, of course, but mostly got the facts right and I left with a greater respect for the media than when I entered.

Were I to be asked which institution is most critical to a democracy, I'd say a free press. Were I to be asked which institutions contributed most to my progress I'd cite education first and the benefits accruing from the protections of trade unionism second.

So it was a bitter disappointment to discover the behavior of the latter within police ranks.

16
POLICE UNIONS

My career in Minneapolis began when I was thrown into the pot, along with my boss and his two bosses, and summarily fired as number two in the New York Transit Police in September 1979.

I wasn't just unemployed. I had been made unemployable in any public capacity in New York. I found that out as I was offered two jobs, only to see the offers sheepishly withdrawn with vague references to City Hall.

I had my NYPD pension, some savings, a son in college and another heading for a similarly costly schooling experience, plus the usual mortgage and expenses. My wife was home.

I was deeply moved when, years after I'd called my son Tony at Amherst to break the news of my humiliating ouster, he confessed that he had silently wept.

When I'd gone to transit three years earlier the bosses there wanted me to forgo my NYPD pension and simply transfer the benefits. In prolonged negotiations I refused, seeking to increase savings through the pension and salary, and they finally gave in to my demands. I saved every penny I could for the three years, but was severely criticized for "double-dipping" in the press and by the mayor—despite it being my perfect legal right to do it. Adding a further blow, they declined to pay me money due for vacation, lost time, and overtime, and I had to sue. It was a glorious moment of triumph when I emerged from the courtroom with a check for $15,000. Management reforms were one thing and legal entitlements another, in my view.

In a further irony, my family and I had vacationed in Cape Cod the previous month and, since we'd been doing that for years, I suggested to my wife that we should buy a piece of land there. This proved enormously profitable and it was a perfect illustration of the truism that we really were in the real estate business, as well as a lesson in the importance of luck. If they'd fired me one month earlier I could never have made this investment; one month later and I couldn't have afforded it.

Now I was out of work, although serving in the role of adjunct professor at John Jay College, and eagerly embraced the offer of chief in Minneapolis in January 1980.

In 1970 the police union's head was elected mayor, and he was reelected two years later. Then a rival overturned him and he overturned the rival.

Over this decade the Minneapolis Police Department was politicized in a way no other law enforcement agency had ever experienced. The most corrosive imaginable spoils system followed the bitterly fought mayoral contests in which there'd be two hundred pros, two hundred antis, and over three hundred in the middle: cops of all ranks, nervously wringing their hands. I characterized this latter group as the man who, having dropped the soap in a Turkish bath, didn't know which way to turn. They electioneered shamelessly, distributed literature, and organized rallies, with no distinction between being on or off duty.

The winners would look a lot like Willy Wonka in the chocolate factory. The losers suffered what they must and awaited the next election.

There had been, in other cities, union officials who'd risen through the ranks to take the reins of CEO but these had been legitimate climbs and transformations into managerial perspectives. In Minneapolis, the vandals entered the city gates. There the union head directly—if not explicitly—sought to have his organization run the police agency for the benefit of his allies.

Every act of government is political, but Minneapolis had brought partisanship into the game with a vengeance, thereby grotesquely skewing the outcome. Unions of government employees were the fastest-growing segment of the labor movement, nationally, over the past thirty years, and nowhere did this growth outpace the swelling numbers of unionized cops.

Virtually overnight, toothless fraternal/benevolent aggregates metamorphosed into moneyed, powerful entities able to hire the smartest lawyers and spin doctors, help elect allies and work behind the scenes to secure favorable appointments, especially in such critically important bodies as civil service commissions, arbitration panels, and other deciders of cops' fates, individually or en masse.[1]

As to which of these applied to Minneapolis, the answer, I was to discover, was all of the above.

The power of the union—the Police Officer's Federation (at least they eschewed the macho Patrolman's Benevolent Association that holds sway in New York City to this day)—had to be curtailed to the boundaries appropriate to a legitimate labor organization: wages, benefits, contracts, and members' welfare.

THE POLICEMAN'S BILL OF RIGHTS[2]

The two shaping influences in my life were education and trade unionism. I really entered the middle class in 1965 when I was promoted to captain in the NYPD, and my salary nearly doubled to the munificent sum of $16,000 a year. This had occurred through the tireless efforts of police unions.

As the chief inspector's aide in 1967, I was seen as little more than an amanuensis by visitors. I attended meetings, took notes, and repressed my voluble instincts. A steady stream of politicos, police executives, union leaders, journalists, and such met with my boss, and I participated as his aide.

The Patrolman's Benevolent Association always had pleas, demands, and grievances and often sought audiences to air these concerns.

At one such, attended by PBA president John Cassesse and vice president Ed Kiernan in New York in 1967, I sat silently and took notes as they complained that the Internal Affairs Division (IAD) was plucking cops out of their beds late at night, holding them incommunicado, even forbidding bathroom breaks, and depriving them of counsel in investigations of police wrongdoing or criminal actions.

The phrase that impressed me was when the union leaders recited a familiar litany: "Cops aren't even given the rights we extend to criminals."

After they left, Chief Garelik and I discussed the meeting briefly, as was our wont—he had a very busy schedule—and I wondered if we couldn't prepare an order outlining investigative procedures that would extend a measure of dignity to cops in these inquiries. The chief inspector encouraged me to look into it.

The problem, of course, was the resistance of the IAD to such reforms and, since they reported directly to the police commissioner, the chief inspector had no direct control over them.

I thought about it and hit on a possibility. The key commander at IAD was Sydney Cooper, a brilliant, mercurial, tough, imaginative, and widely feared corruption fighter who enjoyed his reputation and was attending law school.

I prepared a memo from the chief inspector to Cooper's boss suggesting that Cooper be asked to draft a set of guidelines for investigating police wrongdoing that would emphasize protecting the constitutional rights of the cops targeted for investigation by IAD. Cooper, I was confident, would see it as an irresistible intellectual challenge. Garelik signed the memo and I waited.

Before too long a document came down in rough draft form featuring the guidelines. Since it bore a covering memo signed by Cooper's boss, the objection to it, if adopted without changes, had been outflanked.

Thus was Temporary Operating Procedure 167 of 1967 born.

When the *Daily News* called to ask about it, Chief Garelik had the reporter hold, cupped his hand over the speaker, and told me what the call was about.

"What do we call it?" he asked.

In a flash I responded, "The Policeman's Bill of Rights."

And thus was a monster born.

This reform, I later learned, proved the straw that broke an exasperated police commissioner's back. He'd had enough of his subordinate's upstagings.

The storm finally broke in a form typical of the subtle, indirect bureaucracy we occupied—a snotty little tickler from the police commissioner, demanding to know on whose authority the latest initiative had been undertaken.

My boss' consternation was profound, to put it mildly. I saw it as a not altogether undeserved, or even unexpected, comeuppance. I certainly didn't welcome it but felt—all along—that we were getting away with too much. So much, in fact, that it was my boss, not the police commissioner, whom the mayor asked to join him as a running mate in the 1969 election.

If this were only one shoe it would have been okay.

I set about preparing the usual bureaucratic response, with impressive appendages, but, even before the chief signed it, another venomous missive arrived, with another pointed question.

Over the next year, a state of quiet siege settled stonily as it became clear that a glacial shift had moved the center of power from the Office of the Chief Inspector to that of the First Deputy Commissioner John F. Walsh.

The Manual of Procedure contained enough duties and power to keep the chief inspector not only busy, but at the center of things, whoever might be deciding what those things were. He was the four-star equivalent to the military's chief of staff.

The first deputy could be compared to the key aide of the police commissioner.

I set myself grimly to the task of responding to the blizzard of notes cascading on us from above—literally and figuratively, since the police commissioner's office was just above ours.

It was an excruciatingly painful period, yet I was to draw from the lessons learned in that bureaucratic infighting for the rest of my career. In the end, I was grateful. It seemed that all the useful things in life came in unpleasant packages—like change, unpopular assignments, painful choices, or risky moves or words. The sound bites were muted—or abandoned—but I remembered their worth and employed them when I had the chance. And I never regretted helping to champion the union's cause.

Still, as these pages will attest—in the firings, suspensions, and other penalties suffered—talk, especially punchy talk, is anything but cheap.

If ever the law of unintended consequences needed an illustration, this one would serve.

Over the ensuing years the unions embraced the Bill of Rights, expanded it, spread it nationwide, and even emblazoned it into law.

By 1995 the U.S. Congress was considering a Police Officers' Bill of Rights that would require written notification to a police officer before being interviewed; the complainant must provide a detailed, signed statement and the investigation must begin within fifteen days of receipt of the complaint. Questioning would occur at "a reasonable hour" and at the investigator's office or the officer's workplace. The officer would be advised of the identity of everyone present and the questions would be posed by a single investigator. The questioning would last a "reasonable time" only and allow for "reasonable rest periods." No threats, harassments, or promises of a reward would be allowed. No statement could be used in a criminal proceeding unless the officer had received immunity. All questioning would be recorded in writing or by device and available to the officer. Right to counsel would be guaranteed unless the officer waived in writing. All officers would have the right to a disciplinary hearing and right of access to evidence, witnesses and their addresses, and a copy of the investigative file.

Additionally, the disciplinary hearing would be closed to the public unless the accused officer requested otherwise. No file would be kept unless the officer had the opportunity to review and comment in writing. Any existing Bill of Rights would have to meet or exceed this bill. Contracts would not be affected as long as they were substantially similar to this bill. And all sworn personnel would be covered.

The bill was opposed by police chiefs and not passed, although it is certain to remain a live issue into the foreseeable future.

What began as an attempt to redress wrongs toward the police evolved into Frankenstein's monster.

By 1980 in Minneapolis, the strength of the police union had reached mythic and unprecedented proportions. Sadly, police unions are among the fastest-growing labor force in the country and their increasingly active role in legislative halls bodes ill for the future of investigations into police wrongdoing.

Woven into the partisan political fabric and warfare was a commonly embraced homophobia that saw its expression in bathhouse raids. These were establishments where open gays met for sociability and sex. If the cops were thoroughly distracted by union-political activities and unable to pay much attention to serious police matters, they could at least harass gays.

In Minneapolis, there had been six permanent and two temporary police chiefs from 1970 to 1980, and the former always returned to the ranks as captains. There they'd plot their return or, more likely, the elevation of untainted surrogates who would act as their proxies. The mayor would silently return to the ranks as a lieutenant, except for a two-day period in which he had himself named a deputy chief.

POLICE INSPECTORS

In this bloated bureaucracy I found eighteen captains and five inspectors. The latter were members of any rank who could, by being named by the chief, be elevated as much as four ranks. The five I found were clearly political hacks who'd been rewarded for faithful service to whoever won the mayoralty. I determined to rid the agency of these walking advertisements to the spoils system and began to phase them out.

Most of the captains, tenured and protected as long as they didn't mutiny openly or commit egregious offenses, basically paid lip service to the obeisances and went their ways. A few worked feverishly at subverting and sabotaging everything I attempted.

Nevertheless, these were the men I had to use to command the six precincts, later reduced to four, which were really neighborhood police departments. I had some subordinates acting as community police chiefs whom I wouldn't trust to run a newsstand.

As the years progressed, I grew ever more desperate over the fecklessness of the precinct commanders—and knowing that there were talented young cops I'd have loved to see in those posts, I bridled at the frustration. Suddenly, the notion of resuscitating the inspectors struck me and I promoted a young sergeant and placed him in charge of a precinct.

The union balked—claiming I was using him out of title—and the Civil Service Commission, composed of union allies, agreed and ordered me to withdraw him. I appealed to the court, which was the relief granted by civil service law.

On the stand, the union lawyers struck hard at the out-of-title issue but the three judges' questions indicated this charge lacked substance. So they charged back and hammered at my views of the inspectors—as I had expressed them publicly.

Yes, I testified that the inspectors I found were hacks, the products of political payoffs, useless appendages, and I had eliminated them.

"What happened then?" the cross-examiner asked.

"I changed my mind." This is easier to write than it was to say.

I added, "I came to see that a chief needed the power to select key aides and that a political evil could be turned into an effective administrative tool." I had forgotten that I didn't need to select hacks, in the way of grateful mayors, and could dip into a pool of talent that was untainted by the stains of partisan politics.

An exception to the rule was, ironically, one of the union's officers.

When I arrived in Minneapolis in 1980 the police union newsletter, *Show Up*, was edited by the police officers federation's vice president. He launched a particularly virulent assault on my persona, motives, talents, and experience.

Naturally, I bitterly resented the assaults. My anger was easily outweighed by the sense that he not only had the right, but that my defense of that right would confirm my commitment to the First Amendment, if only in my own heart.

The writer was also at the center of racist complaints, in which black motorists alleged he was singling them out unjustly. I ordered an investigation, which revealed that he was very active and aggressive, but had good, sound, articulable grounds for every stop and was not engaged in racial profiling.

Impressed by his activism and energy, I gave him a more important task, which he discharged ably. I gave him a continual series of key posts that escalated in responsibility and encouraged him to pursue his education.

When a wag noisily accused me of trying to buy the vice president's silence, my answer was simple: "Well, if so, it doesn't seem to be working, does it?" The criticisms did not abate.

He reminded me of what Lincoln had said about Gen. U. S. Grant, when critics lambasted him for his foibles. Lincoln tut-tutted them with, "I like the man. He fights."

I liked this cop, he worked.

Ultimately, I helped him become chief of police of three smallish cities and contributed a section for a book he wrote. I assume he changed his view of me, but I never had much evidence of it—except he did write a supportive letter to the editor of the Minneapolis *StarTribune* when I left that police department.

It was a really difficult lesson—to ignore the form and focus on the substance—but an immensely important one to learn. I had not seen the importance of being able to select key aides for important jobs until I felt the desperate need, years later. The issue of being stuck with tenured executives continues to bedevil chiefs to this day, everywhere.

The judges held for me two to one and, very soon, all precincts were commanded by tough, smart, young inspectors who were in accord with my views of what a community's police chief should be like.

AGEISM, POLITICS, AND REFORM

My wars with the tenured brass continued.

I was sued by a sixty-five-year-old captain I was forcing to retire, as he reached the age limit. He claimed age discrimination, won in federal court, and remained until he was seventy. Congress later passed legislation allowing for a sixty-five-year age limit, but it came too late to help me.

I never, over my nine years, promoted anyone to captain and presided over their attrition with unconcealed pleasure.

In 1980, though, the department was out of control. Political cartoons derided the campaign buffoonery undertaken—in uniform and on duty—by all ranks.

The politicking deteriorated to the point where the more-or-less reform mayor announced, despite being still a young man, that he would not run again and, by then, no one seriously contemplated the return of the union chief—except, very likely, himself.

Donald M. Fraser, a Democrat, had been in Congress for about eighteen years and had, in 1978, run for the U.S. Senate and lost. Now he returned to Minneapolis to run for the seat held thirty years earlier by Hubert Horatio Humphrey.

Fraser was elected handily and began the promised search that led to me. He was sworn in in January 1980—and on February 11, 1980, I took over the department.

As mentioned earlier, my oath had been preceded by the last raid on a bathhouse on February 10 by a defiant group of cops sending me a clear message. I'd made my antipathy for such measures known, and they were responding. The ceremony in the council chambers was notable for the open burning of citations received by gays in the previous day's raid. Trying to use humor as a weapon, I lamented the brevity of my honeymoon.

What followed, however, shook me.

I called in the deputy chief in charge of the vice squad that had conducted the raid and said I wanted the commander and his boss sacked, perceiving the first as a John Wayne type of swashbuckler and the second as someone who masked his prurience behind pious assertions of Catholicism.

The deputy chief's voice audibly quavered as he recounted the horrors that would attend such a transfer. These were well-respected men with tremendous backing in the ranks and a transfer would be the worst possible signal I could send. His voice positively cracked with fear and I was inwardly shaken. I called both executives in to see if I could persuade them to other priorities. Their defiance made me fear mine would be a one-day tenure.

As I shuttled back to my office from another futile attempt at persuading the deputy chief, I found John Wayne with his feet up on my conference table. He did not move as I sat to chat, in unfelt bonhomie, and both were visibly encouraged in their intransigence.

I got up, walked to the deputy's office and said, "I want them out now and replaced immediately. No more discussion." Another bout of unemployment loomed in my imagination.

The deputy complied, the malefactors were dumped, there was a brief press flurry, and it all evaporated. It was the Wizard of Oz all over again and I'd had only to part the curtain.

John Wayne never, thereafter, gave me the slightest trouble. The other guy despised me but gave me no chance to strike out at him, even as I questioned young women I suspected he was hitting on, whether they ever experienced any form of sexual harassment from any source. To my inner regret they had nothing to report.

The raids stopped and the bathhouses, which had resisted the determined assaults of the Minneapolis police for years, finally succumbed to AIDS and shuttered.

A couple of anecdotes will help define the nature of Mayor Fraser, a fine man, with no talent for small talk, and whose life included the ghastly tragedies of the deaths, years apart, of eight- and twenty-two-year-old daughters. Working for him felt like overdue payment for service to feckless careerists. He was, in addition, an ardent champion of human rights and trade unionism.

Early on, in the late summer of a mayoral election cycle, which then occurred every two years, I had become disgusted with the delays and excuses of a timid staff and decided to switch from all two-person patrol cars to a mix of mostly one- and a few two-person cars by fiat. The reasons were easy and obvious. Personnel were costly, about $50,000 to $60,000 a year each, maybe close to twice that today (a whopping $120,000 in salaries and benefits in Nassau County, New York, in 2000), and equipment was cheap. We could respond to twenty calls from a soon-to-emerge 911 system if we had twenty one-person cars, but only ten with all two-officer patrols. Effective and efficient. Classical management. I could almost double our productivity without hiring a single cop, greatly increase their visibility on the street, and it would only cost about $2,000 each—the annual, amortized cost of one police squad.

There would be in Minneapolis, just as there would be in New York City today, pure hell to pay.

As always, I briefed the mayor first and, because of the obvious delicacy of the timing, offered to postpone the trauma to after election day. I warned him the police union would be outraged.

"Don't worry about the politics; if it's right to do, do it now," Fraser said. And I did, and it was hell, but we survived it, if only just barely, since Officer Richard P. Miller was riding in one of the new one-person squads when he was killed in 1981.

The demonstrations, confrontations, calls, angst and turmoil that followed were awful.

We speak of "pressure" or "battling the union" or the turmoil surrounding a controversy, but these are abstractions. The subjective reality always strikes like a thunderous blow.

In the Miller case the union saw its chance to counter my efforts at reform, by then under way for a year and a half of *mano a mano* combat, and played its cards hard.

It began at the hospital, as they uttered whispered poisons into the family's ears as I stood, eighty feet away, in gloomy solitude for over two hours, silently praying Officer Miller—a kindly and respected man—would survive.

He died. I didn't have to be told—and wasn't.

I was excluded from the church at the funeral service and stood on the sidewalk with Erica, my wife, as cops marched stonily past.

Mrs. Miller, the widow, found it impossible to conceal her anger as I attempted to offer condolences. To her great credit she contacted me years later to say she had managed to exorcise her bitterness towards me over this tragedy.

The union picketed and said I was as responsible for Miller's death as the shooter.

At a televised town meeting, a questioner wondered how personally responsible I felt for the officer's death. After I offered a lame response she pointedly said, "I am his daughter."

At the very apex of the anguish, the union called for a "brief moratorium" on one-person patrols but, knowing I'd never be able to reinstate them if I complied, I refused.

No one would ever know if this tragedy could have been averted if officer Miller had been riding with a partner, but I knew we couldn't afford such luxuries.

On a later occasion Fraser called me into his office for advice.

Since I had noticed that he had politely ignored the ceaseless flows of pointers I'd been providing him with for years, I had decided many months earlier to simply stop offering suggestions and just keep him briefed on everything going on in the agency or that was planned for the future. That was my job and I had to learn to stick to it. Fraser didn't seem to miss my ministrations, and I adjusted to the frustrations of silence and lip-biting.

Now he asked me if I'd seen an item he held out. I had. It was a proposed city ordinance[3] sought by some ardent feminists (in this case, literally, since they'd held candlelit vigils, plumping for the law's passage outside and inside his office, which Fraser bore with his customary grace and forbearance). The item would give a rape victim the right to sue a publication like *Playboy* magazine if it could be shown that the rapist had been aroused by its contents and thereby inspired to attack by the erotic material.

"What do you think?"

"It's fascist rubbish," I said. "Veto it."

Fraser responded, "The council passed it thirteen to zero and they only need nine votes to override my veto."

"Veto it anyway and append a strong message. They'll never find the balls to override."

Fraser, who never welcomed my "colorful" language, frowned and thanked me.

He did as I advised and, true to form, the council couldn't find the same thirteen votes, or even nine, to override it. Indianapolis passed it instead and suffered the humiliation of having the ordinance declared unconstitutionally vague on the first review.

In the one-officer-car case, he had defied the union for the sake of doing the right thing and now he had defied a central consistency of his—feminists.

When I finally left the department years later, I told people that Fraser had fallen to his knees, grasped my ankles, and slobberingly begged me to stay. And then, he looked up and said, "By the way, who are you and what do you do around here?"

I had about ten, or even fewer, high-priority items of reform to pursue and the mayor, the best civil servant I ever met, supported me totally.

The former cop-mayor, Fraser's predecessor, was now back in the ranks as a lieutenant but, unlike his former chiefs—some of whom sabotaged and undermined my initiatives—he caused no problems whatever. He had, though, embedded many of the excesses and abuses into the cops' labor contract.

Promotions, in a Ruritanian enclave of proliferating supervisors (112 lieutenants and 23 captains and inspectors for a force of about 700—which, with the many sergeants, made just about every other cop a supervisor) were contractually guaranteed. Additionally, all patrols featured two-officer cars; they wore no name tags (I popularized the issue by publicly saying the cops would prefer to go about in ski masks); and worked in six precincts, which swallowed personnel rather than have them on the streets and when four would have been more than enough.

The force was brutal and racist, regularly stopping or thumping blacks and Native Americans and using racial pejoratives. Cops carried sap gloves (lead lined and producers of a fearful wallop). And there were the bathhouse raids, not to mention an utter lack of focus on, or interest in, priorities or service. Minorities and women were invisible in the ranks.

The problems of the Minneapolis Police Department, in the entire decade of the seventies, could be traced to the city's residents having elected the union president to the mayoralty and that executive's refusal to switch roles.[4]

The problem certainly centered on the gross abuses practiced but they also surfaced, in subtler form, in opportunities ignored or wasted. Foundations complained they'd tried offering the police generous grants, but had been summarily rebuffed because the players couldn't be bothered to do the paperwork. I harvested well over $1 million for such varieties of projects as a robot bomb remover, a physical fitness program, a stress and wellness approach, and countless studies and experiments, most conducted by criminologist Larry Sherman.

The political distractions from 1970 to 1980 were so numerous and pervasive in Minneapolis that even such generally accepted innovations as 911, operative since 1967, were, in 1980, greeted with quizzical glances by a confused and uninformed citizenry.

Control of the Minneapolis Police Department by the police union proved terribly costly to the town.

The unions, however, knew how to meld their actions with the peculiar internal climate of police agencies—and not always for the public good.

17

THE INTERNAL CLIMATE

Most people have jobs and lives, but policing combines both.

Cops wind up not only bonding through the emotional glue of shared dangers, but find that the world they once knew no longer understands them. The police universe they entered is so much apart from the world of civilians that communication becomes an exercise in futility. Cops often have nowhere to turn than to other cops for understanding.

This isolation produces an internal culture that operates under its own mysterious codes. Unlike other subcultures, such as the Mafia, policing pays lip service to openness and works hard at conveying a sense of a professional agency meticulously pursuing its charter.

In 1998 and 1999, I was asked to serve on two cases that illustrate how the inner workings of police agencies operate to secure conformity within the prevailing internal value system.

In the first, a police car with two officers pulled up to a running, parked vehicle late one frigid night. A black male was sitting in the passenger seat. As one of the cops rolled down his window to ask a question, a black female's head popped up on the driver's side. The cops recognized her as a member of their department, greeted her, and drove off.

The next day rumors flew about her being caught giving a guy a blow job. The police radio crackled with slurping sounds and references to the female officer.

At first she ignored the gibes, then tried to laugh them off, but nothing worked. The comments, looks, gestures, and knowing glances continued. She confronted the officers, who denied spreading the rumors, despite the fact that at least one of them had to be guilty.

It got worse and she complained to her superiors, who sloughed her off. Then it got racial and she was engaged in repeated confrontations. The n-word was applied. She was shunned and transferred into an unwanted assignment. Insulting messages appeared, and even supervisors made thinly veiled references to her alleged behavior.

Finally, in what looked like a carefully orchestrated setup, she was intercepted leaving the same bar she'd been parked in front of months earlier, and was arrested for driving under the influence of alcohol, although all indications were that she was sober.

She was acquitted but the harassment intensified. Clearly she was now seen as a rat.

Desperate, at a Christmas party, she complained to the chief and he fobbed her off and told her to go "through channels"—as if she hadn't already exhausted that route. The chief was black.

In a final act of despair, she sued.

I testified at length, being especially critical of the chief, whom I knew well and liked.

She won a judgment of just under $60,000 and lawyer's fees, a paltry sum. I was stunned when the city appealed this mild verdict and inquired as to the reason. I was told the chief felt his mayor would be elected governor in 1998 and he could run for mayor. He didn't want my testimony as part of the public record; it might well have been cited in the campaign.

The mayor lost the governor's race, the chief lost his appeal and the case settled into the dust of civic life without fuss—except for the officer's generously crediting me for the results, which prompted several lawyers to call and offer me more business, most of which I rejected.

An additional irony was that, only a couple of years earlier, I'd had another case involving the same department, with a dramatically different outcome.

A lawyer consulted with me over an incident in which the police had shot and killed his client. The suspect's family sued and I was asked to review the case. The deceased, a disturbed young man living on the streets, had gone berserk and began chasing passersby with a large knife, swiping at them. The cops responded. He lunged at them and they shot him dead.

A totally straightforward case of justifiable homicide, in my view. I told the lawyer the cops had been right and that's how I'd testify. Shooting of mentally disturbed, armed, and galvanized citizens running amok is one of the most perennially controversial aspects of police work. Yes, a severely mentally disturbed person may not have "control" over his actions; however, if he lunges at you or a cop with a knife, the results will be the same: deadly.

It requires no imagination to guess that his enthusiasm for my services evaporated quickly. He packed his things, left and sent me a check for $450.

I was surprised to learn, later, that the city—rather than defend officers who'd acted appropriately—settled with the family for $75,000.

The case they should have settled, the black female police officer's, they fought. And they settled the one case they should have contested.

The public, however, learns only that the police were responsible for a certain number of dollars in a variety of law suits and the cops learn that no one at the top is much interested in just outcomes. With no one to call attention to the abuses, the public silently pays—not just in additional tax dollars, but in the diminished effectiveness of a demoralized force.

In the second case, an officer noticed a suspicious act, investigated, and discovered that a colleague was discarding unpaid and unanswered parking tickets issued to friends. In an agony of indecision and drift, informal and tentative discussions led to his being advised to forget it—nothing would be done to the officer, who was politically powerful and well connected.

Nevertheless the whistle blower persevered and the state police finally launched an investigation. It revealed an interlocking pattern of favors, free meals, and drinks; a criminal's sponsorship of an annual athletic event, ostensibly for a good cause; and a suspicious manipulation of a lottery run by the suspect. The target also served on the pension board, which would decide the financial fate of the informer, as well as that of others.

The case epitomizes the sort of back scratching and favor swapping that often characterizes small departments operating in tightly knit units.

The system, as embodied by the chiefs (there were several over the life of this controversy) and city officials, swiftly closed ranks to focus on the informer—not the wrongdoing alleged and uncovered. The evidence was ignored. The "stoolie" was suspended twice on trumped-up charges.

In one of these, a female charged he'd made a rude sexual comment six months earlier—conveniently straddling the critical discovery of the tickets. He was also charged with speaking to the city's chief executive without permission.

The first was a tortured and ludicrous reach and the second a clear violation of the man's constitutional right of free speech. Yet it is a measure of the intensity of the internal pressures that the whistle blower accepted the patently unjust punishments without complaint, praying only that he could get this ugly business behind him.

A foolish hope. The harassment continued. He was deprived of a promotion to which he was clearly entitled and sent for psychiatric evaluation with an accompanying letter, from the chief to the examining psychiatrist, that could serve as a model of biased, unfounded accusations about such things as how the officer "thought he was so much better and smarter than everyone else." I was totally shocked that a chief would actually append his name to such a damning document without offering a shred of proof to buttress the charges.

By then, the system had become so intent on ousting someone any neutral observer might have judged to be a hero that it had become blind to its own acts. The officer sued.

Even a superficial glance at the structure revealed three distinct strata in this fewer than fifty-officer department.

At the top was the clique or inner circle of good ol' boys who bowled, ate, drank, sometimes slept, and played together. They were linked by blood, friendship, ritual, and self-interest. They ran lotteries for charity that were suspected of being rigged, organized sports events with the town's criminal element, participated in decisions on who should get what in their pensions, actively worked on political campaigns, and ran the police union. These would have been called the "meat eaters" in New York. These insiders automatically included whoever was chief as an ex officio member of the circle.

The second group was the grass eaters. They got along, stayed out of the way, mostly kept their noses clean, and otherwise emulated the bovine ways of the herd. This was, by far, the largest contingent but was refracted and detached from the agency's inner workings.

Third and last, in every sense, came whoever fell into pariah status, against whom all others locked arms. In this case it was my client and, for a brief time—at least until the pressure forced him to rejoin the second group and abandon his former buddy—his partner: the very man who'd brought our hero's attention to the parking tickets in the first place. The only issue of concern to the plotters, in this case, was whether you were with 'em or a'gin 'em in this struggle.

In an eerie echo of this internal culture, a smallish eastern city was found to house an infamous clique known as the Family, which, in addition to pursuing a lot of abuses, practiced bizarre, candlelit initiation or excommunication rites. The situation got so bad that it finally, in 1994, aroused the grass eaters to publicly protest the Family's baleful influence over the agency's workings.

Among the charges were intimidation of other officers, false arrests, physical abuse, using racist language, trying to control promotions and overtime payments, and framing civilians in drug investigations. In this case, a much larger than usual 20 percent of the force were estimated to be Family members.

A grand jury investigation found evidence of abuses and issued a report. The local press covered the story sparingly.

The leader adorned his car with iron crosses and boasted Hitler would've decorated him for his actions. In a city with over two-thirds black and Hispanic citizens, there were four Hispanics and no blacks among twenty-five supervisors, out of a total of almost four hundred officers. The leadership vacuum created by do-nothing chief executives was rapidly filled.

The pervasiveness of such sick cultures is such as to dot the landscape with further examples of the genre.

In 1994, a San Antonio cop arrested a sergeant from his department for DWI. What followed was a nightmarish succession of suspensions for the arresting cop (six upheld, for a total of eighty-six days) by the chief, hang-up calls to his unlisted home phone, his belongings stolen, his car towed twice, shunning behavior by colleagues, threats of retaliation, and general failure to respond when he needed backing up.

He sued and won a $1-million verdict. The city labeled the award "preposterous" and "ridiculous" and appealed. In 1996, the Court of Appeals upheld the jury's "haywire" verdict.

These cases typified, with absolute faithfulness, the police reality nationwide. This is what "professional courtesy" comes to mean in police circles. A curious side effect is that targets were needed, and handy, as a way of reinforcing the value system and to create a rough cohesion as the body united to shut out and, hopefully, expel the interloper.

The above cases are by no means unique. They are profoundly illustrative of the inner culture. It is no great exaggeration to assert that every police department in the nation hosts a minority of employees ready and willing to twist the organization's purposes and practices to their private, twisted agendas.

Not anxious to do such unpopular work, and not needing the money (I insisted on being paid because I had discovered, years earlier, that people listened intently, and even took notes, when they could imagine a giant meter ticking off dollars behind my head), I testified in only the most obviously egregious examples of injustice—yet they abounded.

In both whistle blower cases the officers had broken unwritten rules of behavior that held, first and foremost, that you don't squeal on fellow cops—no matter what. In the other case, the remarkable thing was that the outrage of the majority actually inspired them to public protest, as cops picketed against the abuses of the Family.

A brief news account buried deep in the *New York Times*,[1] early in 2000, offered an unusual insight into the police culture, even as the report simply and straightforwardly offered the facts.

A group of cops in a Brooklyn precinct in an Italian neighborhood were found to have been more than chummy with members of a local social club. The site, a staple of the hangouts favored by street-smart wiseguys who were described as "wannabe" gangsters, became the favored place for cops to coop, lounge, sip coffee, and hang out; run license plate checks; fix traffic tickets; eat "on the arm"; or deal in stolen goods, on duty and off. The place became notorious for the number of police cars parked—as always, illegally—outside, discomfiting residents being tagged for similar violations in a congested traffic zone. And, again, as in the Louima case, the sense of entitlement and impunity had to spell trouble for the systemwide nature of its implications.

The Internal Affairs Division assigned an undercover lieutenant to gather evidence and to set the trap that was finally sprung after the dimensions of the problem were established. A number of officers were up on charges involving a wide variety of derelictions.

A casual reader would encounter the piece and wonder what it's all about.

An insider would conclude two things: The cops who frequented the place were likeliest to be the meat eaters who felt a deeper symbiosis with the suspect denizens of the club than with the law-abiding citizens in surrounding blocks. The others were likely to be scorned as "gloms" and "naive turkeys."

The second important element was the surprising initiative and energy displayed by the NYPD in investigating wrongdoing in the ranks. It was the first such possible harbinger of a tougher approach in battling police wrongdoing, although it was likely it came in response to growing criticism over some ghastly racial incidents, plus the very troubling sense of impunity surrounding the officers' abhorrent behavior in the Louima case. Still, it was very welcome nonetheless.

RABBIS AND THE BUREAUCRACY

Bureaucratic infighting at the top took the form of personal items—like promotions, transfers, or forced retirements (the police commissioner could reduce any high-ranking member back to captain by simple fiat). In this environment reports—even those cloaked in bureaucratese—mattered.

I came to the attention of a high-ranking official precisely through this route in 1957.

An explosion occurred in the form of a pointed inquiry by Police Commissioner Stephen P. Kennedy, a talented, insufferably arrogant man, directed at two-star Chief Francis J. M. Robb. Although the details are lost in the fog of history, the gravamen was why had Robb screwed up the investigation of Jesus De Galindez's disappearance? I was not in Robb's command, but in the 8th Squad—a coveted Greenwich Village assignment. The Village, then and now, was a kind of epicenter of the city's colorful cultural, culinary, and social life. Because Galindez was a Spaniard I had been assigned to look into the mystery.

Robb, who knew me slightly, had to answer the tickler, a dreaded little memo from the police commissioner with Tickler File (T.F.) and a number in the upper-right-hand corner.

Robb assigned his cleverest man to the task of answering this missive—Detective Anthony Ulasewicz, a man as cunning as a shithouse rat and, as the Watergate folks would later discover, outrageously funny. Such idiosyncratic behavior as daring humorous asides was typical of him. Ulasewicz went to Washington, in later years, to serve as a key investigator for President Nixon, and got caught up in Watergate.

But just to cover his bets, Robb assigned me to the task, separately, so he could have two reports to choose from.

I understood the mechanics. Robb would sign and submit his answer to the chief of detectives, his boss, who would endorse it to the chief inspector, who would also prepare a one-paragraph summary, with recommendations, to the police commissioner. By the time any report reached the police commissioner it was dotted with the briefly stated opinions of all supervisors between the report's writer and the department's head.

I figured a very long, tortured explanation would exhaust everyone, driving them to perfunctorily endorse it forward, and no key person would bother to read it. I prepared an answer that ran over twenty pages. Ulasewicz, lacking my bureaucratic Machiavellianism and petty clerical skills, prepared a more succinct reply.

Robb chose mine, sent it forward with, very likely, a silent prayer, and waited. It sailed through and he was off the hook. In a few months I was in the Bureau of Special Services and Investigations (BOSSI) and Robb was my rabbi. He became chief inspector a few years later when Kennedy was succeeded by Robb's rabbi, Michael Murphy.

We all, outwardly, observed the tortured protocols at the top.

When I was forced to retire, following the Yankee Stadium debacle in 1976—discussed later—I had to visit all the upper brass at headquarters and I observed the nicety. My immediate boss, the only black at the top, mumbled clearly unfelt homilies, but failed to totally conceal his glee at losing the biggest pain in the ass in his working life. Chief Inspector Bill Hannan was warm, affectionate, and kind. I'd recommended him for a promotion at a key juncture in his career and he hadn't forgotten.

Then came the police commissioner.

As it happened I had suggested Codd to Police Commissioner Murphy as his four-star chief in the fall of 1970, six years earlier, and Murphy had promoted him to that job. I had no reason to think Codd knew this or even that my suggestion had been central to the choice. Codd had never been comfortable around the beehive that was the Murphy administration but he lent it credibility with the rank-and-file. Codd retired when Murphy left and Cawley was appointed police commissioner but reemerged, like the proverbial phoenix, within months, as the new mayor's police commissioner.

Donald Cawley was appointed police commissioner when Murphy left in May 1973. He and I were contemporaries and rivals, but he was rather brilliant, shooting off ideas like sparks. His talents gave him an assurance no one in public life can afford.

The police commissioner nominally (and the word is critical to an understanding of the role) serves a five-year term but is actually there at the pleasure, or sufferance, of the mayor. Breaking precedent, Cawley announced he'd serve well into the new mayor's term to complete what remained of the five-year tenure he'd inherited from Murphy.

When the new mayor, Beame—a man not known for either verve or nerve—was told, his answer was curt: "Tell him he's fired."

And Codd succeeded the restive young subordinate he'd had to suffer and under whom he'd been unable to continue as four-star chief.

Now I entered Codd's cavernous office. Ramrod straight and imposing, the police commissioner was effusive in his greeting, smoothly ignoring the contretemps roiling both our lives. Soothing music wafted peacefully over the unruffled setting of his room. He enveloped himself in a serenity that rarely cracked.

We observed the hypocrisies such encounters demanded, especially by a police commissioner who wanted no boat rocking around him. I was certain this would be his reaction and was perfectly comfortable with such social feignings of warmth. He wished me well and briefly reminisced about the many moments we'd shared over the years. He expressed a real fondness and I left without a smidgen of resentment over any of it, even though we both knew we were now less than friends. As it happened this, as far as I knew, concluded our relationship, forever.

Codd was not, in any sense, a bad man—and I'd known plenty of those. He had sought peace and it was his misfortune to encounter me instead.

Obeisances were paid to the outer culture's expectations, even as the internal and unexpressed values were reinforced. Playing our roles, whatever the underlying tensions, served as the oil that greased necessary relations between the players.

The climate within, however, got expressed in individual and massive actions that often stunned an unsuspecting public when they spilled out into general notice.

These are mere glimpses at the hermetically sealed inner climate of police agencies. Vignettes help, as does anecdotal evidence, but, for a kaleidoscopic view of the many hues occurring in the internal organizational climate, no opportunity appears to be as rich in promise as Los Angeles. There, the police are almost unraveling under the impact of a scandal that offers an insight into every organizational problem cited in this effort. Through public disclosures we are treated to reflections of the inner, usually silent, culture, but the public rarely grasps the true meaning of these events.

America has long been captivated by the vision of the avenging angel: the hero who sets things right by dispensing a personal brand of perfect justice. We've seen him on the streets of Tombstone and in such emblematic documents as *Dirty Harry* and *Death Wish*.

The city that gave us Dirty Harry will now illustrate the fatal flaw in embracing such notions. The dirty secret is that Harry is not only fallible, but nihilistic and driven by demons that have little to do with notions of justice.

The Code of Silence will receive a rare, but eloquent, exposure and the organization's response to whistle blowers will also be exposed.

All of the early signs—from lawsuits, lawyers' briefs, court confessions, and many personal accounts from a widening circle of participants—point to the most complete picture of the internal workings of a police agency in this country.

It would be a bad mistake to label this a purely local, idiosyncratic problem that has no wider relevance. Such myopia would be the exact equivalent of dismissing evidence of police corruption with the bromide that it only involves a few "rotten apples."

Look to the barrel.

The actions in Los Angeles dealt principally with the agency's attempts to control the underclass.

In other cities, like New York, inner realities often got expressed in different ways.

18

COPS: INDIVIDUALLY AND EN MASSE

Policing is mainly an individualistic pursuit, undertaken by the lone entrepreneur or, more likely, with his or her partner. It is the one cop, or pair, entering upon a wide variety of unknowns, that marks the genre and produces the need for initiative and independent action. Cops have to make split-second, life-or-death decisions that juries and learned jurists spend months unraveling. This is frequently criticized as an oversimplification, or even a gross overdramatization, but it turns out to be true nevertheless.

After months of calls, vilifications, public denouncements, and even unpleasant personal encounters on the street with other cops, my wife would complain, "How can you love these guys?" But she hadn't seen the hundreds of heroic exploits I had. I've always known that cops do beautiful things and policing is a line of work in which ennobling behavior is both likely and relatively common. No one could bear witness to these daily triumphs of courage over fear without deep feelings of admiration for its practitioners.

When cops perform as they should, whatever the public's or the media's take, they must be supported. And sometimes, as in the many times they have to subdue or even kill an aggressive, violent, but disturbed individual, it isn't easy to do. But do it they must.

When cops are obviously trying to do their jobs and make a mistake, we should try to bring understanding to the issue and, where possible, give them as much support as we can.

I had a troubling case in Minneapolis that was roughly, though certainly not totally, analogous to the tragic Amadou Diallo case in New York, but with significantly different outcomes. Of course Diallo was an innocent man and our victim wasn't.

A suspect, who'd mugged one of our decoys, was being frisked after his arrest by cops with shotguns. A sudden movement on his part led to the accidental discharge of the firearm, killing him instantly.

I investigated swiftly, even insisting on blood samples of the cops for any trace of alcohol, despite the fact that they were obviously sober and on duty. Although the Fourth Amendment protects everyone against unreasonable searches, I believed that drug or alcohol testing of cops, in such circumstances, was perfectly legal.

The cops made no secret of their chagrin and made no attempts to fudge the facts. They readily admitted their mistake. It was a tragic accident.

The cops were white and the suspect was black. He was not armed and had a long and impressive criminal history that was totally consonant with his actions in this case.

I had the case presented to a grand jury, who found the cops innocent of any wrongdoing. Grand juries can be eloquent voices of the people in controversial cases. Whenever a bodega owner in the Bronx, shot a robber with an illegally possessed gun—a crime by the victim—rather than arrest these people who were, in my view, defending themselves and their families, I had the issues submitted to grand juries, who invariably failed to indict the bodega operator.

These shootings by these grocery operators were rare enough, but a National Rifle Association that desperately sought examples of the effective use of firearms surprisingly passed on the opportunity to extol and publicize these heroes. The NRA was, instead, supporting ersatz studies that presumed to speculate on the thousands of occasions in which guns had been used in self-defense.

The NRA's arguments were, basically, that guns served a free people to defend themselves against tyrannical government—an argument that, however absurd, resonated with gun-show, camouflaged, conspirationalist thinkers like Timothy McVeigh—the Oklahoma City bomber. Related to this was the self-defense issue, in which a woman fends off a rapist with her trusty revolver.

Bodega owners—with sometimes illegal guns (the NRA has stridently called for strict enforcement of existing laws, saying that we don't need new restrictions) and being mostly Hispanic—were not about to be chosen as NRA poster boys, despite the paucity of other examples of effective use of firearms. These were struggling, striving stalwarts trying to climb out of poverty and frequently brought checkered personal histories with them.

My own tough gun control stance was, in no little measure, buttressed by a personal experience that included very few examples of effective employment of firearms. In fact, I could remember only one case, over my nine years in Minneapolis, in which a citizen had used a weapon effectively—and I gave him a medal.

He was a pharmacist and a gun enthusiast. Two robbers came into his shop, with guns, to hold him up. He pulled his magnum, shot one dead, and captured the other.

I believed strongly in a citizen's right to defend himself and awarded another medal to a young woman who had been accosted by a knife-wielding rapist who punched her in the face, knocking her down, and who stabbed the ground with his knife as he undid his pants. She staggered to the knife, pulled it out of the ground, stabbed the assailant in the arm, and ran away.

I told her I'd have given her a bigger medal if she had killed him. Such events of heroic and successful self-defense were as rare as the abduction of a toddler by a stranger.

The police are toughened and inured to violence—indeed, they peculiarly appreciate a truism that is a cornerstone of Realpolitik wisdom—that violence can be an effective tool when appropriately used, in measured cadence, to bring about a positive result. Thus is another dissonance created between the outside world—which at least pays lip service to abhorring violence altogether—and the insider cop's world that sees violence as an essential accouterment to solving a lot of problems. Violence, appropriately used, can be as effective as most other approaches. In fact, a large share of our movies center on the positive uses of violence. Cops know this and a lot of our thinkers don't.

Unfortunately, this growing predilection for violence spills over into personal lives, and domestic abuse—a delicate little euphemism for the beating of women by men—is a very serious problem among police families, as are suicide and alcoholism.[1]

One of my most powerful experiences in Minneapolis was when I had to respond, late at night, to the boonies. One of my cops, in a drunken rage, had smashed into his estranged wife's house, where he choked her teenaged nephew until she blew the cop away with a shotgun blast.

There was a long, painful record of escalating violence leading to her desperate attempt to escape.

I made no friends in the ranks by coming to the wife's defense. She was not arrested and the case was presented to a grand jury, which found it to be a justifiable homicide. This was another of the very rare instances of a useful employment of a firearm, but who could have made that assertion in public? She did not get a medal.

Had it been my experience that guns were being effectively used against criminals I'd have supported the arming of every man and woman in the country. This assertion is a blatant and demonstrable NRA fiction.

In the earlier Minneapolis case I had come to the cops' defense and said publicly, after admitting the accident, that we hadn't, after all, "killed him in church or in the bosom of his family. He was mugging us." Despite a lot of anguish, my comment served to cool the controversy. The city made a modest settlement on the suspect's mother and the issue lapsed into the dustbins of history.

It was just about as simple and straightforward as that.

Though there were stark differences with the Diallo case, there were some surprising similarities, too. In the end, the viewing public—the final arbiter in these controversies—responded very differently to the events.

Cops stereotype and act on these shorthand templates. One big problem is that biases occur and they lead to errors. Cops not only work in a racist society, but are often asked to enforce the overclass's need to keep the underclass out of sight and under tight fetters.

In the simple world of the cops, there are about three categories of humans:

(1) The Brotherhood—those in the job and thus in the know
(2) Citizens and other tolerated outsiders
(3) Scumbags, humps, and assholes

The last group comes in for a lion's share of police attention.

It is not safe to fail the "attitude test." This is another way of describing defiance, the questioning of an officer's authority, or even failure to demonstrate appropriate levels of deference.

Since traffic citations are issued "in lieu of arrest" recipients play with fire when they balk during this process. Many who would be well-advised to choose the "in lieu of" are tempted to test the limits, with fateful and unfortunate results. In other situations there are catchall provisions that are easy to steer an obstreperous asshole toward, such as disorderly conduct laws or "failing to comply . . . ," and so on.

It is hard to imagine a citizen winning these encounters, which is the principal reason I appear as an expert witness in the few cases in which the aggrieved citizen sucks it up and sues. Abuse of power is one of the nearly irresistible temptations of policing. Asserting authority and otherwise showing scumbags who the boss is constitutes another. The first has to do with the intoxication of power and how it tempts all humans to abuse it. The second relates to beating back a real or imagined challenge to authority.

The confrontations between police and their targets is where the rubber of authority meets the road of law. And this is the area so dramatically covered by the Earl Warren Supreme Court as it established the rules governing such encounters.

In a series of decisions in the 1960s, the Supreme Court guided cops' actions in searches, questionings, access to attorneys, the admissibility of evidence and confessions, and other enforcement actions. It is not too grand an assertion to hold that the principal agent for reform of policing on the street in the latter third of the twentieth century was the Warren Court.

The individual actions of lone cops or pairs on the street, even late at night and in secluded places, can be controlled if the cops are inspired by the fear that their actions will be carefully examined by a determined chief and that they will be called to account for their behaviors. That is the final inhibitor of brutality, even as such powerful tools as Supreme Court decisions, litigation, outside review, or FBI inquiries also came into play.

EN MASSE

Cops love to compare their organizations to the military, glorying in the titles, insignia, forms of address, uniforms, salutes, and a supposed but nonexistent discipline. In fact, except for the outter trappings, the military and the police could not be more dissimilar. Where cops operate as lone wolves, exercising judgment and initiative in ad hoc actions adapting to ever-changing circumstances, soldiers operate en masse and are forbidden to undertake the individual actions that are the very hallmarks of police operations.

Cops rarely operate en masse, or even frequently find themselves functioning as parts of a larger group, either formally or, as we shall see, off duty. There is the very occasional parade and such demonstrations as attended the December 1999 World Trade Organization conference in Seattle but, as this event again proved, they're not very good in these exercises. And in others they can be worse.

When political considerations get mixed with race, as they did in the Harlem rally in the summer of 1998, the results can be really unfortunate.[2] In that event, a demonstration featuring highly controversial— some anti-Semitic—speakers in an all-black setting, the police moved in very aggressively, precisely at the 4 P.M. scheduled ending. Such punctilious observance of time constraints might be said to have been unprecedented in a department accustomed to massaging such ceremonies and letting them meander to peaceful conclusions.

In this incident helicopters swooped down precisely at 1600 hours and riot-equipped police stormed the platform. It would not be hyperbole to hold that the cops, by their overreaction—which had quite clearly been thoroughly planned in advance—provoked a confused melee in which a couple of meaningless arrests were effected and in which an already tattered police reputation in Harlem, to be sure, lay in further ruin.

What might have been behind this surprising and dismaying action? A mayor planning to run for the U.S. Senate—being in the second term of a two-term-limit office—who never counted on a black vote and who was prepared to sacrifice any such gain in order to retain the support of an adoring and voting white majority.

Attacking an event stained by anti-Semitic overtones was sure to play well in the Jewish community, an integral part of a plan to cobble a winning coalition of voters together. That the action confirmed the worst suspicions of angry black folks would prove of little concern to the actuaries calculating the electoral numbers.

When asked for my reaction, I told the *New York Times* that the NYPD owed the Harlem community an apology.

These very same cops blocked traffic, stormed the Brooklyn Bridge, laid siege to city hall, and pointedly hurled racist epithets at their own black commanders in a 1993 dispute that coincided with the mayoral election in which the mayor in this case, Rudolph Giuliani, won over an incumbent black, David Dinkins. That Giuliani was both a beneficiary of this action and an untroubled witness to it didn't seem to bother him excessively. He did little to alienate the core support behind the police faces. I had to wonder at his thoughts over having a rare chance to see the underbelly of the beast he so proudly extolls and whose actions, even obviously questionable ones, he so stoutly defends. In another of history's unexpected turns, Mayor Giuliani was discovered to have prostate cancer, was accused of two separate series of adultery, and, on May 19, 2000, withdrew from the Senate race. His humble and introspective behavior now stood in stark and vivid contrast to his previous bellicosity.

I became very wary of the cops' predilection for lawbreaking, especially en masse. There was a strong element of nihilism rooted in a "we're above the law" psychology that seemed to grip cops when they were together and angry.

The durability of this syndrome became evident to Louisville, Kentucky,[3] citizens when uniformed, on-duty cops rampaged and blocked traffic in downtown streets on March 3, 2000. They were protesting the firing of a police chief who had, without the mayor's knowledge, approved awards for valor granted to two officers who had killed an unarmed car theft suspect in May 1999 with a barrage of twenty-two shots. The officers were white and the suspect was black and the African American community vigorously protested the act at the time and was outraged that the officers were commended for their actions.

When the mayor belatedly learned the cops had been awarded medals, he saw it as a slap in the face to the black community and fired the chief. Police commanders attended the police disorder and threw their badges down in sympathy with the chief. As the cops stormed about, the mayor asked, "Who's watching over us?"

The police union planned another demonstration to support the chief. The event served to illustrate to me the danger inherent in failing to control the cops. It was another reminder that the chief, who is supported by the union and widely loved by the rank-and-file, will likely be betraying the interests of the people he is sworn to serve.

As noted earlier, one of the key litmus tests that a chief is doing his job is, unfortunately, a vote of "no confidence" from police unions that have become apologists for wrongdoers in the ranks. The union's interests and the chief's diverge, since one is management and the other labor. That is not to say a positive and constructive relationship is not possible, but that the realities must be recognized if the people are to be served. This is the essential choice for the CEO—to throw yourself into bed with the union or serve the people.

The local newspaper, the *Courier-Journal*, later found that more than one-third of the cases involving the use of force by the Louisville department were not properly documented.[4] This sort of omission prevents the discovery of incidents of abuse by the police and illustrates the pernicious effects of having police executives who are mindlessly protective of the troops at the expense of the public's protection.

"Policemen's Brawl" was the descriptive used in Indianapolis newspapers[5] for a drunken celebration by cops on August 27, 1996, in which women were allegedly harassed and two men beaten. The officers had attended a baseball game with their chief, who left before they went off to the bar. The chief offered to resign but was urged to stay on until the mayor discovered that he attended another game with some of the implicated officers two days after this violent display of above-the-law tactics. The chief's resignation was accepted. It served as another illustration of the sort of oversight exercised by many police executives. You can't be one of the boys if you expect to be able to discipline them when things go wrong.

Although many, on both coasts, would be hard pressed to distinguish Indianapolis from Minneapolis, differences do exist.

By way of contrasting the chief of the former from my tenure I'd cite the appearance of a clearly uncomfortable officer who came to see me, in the mideighties, to apologetically advise me I would not be welcome at the union's family picnic.

I never did make them—nor any of the beery retirement parties, after the first, to which they asked me while still in the rosy glow of hope that I wouldn't turn out as badly as I did, in their eyes. The commentaries about me in the union newsletter *Show-Up* were classics of inspired invective.

New York's Rudy Giuliani was one of the few outsiders who had a chance to see, up close and personal, this darker side of American policing, but all the evidence reflects his having ignored the issue to accommodate broader interests. Despite a dramatic nationwide decline in crime—powered by varied and not always totally understood forces such as a roaring economy, benign demographics, the peaking of the crack epidemic a decade earlier, and myriad other known and unknown factors—Giuliani was quick to demand credit for the decline and strongly supported the cops he claimed had brought it about.

As Napoleon put it, when asked which soldiers make the best generals—"lucky ones," he'd responded. The same was certainly true of chiefs and mayors. Giuliani looked very much like the man who, having been born at home plate, assumed he'd hit a homer.

YANKEE STADIUM—1976

From 1967 onward I had what might be called a catbird seat over the NYPD's inner workings, and they were labyrinthine. Over the next ten years I was at the epicenter of the department's hierarchy—either as a key aide or as a result of holding important commands.

It was curious that I had really been a bust as a cop and as a detective. I never made the psychic leap from chronic and inveterate order taker to sudden and confident order giver as a first-line supervisor (sergeant), always fearing that those cynical cops would just say, "Fuck you, no, I ain't gonna do it."

I was pretty well up the ladder before I was inwardly convinced they wouldn't say it, at least outwardly, and so became a slightly more assured supervisor. Nevertheless, having been a really feckless scholar through high school, I felt unprepared for real management.

I sought managerial experience in the assignments; closely studied the department and, especially, its key or promising stalwarts; and went to school. Strangely, where I'd found police and even investigative work—for which I had no real talent—boring, I took to abstract administrative problems with élan.

By the time I was "given the Bronx," in the parlance of the trade, I'd been through a pretty comprehensive initiation. I'd stumble again, seriously and repeatedly, but I was, at the very least, really interested in management's arcana and had a bent for introspection that proved a boon.

I can recall one day, in uniform and sporting two stars, sauntering up to a very young cop during a demonstration in which hundreds of unhappy Puerto Ricans, angry over a lack of construction jobs, were blocking the Willis Avenue Bridge and hundreds of delayed motorists, furious at their wheels. Knowing that I was not going to call the scores of cops present into action, I softly said to him "What do you think I ought to do, Officer?"

"Jeez Chief," he stuttered, "I thought you'd know."

But the gods watch hubris jealously and move swiftly to punish its arrogant practitioners. Noticing one rabble-rouser exhorting the demonstrators to block more lanes of traffic, I thought he'd better be interrupted and ordered his arrest for disorderly conduct.

As he was being hauled away I was seized with a familiar and unsettling sensation as one of my aides whispered in my ear, "Do you know who that is, Chief?"

No, but I could guess it spelled *tsouris*.

The mufti-clad militant was, it turned out, the revered local Catholic priest.

I immediately dispatched the aide to the precinct to tell the priest we'd release him without charge if he'd promise he wouldn't sue for false arrest. He graciously agreed and a minor controversy was averted. The Harlem and East Harlem riots of the 1960s made us all very wary of "long, hot summers." The streets of the Bronx were crammed with folks escaping tenement heat and enjoying a few beers. Crowds of hot, unemployed people drinking beer and wine make cops nervous. It was this fear that had moved a mayoral aide to slough off Frank Serpico. That was the party line—don't make the cops unhappy with a tough summer ahead. In

1976, I nervously watched the summer calendar make its tortuous way to fall and had no trouble grasping City Hall's reasoning, even as I failed to agree with it.

THE BRONX

Whistlers through graveyards spoke of the Bronx's rebirth whenever a green shoot sprouted through the scattered bricks, but I saw a wasteland of burned buildings, empty lots, shattered glass, potholes and water pools, packs of wild dogs, shaking figures around oil drum fires, and an eerie emptiness that made infrequent visitors wonder if they could still be in America.

The one and a half million residents—one-third black, one-third Hispanic, one-third other—lived amid urban devastation of a sort known only to Detroit and Newark. Yes, there were enclaves of tranquility and prosperity—Riverdale, the northeast Bronx, and the miraculous City Island—but, in the 1970s, the south and central Bronx were ablaze.

I allowed cops to shoot the wild dogs and rarely did more than the most perfunctory inquiry into such socially useful acts.

Bill Moyers did a documentary called *The Fire Next Door*, and there was the classic *Police Tapes*, both of which captured the ugliness, decay, and despair.

I wondered what I might do and, in 1976, asked, "Why doesn't President Ford come to the Bronx?" The comment received some press but no action for months.

One day I received a call that Gov. Jimmy Carter's son wanted to see me.

Either he had a tough schedule or I was duller than usual, because Chip Carter's head kept sliding off his hand in desperate dozings as I described the horrors of the Bronx. I was totally confident I'd heard the last of this and assumed Chip would look me up again only if he needed to get a sense of prolonging his life through excruciating boredom. So I was surprised to see the national media's celebration of recently elected President Carter's alighting on Charlotte Street's rubble. He uttered the usual bromides and promises and left.

This visit proved such a stunner that it became part of the presidential formula. Ronald Reagan went there in 1980 and engaged the feisty residents in a widely covered give-and-take in 1984. A sort of Potemkin village of model one-family homes sprouted in this unlikely spot but, otherwise, the visits accomplished nothing more than to gather the much sought after media attention.

The gradual regeneration of the Bronx would occur through pressing housing needs during a prolonged economic boom that made the refurbishing of the burned-out hulks feasible. In the end, I inwardly regretted having raised hopes, only to see them met with empty promises.

During these almost four years in command of Bronx forces I grew desperately anxious to focus America's attention on the desolation surrounding me. It looked like the Bronx—not Vietnam—was the battle for the country's soul.

When Susan Raymond called in 1975 to seek my advice on a police documentary she planned to shoot, I saw another chance. She and her husband, Alan, had just done *An American Family: The Story of the Louds*. I'd thought it a gripping document of a golden family's dissolution. She said they'd contacted the police commissioner's office and, while they'd been denied permission to film the NYPD, they wanted to talk to me to get some ideas of where they might do their film.

"Come to the Bronx and film the Forty-fourth Precinct—the center of action," I offered.

"I'm sorry, Chief, I guess I wasn't clear—the police commissioner has said no to doing any part of the NYPD."

"Come anyway. I run the Bronx. Film anything you want."

They came, did about one hundred hours of film, and edited down to a ninety-minute documentary—*The Police Tapes*, which won Peabody, Emmy, and Du Pont Awards and which was reported to have inspired *Hill Street Blues*.

When Police Commissioner Codd was given a private showing the only comment attributed to him was, "Their tunics were unbuttoned"— speaking about the casual approach Bronx cops took to their uniforms. The Raymonds also won an Oscar in 1995 for a documentary on Philadelphia school children, and an Emmy in 2000 for their searing indictment titled *Children in War*.

The disintegration, however, continued unabated despite such an eloquent clarion call to reform.

BRONX AND RENT CONTROL⁶

If there was one villain in the destruction of the Bronx in the 1960s and 1970s it was, ironically, rent control.

As thousands of families got up and abandoned the Grand Concourse for Co-Op City virtually overnight, a vacuum was created that was sporadically filled by less stable occupants. Squatters invaded; looters stripped plumbing; water cascaded and froze, driving paying tenants out. Others withheld rent. Landlords, faced with rising taxes, more costly services, and demanding mortgage payments, bled cash. Rents, when collected, were low and fixed. The moment of truth finally came—pay an arsonist a few thousand to torch the place or simply walk away from the building.

Soon the borough was ablaze.

Orchard Beach was one of the key summer amenities to which Bronx residents hied during the tense summer months. So when the lifeguards went on strike in 1975, and the Parks Department closed the beach, I ordered it reopened and decided to take the risk. As it happened a drunken lady did wander into the surf and perished, but I wasn't even mildly tempted to rethink my resolve to keep the place open.

On another occasion at the same beach I responded to a Fourth of July "celebration" that boiled over into a riot of assaults, bottle throwings, fires, and arrests. I made points with City Hall by playfully referring to the event, on the TV news, as "holiday hijinks." The mayor had had his fill of rioting after the street disorders in East Harlem in 1967 and 1968.

As my fourth Bronx summer was winding to cooler levels, I began to feel the annual relief of another crisis avoided. Predictably, the sense of euphoria was shattered by the unexpected event of cops on a rampage.

Traditionally, the expiration of the police contract was followed by months and months of desultory negotiations and escalating rhetoric until the inevitable denouement of an agreement. Cops were legally forbidden to strike—and there were stiff penalties for violating the Taylor Law—so compulsory arbitration became the alternative, although nobody much liked that route. The agreement would be followed by a fat check for the money due, retroactively, and calm would return until the next expiration.

Sometimes the negotiations would get tangled with union elections and this raised the stakes as incumbents fell prey to charges of foot drag-ging, or worse. Mostly, these protracted dealings went smoothly enough, given the volatile setting.

And the presence of a good, gray, career civil servant—Abraham Beame—in the mayor's chair boded well for accommodation. The police commissioner, Michael Codd, was very old-school and loved the troops, so there was little concern on that front. The scenario seemed ideal for a positive result.

But it didn't happen.

The cops' exasperation grew as the months lapsed into years and internal union rivalries, always hot, began to seethe. There were angry meetings, demands to strike, threats of "blue flu"—where officers would call in sick in large numbers (they had a very liberal sick policy that essentially gave them virtually unlimited full-pay benefits)—and other job actions.

Cops began to demonstrate, at first picketing, leafletting, and stomping. Their union hall meetings, rarely models of decorum, became downright raucous as the meat eaters took charge. The diminutive mayor—he was under five feet tall—and the police commissioner's name came into play in the imaginative way of New York name calling—in an inspired bit of street theater when the picketing cops chanted: "Codd is a fish and Beame is a shrimp." The demonstrators, emboldened, escalated the actions and were joined by more and more colleagues.

By the fall of 1976 an operatic pitch was reached as they marched in a large body to Gracie Mansion—the mayor's residence on Manhattan's East River. There they chanted threateningly and pointedly, en masse, urinated on the grounds. Then, in actions that would prefigure events at the Brooklyn Bridge years later and be repeated in Louisville and other places in America, they marched riotously through the East Eighties in the street, blocking traffic and setting off a cacophony of horns.

It all proved a field day for the press and acutely embarrassing to a police commissioner who had no enthusiasm for disciplining cops. Codd uttered the usual stentorian bromides but the needed resolve and actions were missing—and cops never respond to imprecations or predictions of dire consequences.

On September 28, 1976, Muhammad Ali was to fight Ken Norton for the Heavyweight Boxing Championship at Yankee Stadium, and the

Patrolman's Benevolent Association promptly announced they'd picket around the Yankee Stadium site. Given the actions of recent days, we all knew this meant trouble.

The police commissioner convened a planning session to cope with what was developing as the focal point of the dispute.

I knew that on-duty cops would not act against the demonstrating off-duty officers they'd be joining just as soon as they could. My only chance lay in getting teams of supervisors to film the actions and then later move against the offenders with the photo evidence. I could at least threaten supervisors with sanctions for failing to act. Codd immediately and reflexively nixed my proposal, not concealing his distaste for such tactics, and ordered a large body of cops to contain the pickets behind wooden barriers.

I was well aware I was heading for a disaster and decided to intercept the marching cops as they walked across the McCombs Dam Bridge to the stadium, their announced route. I'd be in uniform and at the head of a substantial body of cops that I hoped to suck into a melee with the advancing horde of demonstrators.

The best outcome, for me, was to get knocked on my ass, my uniform torn, with a few bruises, and thereby provoke the cops behind me to fight. It would all make exculpatory footage for my failure and we'd all have good excuses for the fiasco sure to ensue.

The demonstrators saw this and reversed plans, taking the subway to the stadium where they noisily tramped and chanted. This was fine, but the crackling police radio informed me they'd "broken out" of the barricades, and now about thirteen hundred of them circled the arena as thousands of prominent folks and celebrities arrived for the fight.

Confusion abounded and enterprising young muggers of the Bronx saw their chance and pounced, snatching jewelry, watches, tickets, and more from the well-heeled crowd. Kids clambered over buses and tore about. One came within inches of snatching Howard Cosell's toupee. Powerful citizens boiled. There'd be hell to pay.

We made a few arrests of the denizens—not cops, who gleefully chanted and sowed chaos under the benign gazes of their colleagues.

I feared even for the fate of the bout and was relieved that it came off. Ali won. I lost.

I had scurried from place to place, frantically and futilely barking orders at deaf cops. My 1958 nightmare, as a first-line supervisor, that the cops wouldn't heed my orders was now a reality.

By the end I was exhausted and drained. I could barely walk. My legs were cramped. It was 2:30 A.M. on September 29 when I finally left the deserted scene for home, where I received an ominous summons to appear at the chief of operations's (the title had been changed from chief inspector) office at 8 A.M.

The four-star chief, James Hannan, had been a friend as well as my subordinate only four years earlier. An avuncular figure, he'd been chosen because he was our supreme mechanic, the executive who could tinker and fuss and tweak the engine to keep it running without introducing troubling and newfangled notions. I had, in fact, predicted his appointment by way of demonstrating to my close associates that I had Police Commissioner Codd figured out, even though the others didn't, at the time, agree with me that Hannan would be the anointed one.

Now, amid news reports and headlines of chaos in the Bronx, he simply wanted to communicate the police commissioner's displeasure. "He's very unhappy with you, Tony," he said, and then he added the words that spelled my doom: "You can't afford another mistake." My failure lay in my having allowed the cops to rampage, not curbing the kids snatching at tickets and watches, and, especially, allowing the rich and famous to get a glimpse of society's underbelly.

How the hell was I going to avoid another mistake in the Bronx, where every day brought three or four that I'd been able to motor over only because no one wanted to know and there were no volunteers for my post? Now they would want to know and would be watching.

The story dominated the news over the next six weeks. All kinds of accounts—a grand jury was going to be convened; a confidential report blasting my handling of the event was "leaked from police headquarters." Demotions or indictments, or both, loomed.

In the heat of the inquiry I was invited to offer up the man I'd put in charge of the stadium while I was at the bridge and on whose watch the cops had broken out of their barricade-confinement. I'd have none of that; the man worked for me and was following my orders. It would be my head or no one's.

Incidentally, that officer, Inspector Fred Heineman, went on to become chief of police of Raleigh, North Carolina, and was elected to Congress from that district.

The controversy flared on without abatement. The denunciations were reaching levels of time and intensity as to make me unemployable, and I'd soon need another job. I certainly understood the virtues of silent acceptance of my fate but I came to see that the policy of forbearance and submission had limits.

By mid-October my spirit was bent low. I'd been hammered repeatedly in public and in the press and harassed mercilessly in the endless internal inquiries. Coming home from a dinner party at a neighbor's house my wife, a tough and spirited militant, uncharacteristically burst into tears over the questions and scrutiny to which we were all being subjected.

I had a speech commitment at the City Club, an influential group interested in sound government, around that time.

A few days earlier I had a Paul-of-Tarsus-like epiphany. As if clouds parted to reveal the truth, I had a flash of insight—I'd fight. I'd take them down with me. No two-star chief—who could be reduced four ranks to captain with one stroke of the police commissioner's pen—had ever openly defied the commissioner. I decided I'd do it, secretly suspecting Codd would have no appetite for a public struggle. It was a high-stakes gamble but I relied on an analysis of the man that had so far proved accurate.

Before the counterattack, I had to somehow stop the music—arrest the unending drumbeat of criticisms washing over me.

My chance came when Selwyn Raab of the *New York Times*, called for one of those analytical pieces the paper does so brilliantly. I pontificated at length, including a pointed reference to "the feral children of the Bronx" and the horror experienced by the celebrities attending the fight at encountering this sociological phenomenon.

Several hours later, Raab called back. Was I sure I wanted to go with this quote? It made me sound racist.

"What is the quote," I asked.

"Your reference to the 'feral youth of the Bronx.'"

"No," I corrected, "I want it to be 'feral children.'" I thanked him for his really gracious solicitude and he wrote it.

The music stopped.

I referred to the wild kids attacking the stadium attendees that night in such stark terms in order to shock the audience into a moment of paralysis. My real objective was to shift the debate into the arena of the NYPD's internal management problems, which, for example, has resulted in the layoffs of thousands of young cops the year before, in 1975. The band suddenly struck up a new, sociological tune.

I delivered my speech.

The police commissioner awoke on October 16, 1976, to a front page story in the *New York Times* blasting the management of the department. Cops were not working eight-hour days; they all rode in inefficient two-person cars; there were too many precincts. I unburdened myself of all the grievances and observations that had been bugging me for years—and which I'd face and address in Minneapolis three years later.

The outburst was followed by a cacophony of questions from the press, myriad appearances by me in which I buttressed and expanded the charges of mismanagement. An eerie silence emerged from headquarters.

Codd would not respond directly, I felt, but would await a chance that, given the realities of Bronx policing, was sure to come. What the police commissioner didn't know was that I was secretly plotting my exit. My negotiations with the transit police intensified and I made ready to jump. At that time transit was an entirely separate agency but it has since, quite rightly, been taken over and absorbed into the NYPD.

An unbelievably lucky break came when the Fund for the City of New York announced that I was one of five government officials chosen for their Public Service Award, which also carried a $5,000 prize and received wide publicity. Suddenly, a public that was trying to figure out whether I was a hero, villain, or boob had the prestigious organization's answer.

I accepted the number two post in the transit police—a three-star rank and, hence, a promotion—and filed for retirement after twenty-four years at the NYPD.

The cops settled their contract dispute, disbanded, and returned to their precincts much in the manner of juntas returning to barracks. They'd be a lot easier to control individually.

My own assessment of my performance was that I had responded stupidly in an unwinnable situation without being able to figure out what I might have done differently. I knew just how able and devoted generals felt who, having done everything possible, nevertheless were defeated in battle.

I left with a deep and abiding affection for an institution that had nurtured, protected, even cosseted and educated me—the NYPD. I'd had other offers and turned them down because I loved "the job" and would have happily remained if I'd been allowed to. Still, I left without rancor to a better-paying job, transporting a pension and ready to make hay.

Codd retired as Ed Koch was elected mayor in 1977, and died not long thereafter.

POLICE STRIKE

There is probably no more unthinkable a prospect in policing than the idea of a strike. Not since the 1919 Boston police strike catapulted Governor Calvin Coolidge into the presidency, through the vice president slot and the death of President Harding, have the police even considered such militant actions. Coolidge fired hundreds of strikers and refused to take them back. It was as seminal an event as President Ronald Reagan's firing of air traffic controllers two-thirds of a century later, and similarly refusing their return.

Nevertheless, legislators have moved to impose grave and costly sanctions in the event of the unmentionable, and compelled arbitration when disputes arise. Why such drastic action to confront a nonevent?

The absence of any major police strike has not precluded mass sickouts—the so-called blue flu syndrome—when cops are unhappy, en masse, and we've seen just how militant cops can become when disaffected as the law enforcers ironically surrender to nihilist instincts.

Having confronted the really frightening sight of militant cops on a rampage led me to think of how I'd deal with a police strike. I thought long and hard about the issue and finally devised the approach I would take, without ever discussing it with anyone until this moment. Fortunately, the scheme never came to a test, but the unity and militancy of the Minneapolis cops certainly had me fearing they just might resort to such a showdown as I rammed reform after reform down their collective throats.

I'd have to determine who was out and who would remain. A clear policy statement would have to be issued that must frighten the strikers without irrevocably wedding me to a straitjacket. Whatever I threatened would have to be pursued.

I'd hope for retaining a cadre of supervisors around whom I could fashion an organization, but I'd prepare for the worst-case scenario of a total stoppage.

First—having issued a statement—I'd ask the mayor to declare a state of emergency and call in the National Guard, envisioning about a three-month takeover to allow the governor to deploy the Guard for a long-term assignment. This might well mean staggering call-ups to accommodate the normal life and work cycles of those recalled to serve.

Second, I'd be conciliatory and patient. I'd beg the cops to return, promising rehiring, although we'd impose a suspension of two days for every day out and permanently add a reference to his or her participation in each cop's personnel folder. As an act of mercy these latter penalties might be softened at some critical juncture.

Meticulous records would be kept by city employees of all events and participants to allow us to present articulable grounds in the lawsuits certain to follow.

It would be critical to bring the public along in fashioning a solution and this would have to involve exhausting their patience with the strikers.

I envisioned days of escalating rhetoric and swelling public exasperation as the cops continued to break the law. The passage of time would also exacerbate the economic problems certain to beset the strikers.

This temporizing would tax my nerves but it was essential to any prospect of a favorable outcome. Caving to the militants would guarantee a reprise.

The airwaves must be dotted with statements that contrasted the chief's reasonableness with the intransigence of the cops on strike. Their breaking of the law would put them at a tactical disadvantage from the first, and all that followed would have to underline and deepen that weakness.

As tensions would escalate and politicos and editorialists would demand action, I'd make one final offer of return, with minor concessions, and with a fixed deadline. Here I'd hold the line. Anyone not back at the appointed hour would be permanently fired.

Since Minnesota has just about the highest requirements in the nation to be a cop, there was a ready pool of candidates in community colleges throughout the state. These would-be law enforcers were taking two years of criminal justice courses and the eight-week skills course—which topped off the training—or had already graduated and were looking for jobs. Then there were the instructors, those with military police experience or members of other departments—locally or nationally. A scale system of points—for experience, training and background—would be employed to determine the level of entry.

Once embarked on this course, the rubicon would be crossed and total war declared. There'd be no turning back nor would anyone be taken back. An entirely new department would be built from the ashes, with the National Guard in place for at least about three months to get over the initial bumps.

In terms of time, I envisioned a process of pleadings, hectorings, and exchanges ranging over the first two weeks. Planning would have begun, secretly, with the threat or possibility of a strike surfacing.

It is painful to admit, but an essential feature of the entire program would be the escalation of the people's angst, fear, and disgust to the level where they'd demand action and support it energetically when it came. To move prematurely to a solution absent public understanding and backing would be to ensure its failure.

I have no way of knowing how it would all conclude. Thankfully, it never came to that, but I was determined that such an event would not go unanswered.

Any hope of reform would have to take the individual and collective proclivities of the troops into account, as well as the organizational problems requiring attention. As we've seen, cops can be very tough and militant. Citizens can be uninformed and the press will focus its lights on those making the noise. Controlling such actions as we've seen described here is a tough assignment.

19
REFORMS: WITHOUT AND WITHIN

The Minneapolis reform agenda was a full plate but I determined to keep the list as short as possible, to seek the public's support for every reform, and to sweeten every pill for the force with such concessions as wage increases, the creation of elite and energetic new units and reward systems that included medals and other forms of support and recognition. I wanted the cops to know that I'd support them when they did good work and that I'd try to give them the benefit of the doubt when they tried to work in good faith—even when they erred, as cops on the street sometimes do. Some mistakes, as the Diallo case in New York so well illustrated, cannot, however, be either forgiven or overlooked. Acts of bad faith would receive tough treatment.

In my public comments I always praised cops generally, especially when I had to impose discipline on a few individually. In one notably egregious bit of police abuse I publicly accused the cops of "[taking] the U.S. Constitution and wip[ing] their bottoms with it."

In many ways, my approach was Machiavellian but I had a lot of faith in that author's words.

Over the years each and every item got adopted, often bloodily. There were "no confidence" votes by the union (it's hard for me to imagine to this day any chief doing his job appropriately who hasn't been publicly chastised by the police union in this fashion—it ought to be one of the rites of passage to a Chief's Hall of Fame, if they ever construct one) and phoned death threats to me and my wife (my phone number was always listed—I was not going to cower before the assaults, picketings, protests, denunciations in the press, awful charges in the union newsletter, and frequent recruitments of politicos to take me on). But with the mayor's unswerving support and a public that positively doted on me and strongly aided my efforts, I managed to cling to office. Again, the power of an aroused and focused citizenry in a democracy is not to be underestimated, and it nourished and supported me.

The issues of openness and accessibility deserve some extended commentary because, as I assessed the impacts of these approaches, I learned of unexpected benefits accruing from the tactics.

Being a populist, I thought that any citizen, however humble or weak, ought to be able to reach me, for any reason, any time he felt the need. Populism, to me, meant looking after the interests of the powerless.

While the reforms required battles in courts, before arbitrators, in contract negotiations before the council or Civil Service Commission, and in the press, the depoliticization of the agency simply required us—the mayor and me—to do nothing.

The cops could, on their off time, politic all they wanted but there'd be no rewards or punishments following the elections as long as Mayor Fraser and I were there. There were elections for mayor and council every two years then, but following each of these, none of the cops were promoted, demoted, or transferred, as had previously been the invariable practice.

The removal of incentives killed partisanship virtually overnight. The corrosive politicking vanished as if in evaporation. It wasn't even remarked upon. It became, in essence, a nonevent.

Even as I failed to touch their attitudes—and soon recognized the futility of even trying—I knew how to change their behaviors on the street and it rested on one word: fear. Chiefs could motivate, exhort, encourage, cajole and even threaten or reward all they wanted, but baleful and cynical cops would just nod "yes sir" and go right on doing whatever they pleased.

The only way I ever discovered—or ever observed—of effecting a change in police behavior was to define impermissible limits very starkly and investigate and punish transgressions swiftly and surely. Once they got this message—in the form of actions that buttressed the words—even the worst, with occasional lapses to be sure, conformed.

Anxious to evade the deadening embrace of sycophants that surround every CEO I sought reality in the roll calls and training sessions I attended almost every day. There, in a setting where officers could say or ask anything, my ego took a daily pounding that reached its nadir when an officer bluntly asked when I'd leave and added, "You're nothing but a New York fucker."

A rush of violent emotion swept over me as I slowly moved back, surreptitiously, to grasp the desk behind me for support. I mumbled a bit of recitative psychobabble as I inwardly struggled to avoid actually fainting and gradually regained my balance. I finally managed a calm, discursive reply, staggered to the end, and left, shaken and disturbed, but determined to return. I did, again and again.

One such session, to demonstrate the officers' lack of inhibition, became part of the documentary *The Police Chiefs* in 1987. Viewers were appalled at the uninhibited animus expressed at me by the cops at roll call, even with cameras whirring.

So I left these sessions battered and bruised, yet grateful. If ever there was a character builder this was it—a sort of twisted version of the Carnegie method. How much healthier, though, to my functioning, than the blandishments of the pilot fish attracted to every chief?

The people had loaned me their strength and support and I'd keep it until they perceived I'd broken faith with them. I meant to guard such great power jealously. This tome is splotched with examples of how a threat, by me, to "go public" usually brought surrender.

I couldn't be perceived—or substantively act—as if I was trying to preserve my persona. Every battle had to contain the essential element of the people's good.

I did nothing to the guy who shook me so profoundly. When I attended a training graduation ceremony, however, I faced another challenge. I arrived to award the certificates to the graduates. An aide informed me that one of the students would refuse to salute me or shake my hand during the ceremonies. I was internally conflicted. I was furious, but the fury had to give way to reason. I thought hard.

I decided control was the issue. The police department was not a democracy, but a dictatorship. I encouraged dissent, but this was permission, not a right. I hoped I submerged my ego and told the aide to tell the officer that I was ordering him to step forward, salute, shake my hand, and accept the certificate. Failure now constituted clear-cut insubordination.

The man came forward, in his turn, saluted, shook my hand, accepted the document, turned smartly, and marched off.[1]

Some events are best described and left to the reader to judge dynamics and justifications.

There was little doubt in my mind that a lot of my probity rested— just as in my control of the police department—on fear of my willingness to impose discipline rather than a love of virtue.

Besides the cops, there was the council, a minority of whose members were eager to pounce on every misstep of mine. When I went to Europe for an international police conference, the city's fiscal officer was summoned to a council hearing and asked who was paying for the trip.

"I don't know," he responded, "but I know it isn't the city."

"How could you know that?"

"Because Chief Bouza has never submitted an expense voucher for anything."

The result was the ordering of an audit of a fund I used. When the report came back that I'd contributed $54,000 in honoraria and grants to the account I used for police purposes, the council suppressed the results of the inquiry without a word.

I must admit to some disappointment that the press had no interest in the matter.

FEEDBACK

In the twilight of a long career, I despaired of getting useful feedback from my aides. Instead—whether in the NYPD, the transit police, or Minneapolis—they strove to catalogue my wonderfulness in ways that would cleverly sneak under my defenses. It was no use to plead.

"Of course we'd tell you if we thought you were doing something wrong, Chief, but . . ." That was the litany.

I discovered the need for tough, useful insight when Pat Murphy took over the NYPD and launched what many considered a reign of terror that featured transfers, demotions, and hasty retirements. My own ascension to command the Bronx forces occurred precisely because of one of those encouragements to depart, when an inspection of the command revealed management lapses at the top, forcing my predecessor to retire.

During one meeting attended by about thirty of the key insiders, Murphy said he was thinking about authoring a newsletter to the troops. Everybody nodded enthusiastic support.

I said, "You'd better write it yourself, Commissioner. If you have a lieutenant do it the troops will see it as bullshit." This was followed by a shocked silence, finally broken by Murphy's mild agreement. The anecdote made it into *Target Blue*, a memoir of the NYPD.

So I learned that the only useful feedback I'd get was by going out and listening to the cops every day. They gave me an earful. Any hope of reform had to start with a chief's willingness to submit to scrutiny and criticism.

At the end of nine years I had the full support of the mayor; eight and sometimes nine votes in a thirteen-member council; the open hostility of the union and its handmaiden, the Civil Service Commission; the public's affection; and press treatment that was, if anything, overgenerous. I could also claim the contempt, scorn, and detestation of a huge majority of the rank-and-file, all of whom bitterly resented the very short leash on which I held them.

And another irony lay in the fact that, for those nine years, there wasn't a major lawsuit won against the agency and no real scandals—though there was a continuous bubble in the pot I was stirring. We'll never know how many cops were prevented from committing how many atrocities, but it is on that unknowable factor that I'd stake my fate.

When asked, as I began my stint, how long it would take me to reshape the Minneapolis Police Department, I said, "About three years." And thereafter? "I'd be taking money under false pretenses."

Years later, as I approached the end, this quote (one of many such dotting my public landscape) was framed as a question. What about it?

"I never said I wouldn't take money under false pretenses," I said.

All of the major objectives, save one, were realized. I failed to hire enough black males even though, through affirmative action, I reached every single one on every hiring list presented to me. And I pursued aggressive recruitment programs to entice black males into the ranks. The racism of the institutions controlling the flow—all of them—was palpable. Black leaders who blasted the police and scorned the agency didn't help either.

The mayor and I had tried—we'd hired a lot of women and institutionalized the acceptance of gays in the ranks (in another intemperate outburst and trying to entice gays I knew were already there, I said that I'd come out of the closet if they would and we could establish a precedent—a bit of humor that didn't work), but we failed on the central issue of hiring black males.

Knowing the width of the chasm between public knowledge and the inner reality of the police world, I distilled every issue into catchy and hopefully clarifying sound bites. Every initiative was preceded by a public debate. Why one-person patrols? Why were four precincts better than six? What makes name tags important? What is 911 and what can it do for me?

Every such initiative produced vicious controversies that could not be won without the public's backing. This might take the form of comments to the press, election outcomes, letters to the editor or simple nudgings across backyard fences or in the supermarket checkout line. This was what public discussion was about and its power has to be felt to be known.

And so Minneapolis became the only job I was either able to get or leave voluntarily of the ten or so I sought or held from 1976—when it all started—to 1994—when I faced ignominious defeat in a governor's primary. And still, my ego remained swollen and distended through it all, an unconquered monster.

EGO

A digression is needed to address the subversive power of ego and how it can undermine reforms.

I remember identifying a problem while in Minneapolis, the answers to which hadn't come. I can't recall the specifics, but I called a meeting of key aides to discuss the issue. In the interim, over a weekend, my inner dialogues led me to the answers.

"Brilliant," a cunning inner voice uttered, "now you can dazzle them with your insight. Now they'll know why you were chosen chief." I was gleeful.

Then a very soft inner voice asked, "Is this why you came here, to show them how smart you are? And how will your associates react? Sure, they'll flatter you and walk off, washing their hands of the issue. How do you get them to feel they have a real stake in the outcome?"

I attended the meeting, described the problem, and stimulated a lively discussion. Sure enough, the group came up with the answers, aglow over their prowess. They'd work to implement the plan. I congratulated them and thanked them, with a silent thanks to the tiny voice that had alerted me to my ego's hubris.

Manipulative? Of course, but it proved the best example I ever had of a lurking menace that may have gained me great satisfaction at the expense of whatever progress I hoped to achieve. My ego had been loudly insisting I show them how clever I am, but the tiny voice of reason and humility helped me to see the light.

Reforms required a recognition of the problems, their prioritization, the development of a plan, the generation of public discussion, and securing of a wide consensus before adoption. This doesn't mean necessarily convincing determined opponents of the reform—the battle is for the minds and hearts of onlookers, usually the people.

Reform must flow from sources of unquestioned integrity and good faith. If motives can be successfully impugned the effort will founder on the shoals of public skepticism.

Reforms should be aimed at important problems; the pain involved in their adoption is too great to be suffered for frivolous pursuits.

Entrenched interests will battle progress, and the fight for the change rarely enlists even potential beneficiaries because they haven't experienced the benefits yet.

A cleansed agency automatically produces high morale, but the cleansing involves tough actions. It is certainly safer and more comfortable to go along, but that isn't what public service ought to be about.

A lot of the big national issues will raise the question of reform. It is hard to think of any that won't provoke controversy.

20
ISSUES ACROSS THE LANDSCAPE

Generalizations are treacherous, but necessary. They need to be questioned carefully, yet they are useful instruments. Understanding the internal workings of police agencies necessarily involves lapsing into broad assertions—but these must still be challenged. And issues surface in unexpected and often unbelievably controversial ways.

Cops once had to arrest abortionists who often endangered or inadvertently killed their clients and, overnight, had to protect doctors performing them from the assaults of right-to-lifers, even as they excluded the butchers with hangers. The constant is the primacy of the law. If you can't enforce it, you've got to quit. Another constant is the ability to adjust and eliminate partisan views and party politics from within the ranks—particularly when the police must recognize that, being in government, they are inescapably engaged in political acts. The simple fact is that cops must enforce the existing laws, even when they undertake 180-degree turns. If such enforcement ultimately violates the conscience, the only recourse is to resign.

This is a tortured locution but we've seen, especially in the LAPD and Minneapolis, how the issue of politics can be twisted to conform to personal aggrandizements. Demagogues will shout, "Get politics out of the department!"—when their real aim is to insert their own brand.

The police have to understand the complex forces at work in society.

241

A study announced in 1999[1] addresses the question of how the performance of abortions on impoverished teenaged females impacted the crime rate about thirty years after adoption. Their conclusion was that it had, and significantly. Publication of the study is certain to create a furor.

What is the impact of a fast or slow economy on crime rates?

Why is street crime centered in cities?

How do racism, ageism, economic disparities, and addictions impact on crime?

What are the forces at work in the ghetto culture and how do they contribute to raising or lowering crime levels?

Are the police the only crime fighters, or do, and should, others play a role?

How do we prevent crime? More cops? Bigger prisons? More mandated sentences? Tougher war on drugs?

What works? What doesn't?

The sad truth is that police chiefs and mayors—and even presidents, like Clinton—have furnished simple answers to these questions. It is they who hold the answers. And the answers usually involve more cops, bigger prisons, tougher laws. When crime—serendipitously and inexplicably— declines, there is no dearth of claimants for the credit. The cock crows, the sun rises, and the rooster claims a cause-and-effect relationship.

We want answers and the system will produce analyses and studies that accommodate private ambitions, in the name of public good, but the slippery social factors vary in size, shape, and importance in unseen and unmeasurable ways. In the end we are left with the street criminal and the two thousand blows that shaped him into a monster.

Go to the Woodbourne Correctional Facility in New York State and visit the man regarded as the most dangerous of all, Willie Bosket[2]—now around thirty-eight and black—and analyze his life. Or another—the infamous Willie Horton, who helped George Bush get elected president in 1988—and be appalled and repelled. But who ever asks how white society contributed to create these criminals? And therein lies the conundrum at the very core of American society.

Who waxes febrile over the vast depredations of white-collar criminals, who are often white, well educated, and identifiably of the overclass? And those white criminals who dump drugs on the underclass?

GUNS

What can be said about guns that doesn't wind up sounding like another stentorian Handgun Control Inc.–National Rifle Association[3] debate? And why can't the NRA remember its middle name?

America wakes up to the shooting deaths of its children in schools, and other First World nations do not. Our landscape is going to be dotted with such tragedies as occurred at Columbine High School on April 20, 1999, where thirteen kids died. They were shot with firearms bought illegally at a gun show. Other nations simply don't encounter those shocks because of tough gun control laws. The shocks will continue for us.

The response to a ghastly series of firearms tragedies in our schools was to convert them into garrisons, replete with security devices, cops, a climate of paranoia, and public hysteria.

Lost in all this is the statistical reality that schools are among America's safest havens and the home the most dangerous, followed closely by the workplace. Notwithstanding the awfulness of being told your child has been killed by another sick child with one of the ubiquitous firearms, the reality remains that it is in familiar places that we face our greatest dangers, from familiars.

What makes the school tragedies particularly poignant is their preventable nature—first, by essentially eliminating concealable firearms from society, and second, by responding to the warning signals emitted by troubled kids and adults more effectively. We mustn't lose sight of the fact that many of the problems that trigger violence emanate from drugs, alcohol, disordered homes, and mental illness.

Cars can be controlled—licensed, registered, and monitored—and so can guns.

Sex, drugs, gambling, tobacco, and alcohol cannot be interdicted but they can be controlled to irreducible minimums, at a heavy cost. These are addictions and inherently ineradicable, although they can be reduced. Guns are like autos and amenable to regulation.

We need to recognize the distinction between controlling traffic in substances and controlling human behaviors awash in addictions.

The Second Amendment argument—what we derisively can call the "right to arm bears" section—has, first, been found to apply to "well-regulated militias," and even were that long-standing Supreme Court ruling to be revised, it would still be amenable to restrictions, through laws, in exactly the same way we allow free speech but forbid inciting to riot; or freedom of religion, but without human sacrifice.

We are alone, among industrial nations, in allowing troglodytes to be armed to the teeth without limits. Almost as many Americans die from firearms deaths—accidents, suicides, and murders—as in car crashes. The manufacturers' response has been to increase production and heighten firepower and magazine capacity. The result has been a higher percentage of deaths in shootings that formerly resulted in woundings.

Machine guns have been prohibited for almost seventy years and they don't exist in our society. Hunting weapons can be manufactured to preclude their conversion into assault guns, and heavy penalties can be imposed on those who saw off and shorten shotguns.

The rights of hunters, sportsmen, and defenders of person and home would not be impacted by laws that allowed the free ownership of registered long guns (rifles, shotguns, and so on). Concealable weapons (mainly handguns) must be registered and licensed, and licenses be granted only to law enforcers and those exhibiting a true need and demonstrating proficiency in their use. After all, America's most determined "gun grabbers" would be happy to allow Charlton Heston to keep his shotgun under his bed.

In the meantime, the United States plays into the hands of the NRA by nibbling at the edges with Mickey Mouse requirements supposedly making guns safer.

The evolution of America's cops on the gun issue is rather like the shifting of tectonic plates. They moved, ever so gradually, from marriage to the NRA to the divorce of gun control advocacy—though by no means, yet, as radical as proposed here.

Sarah Brady's emergence as gun control's poster woman created a credible logo with which most police chiefs could identify.

The NRA's assertion that guns are being effectively used in self-protection is a tortured extrapolation equivalent to deducing that, if one of a hundred people going out to buy a carton of milk finds a bag with a million dollars, it follows that 1 percent of such folks on that errand would be similarly blessed. They take an aberration and conclude that it must occur repeatedly. It is a transparent piece of sophistry.

The NRA seizes on an incredibly rare exception and converts it into a rule.

In unarmed societies criminals, the mentally disturbed, and ordinary citizens all lack access to firearms and have to resolve their disputes and challenges more creatively.

CAPITAL PUNISHMENT[4]

Studies show . . . what?

In criminal justice the answer is—pretty much anything you want.

Someone shoots a rapist in self-defense and the NRA will commission a study that proves the wisdom of arming everyone. Invention by extrapolation would be putting it too kindly.

Opponents err with equally embarrassing analyses when, ignoring the transborder ease of purchase and traffic in guns—they hold that communities that enacted tough gun laws are safer. New York has had tough gun control laws forever and no one in the 1970s, 1980s, and most of the 1990s would have held it up as a paradigm of citizen safety—involving guns or any other weapon.

Capital punishment is the same.

The only persuasive finding is that executed persons don't recidivate. Unfortunately, the system is so sloppy—to be generous—that a lot of errors occur. In 2000 a Republican governor in Illinois, appalled by tragic mistakes, suspended executions until more certainty could be introduced. He found that thirteen people had been wrongly sentenced to die between 1977 and 1999.

What cops don't realize is that careless work—and, as we are seeing in Los Angeles, worse—undermines the very objectives of tough enforcement they so keenly desire.

In shaping human behavior, two forces work—rewards and punishments. These need to be measured, appropriate, relevant, and rational. Death is the ultimate penalty and, if punishment works at all, why wouldn't it deter onlookers when all other sanctions are presumed to condition human behavior?

Death not only protects society from the violence of the executed but serves as an object lesson to onlookers. There's a reason why thrillers in the '30s carried the tag line, "You'll get the chair for this." Nevertheless, the practitioners in the criminal justice system—cops, prosecutors, judges, and so on—have, through abuse and misuse of power, managed to give capital punishment a bad name. It is almost as if they blindly execute the poor, black, retarded—or even the innocent.

Until we adopt a sensible reform, there ought to be a national moratorium on executions. The federal government—through the example of its comprehensive Crime Control Bill of 1994—moved energetically in the other direction by greatly expanding the number of crimes calling for the death penalty. It was a great example of President Clinton pandering to strident law-and-order demands. And yet, when the first suspect was to be executed under this law, President Clinton stayed the process, leaving it to his successor to carry it out.

In July 2000, the newly elected president of the American Bar Association, Martha Barnett, called for a moratorium, citing social profiling, the execution of the mentally retarded, racial bias, and the results of DNA tests.

The demonstrated fallibility of the process is so great that a suspension of killings needs to be undertaken until a system is produced that reduces the possibility of error from "beyond a reasonable doubt" and into the realm of "beyond the shadow of a doubt." This requires an additional legal proceeding, but the flawed—and corrupt—administration of justice now demands it. Presidents and presidential candidates need to put their jingoist law-and-order rhetoric aside and look at simple justice's requirements.

It is indisputable that the U.S. Constitution, by holding that we may be deprived "of life, liberty, or property" under due process of law, allows for the state's taking of life.

I've been an advocate of the death penalty all my life but would now—very late in the game, to be sure—call for a moratorium and reform. There should be a second proceeding in capital cases in which the guilt of the accused is conclusively proven before a sentence of death can be imposed.

I feel driven to a position I never thought I'd have to contemplate but I can always claim my colleagues, not the devil, made me do it.

DNA[5]

The advent of DNA, in which analysis of the genetic composition of bodily fluids, tissues, and even hair serve to exclude a suspect from complicity in a crime—or inculpate him—has produced a revolution almost equivalent to the introduction of fingerprint identifiers.

Courts were understandably reluctant to accept DNA as indisputably linking a suspect to or excluding him from a crime. Gradually, the march of scientific reliability persuaded more courts and, by the end of the twentieth century, it was widely accepted. Its use in the O. J. Simpson trial, despite the attacks on DNA reliability, actually served to clinch its status as an acceptable indicator.[6] The infamous stain on Monica Lewinsky's dress probably sealed the question of DNA's forensic acceptability.

The revolution that DNA produced, however, has been greeted by near-total silence by the police establishment, even as further evidence is presented of the gross fallibility, or worse, of street justice—even as it applies to capital cases. As the twenty-first century began, police departments shuffled reluctantly to using DNA testing.

As DNA demonstrated—in the few cases where it was relevant—the criminal justice system had railroaded weak, scorned, or defenseless (literally and figuratively), often black suspects onto death row.

It was this shocking development that led the pro-death-penalty governor of Illinois to suspend executions and forced me to rethink my advocacy of the death penalty.

The ugly truth is that the excesses of street justice revealed in the year 2000 LAPD scandals and the overturning of capital convictions across the land has metastasized into the most damning indictment of criminal justice processes imaginable. Such a horrendous outcome ought to produce a call for a national debate—such as might be sparked by a President's Commission on Crime and Justice—but has, instead, been greeted by a deafening silence.

A quarter century ago, executions were suspended because of their unequal application on the basis of race. Now they ought to be suspended on the basis of justice.

DNA as a unique identifying marker—where blood, semen, bone, hair, teeth, nails, tissue, saliva, or other bodily parts, through the analysis of cell compositions, point to a specific person—has served to unmask the grotesque injustices wrought by our criminal justice system even in an age we heretofore labeled enlightened.

We have, after all, been blessed with Supreme Court decisions, civil rights laws, and reforms across the board. Indeed, some decry the "bleeding-heart liberalism" that is so gentle on desperados.

Really?

We have people in California prisons who were coerced into pleading guilty to crimes they didn't commit. The Illinois governor[7] was amazed to discover that thirteen inmates had been wrongly executed since 1977. Every day brings new revelations of how the system twisted the processes to produce the expedient and desired, albeit wrong, result.

The advent of DNA has served as a wake-up call to adopt more reforms to ensure the integrity of our processes and teach us to be both tougher and smarter.

The political answer has always been—from former President Clinton to Mayor Giuliani and his peers and their chiefs—to hire more cops, pass tougher laws, and fill more prisons—and even to proceed with the killings, even as they wash their hands of complicity in the process.

Internally it looks a lot like the hysterical response to communism that sparked a military/industrial complex of bloated and hugely expensive dimensions. Advocates could hold, at the collapse of the Soviet Union, that communism's downfall had been brought about by its futile attempt to match capitalism's expenditures on armament. This is surely partly true, but what a notion—to up the ante until the opponent is bankrupted. Where does this leave our responsibility for impoverishing the hundreds of millions living under communism and now struggling with nascent capitalism? And where does it leave the capitalists who shelled out thousands of billions in a sterile effort that housed, clothed, or fed no one?

A larger reality is that communism was overborne by the twin appeals of freedom and prosperity, but we find it difficult to intellectualize issues into victories for ideas. This is a matter that goes beyond the confines of this book so we need to return to the troops and the system in which they work. The lesson we need to apply is that the "Red scare" panicked us into costly and irrational responses, and law and order produce the same result.

Now we lavish our wealth on hiring more cops and the fact is, ironically, that hiring all those cops doesn't provide much additional coverage despite gargantuan costs. Inefficiencies get built in—the union secures sick leave, retirement, days off, and benefits that eat up large chunks of the increases. Our defense establishment didn't bring down communism and our expenditures on prisons and cops won't bring down crime.

The NYPD—and every other police agency I've studied—could generate much greater coverage by going to an eight-hour, five-day work week and one-person patrols; consolidating the number of precincts into about two-thirds of the current total; tightening sick leave policies; controlling overtime; and returning to really aggressive police tactics such as decoys, stings,[8] and, in special cases, even stakeouts. There are safety and political—as well as racial—risks in replicating victimization patterns, facilitating the commission of crimes, and having cops shoot robbers in shops, but really aggressive policing requires nothing less. Obviously, the policies need to be monitored closely to avoid abuses—or worse, as in Los Angeles.

The political will for such external reforms is lacking, just as the internal will to root out corruption and brutality through, for example, the use of spies in the ranks, is lacking.[9] For example, the killings of black males by white cops had brought nearly intolerable strains to an already taut relationship between the NYPD and the African American community it presumably served.

Race—in a racist society—becomes a white-hot issue when applied to the police, who are society's agents in the ghetto. And so much rests on such imponderables as a word seeping increasingly into our lexicons—attitude. Had black leaders detected a subtle shift in the attitudes of black males toward their responsibilities as fathers and providers when they organized the surprisingly successful Million Man March? Do blacks hunker down and collectively attempt to survive such blizzards of white resistance as evidenced in welfare reform and related legislation? It is one of the great unspoken tragedies that black and white economic and educational disparities were narrowing significantly through the '70s and '80s until white America abandoned the effort with the advent of President Reagan and his economic policies.

What caused the crack epidemic to peak in the mideighties and decline thereafter?

Some hold that the answer to reducing street crime is the incarceration or control of able-bodied black males.[10] By 2000, one-third of such males were, in fact, under some sort of criminal justice control. Many of these, as we've seen in Los Angeles, are actually innocent and many others are incarcerated for long periods for nonviolent drug offenses that might be addressed through treatment.

How has the rising economic tide affected black families? We know that the unemployment rate plummeted, but that of white males is always below the average and that of black males triple the averages of their white counterparts.[11]

What factors went into the explosion of glee in the black community over the O. J. Simpson acquittal and what did the white community think about that? Although old news, it was a flashing insight into the massive oppression felt by blacks in America.

How can the police be trained and controlled to treat blacks with respect?

How can the response of black males to police encounters be generally made more positive?

What is the role of government in addressing societal ills and how does the attitude of white America shape the response?

The police are the elephant in the room of white/black relations, yet the pachyderm is studiously ignored by those present. We don't want to discuss the widening chasms between rich and poor, white and black, young and old, urbanite and suburbanite, or educated and excluded. In its 1999 report, the U.S. Census Bureau reflected the wide gaps between white and black, the stubborn nature of black poverty, and the widening chasm between rich and poor.[12] We prefer instead to express our attitudes in such attempts as the one to eliminate the one agency engaged in redistributing income from rich to poor—the Internal Revenue Service—everybody's bête noir.

In the distribution of our resources, the cops get the lion's share. Nearly everyone wants a cop in front of their door. It is only in relatively recent years that prison builders have begun to compete more successfully for criminal justice dollars. This has led to an enormous building boom that still fails to target the violent menaces. At least half the prisoners are there for nonviolent crimes.

The true irony is that, following a Cold War–like bloating of the defense budget, we are now engaged in an explosion on criminal justice accouterments and in self-congratulatory encomiums claiming they've brought crime levels down. You can bet the chiefs and mayors will trot out socioeconomic indexes when the inevitable reversal appears. They can hope, often successfully, they'll be gone by then anyway.

And little thought is given to such costly inefficiencies as a growing geriatric population of toothless prisoners, the majority of whom are there under harsh mandated sentences for nonviolent drug-related offenses. Such myopia enables the true predators to squirm through the net to strike again.

The creation and toleration of a homeless mob that needs such a panoply of services as would accommodate single mothers with little children (the true victims of society's cruelties); petty, repeat criminals; drunks and druggies; and the dangerously, and not so dangerously, mentally disturbed,[13] who must be controlled if we are to prevent their pushing innocent bystanders in front of oncoming subways, perpetuates the danger and exacerbates the problems when the new wave of crime appears.

Drugs, including alcohol, offer the hope of escape from the awfulness of ghetto life and the pervasive miseries afflicting the underclass. Drugs and booze abound in the white suburbs, too, but their use doesn't result in a burst of violence produced by racist oppression, though we've seen it erupt in domestic abuse and murder-suicides.

The riots following the assassination of Martin Luther King Jr. in 1968 sparked the creation of a national commission on violence and race that ominously predicted a widening racial chasm. The war on poverty narrowed that chasm and its abandonment accelerated the separation again.

A third of a century after the Kerner Commission we can point to obvious signs of progress, but less obvious is the oppression, exclusion, and exploitation of blacks that the rest of us see only occasionally, as in the polar responses over the O. J. Simpson acquittal or the riots following the original Rodney King verdict favoring the cops. There are black mayors and police chiefs; Supreme Court decisions have bolstered the black community; the criminal justice system has improved by mostly eliminating third-degree methods, providing attorneys, and insisting on due process; unemployment is down and some are making it.

Nevertheless, the plight of blacks worsens. Employment, poverty, imprisonment, family cohesion, and even mortality statistics underscore the continued existence of the chasm depicted by the Kerner Commission in 1968.[14] We reached two million prisoners in 2000, a tripling over the last decade. Black males, one-third of whom are under some kind of criminal justice control (parole, probation, or prison) are unemployed at three times the rate of their white counterparts. Income figures are more dismaying, as are educational factors.

Rioting and crime are wrong and need to be punished, but they need also to be understood as protests and cries from the heart if they are to be prevented. Police behavior can be channeled and controlled to reduce brutality and corruption as well as racial profiling and all-out racism.

The underlying problem can be understood when examining a distant paradigm that affords the possibility of a more objective perspective. There is nothing quite like looking at a neighbor's problems to facilitate the fashioning of solutions.

Germany, following World War II, had its collective face rightfully rubbed hard into the muck of Nazi atrocities. The Nuremberg trials were just a dramatic example. Those who had fought the Nazis came to high office; Germans made reparations to Jews, Slavs, gypsies, and other victims and confronted the Holocaust; denazification became a descriptor of a wide variety of programs. I think we can assert that the nation was, to the degree possible, cleansed through these crucibles. Yes, restoration was impossible, but contrition at least pointed to a more helpful future.

Austria, equally guilty, was cheek-by-jowl to the Red menace and, hence, sheltered and protected by the West and given a free ride on denazification. The West even seemed to buy into the fiction that it had actually been the Nazis' first victim.

The result? Waldheimer's disease, in the form of raising a Nazi official with a very suspect record to the highest international and national posts, even as his status as pariah came to be recognized. And more than half a century later, the surfacing of a party leader with kind words about Adolf Hitler, cruel words about immigrants, and simple answers for all.

Nations, like individuals, who do not acknowledge, understand, and confront their sins are doomed to repeat them. The lesson to us? If we don't confront ours, we are doomed to a perpetual plague of racism, crime, and social dissolution.

HOW TO COMBAT CRIME

The skies are crowded with mayoral birds crowing about their successes in fighting crime. This is a dangerous illusion. Tough tactics continue to be aimed at drug deals, at black males everywhere, and at what are laughingly called "quality of life" offenses. Yes, these need to be addressed, but not at the expense of aggressive tactics aimed at street crime.

The skies have cleared and a brilliant ray of pacific sunshine bursts through. There is no shortage of claimants to having produced the weather.

But we're seeing how police departments everywhere have abandoned stakeouts; decoy operations—whoever reads of muggers being intercepted by cops posing as victims anywhere, anymore?; stings, making it possible for burglars to sell stolen goods; and, save for organized crime, infiltrations. And we continue to hire more and more cops, build more and bigger prisons, and pass tougher laws.

Parenthetically, let's add here that the privatization move—like outsourcing in the private sector—is not popular with civil service types who vigorously oppose any reforms. We are seeing some promising initiatives in the private management of prisons, but education—with its Ivy League and prep schools—provides the best example of the healthy effects of competition. My own disgust with police unions that have evolved into apologists for criminals, psychos, degenerates, and druggies in the ranks, and who wrap themselves in the mantle of civil service's protections, is such as to have turned me into a reluctant convert to any approach that introduces competition and alternative possibilities.

At the very time that former President Clinton crowed about the impact of his policies on the crime rate, America's police are at their flaccid worst. Where, in the '70s and '80s, the cops pursued tough, aggressive, imaginative legal strategies, recently and today they pay lip service to toughness and shoot innocents because they happen to be black. That these males are the targets of racial profiling in drug and traffic enforcement is the reason the events occur.

In the unlikely event that a president were to reconvene a commission on crime—an outcome to be devoutly wished for, but not one on which to pin any hopes—what might I suggest they consider? Since the underlying causes of crime—poverty, racism, and so on—remain largely untouched; since this blissful period of peace is likely to end—and soon, what ought such an august body of experts debate?[15]

Street crime can be fought successfully by the criminal justice system within the confines of the U. S. Constitution if consideration is given to these factors:

(1) By the time the cops are involved, the criminal has been shaped and the crime committed. Prevention means looking earlier.[16]

(2) Racial politics have to be discussed.[17] Whites must acknowledge how their oppression makes black life intolerable. Blacks need to confront crime and violence in their ranks.

(3) Police departments must be reformed and controlled and they must reflect the communities they serve,[18] including tough internal tactics to test integrity and the hiring of women, blacks, and gays.

(4) Aggressive police actions need to be based on information, research, and analysis. Police action must be thoroughly informed by reliable, relevant data.[19]

(5) The involvement of the people is critical. Would the Unabomber have been caught if his brother hadn't turned him in? How come no one informed the cops of the Son of Sam's bizarre behaviors?

(6) The investigation of crime must be careful and aggressive. Suspects must be lawfully pumped for information—they have it. Evidence must be gathered with care. Such innovations as DNA need to be pursued, even to the point of reopening old cases (e.g., where blood or semen were collected).

(7) Crimes are not equal. Evaluation is critical and energies should be concentrated on the more important cases. Crimes between familiars have a smaller impact on the public than between strangers. There is a reason why murder and most other crimes have escalating degrees of severity and punishment.

(8) Deals must be struck but they have to lead to bigger, better results. Plea bargains are valuable, useful tools—if the right bargains are made.

(9) The criminal justice system has to learn to coordinate its action. Having a common computer system that tracks crimes, suspects, warrants, and other data would be a useful start.[20]

(10) We are suspicious of national, centralized efforts but we desperately need coordination and dissemination of data across the county and from one source, by criminal record, warrant, gun, automobile, and related data. The FBI has to be more aggressive and demanding in its collection of crime data.

(11) Aggressive tactics such as decoys, stings, infiltrations, and stakeouts need to be restored to the arsenal of approaches used by cops. Precautions are needed and these should be based on articulable grounds, meticulously documented and abandoned where shown to be unnecessary. Terrible abuses by cops—both at the national and local levels—have led Americans to both skepticism and curtailments of these actions.

(12) Qualify-of-life problems—such street conditions as aggressive begging (called "rough tailing" in the Midwest), graffiti, squeegee men, truants, public and disorderly drunks, street peddlers, and other actions that convey notions of disorderly bazaars or an "anything goes" attitude or a sense that the vandals are within the gates—need to be attacked.

(13) Community policing shouldn't be—as it currently mostly is—either a subversion of 911 or a touchy-feely public relations effort. It ought to be a partnership between the cops and the community, aimed at analyzing chronic local irritants and preparing and implementing solutions.

(14) Studies in Minneapolis and elsewhere have shown that a tiny proportion of people and places are responsible for the overwhelming majority of police problems, such as frequent fights, disorders, assaults, and other summons of aid. These "hot spots" need to be analyzed and discretely addressed. Consulting with residents about these social cankers, together devising approaches and solutions, and following through is one true meaning of community policing.

(15) The gun issue has to be addressed. Muggers, robbers, and rapists in other countries are much less likely to be armed with guns

than in America. Concealable firearms must be nationally registered, licensed, and dramatically limited. Although citizens draw little comfort from such realities, they have a much better chance—of surviving, escaping, or even overcoming their assailants—when facing knives, clubs, or rocks rather than guns.

(16) Traffic enforcement is central to fighting crime and controlling the streets.

(17) Executing warrants energetically and efficiently brings important consequences to bear on repeat violators.

(18) Mandated sentences[21] are stupid responses to real problems and put one class of criminal—usually drug addicts—ahead of potentially much more serious menaces, like muggers and other violent offenders. Legislators must abandon the temptation to pursue the crime du jour. Judges must judge.

(19) Sentencing guidelines constitute a sophisticated approach to prison crowding and seriousness of offense and shouldn't be given a bad rap. These guidelines take the system's capacity into account, evaluate the seriousness of the crime and the danger posed by the offender, and tailor the sentence accordingly.

(20) Just as some crimes are more important than others and require more devoted attention, a minority of criminals pose a much more obvious threat to public safety than the casual, ad hoc, unfocused majority. These are the recidivists—predators who repeat criminal behaviors and who commit great numbers of crimes. These should be the targets of the criminal justice system and these are the ones who should constitute the bulk of our prison population—but they don't.

(21) The mentally disturbed can be dangerous. Emptying our asylums, as behavior-controlling medicines were developed, didn't help to coerce the mentally disabled to take their dosages. We need to create consequences for not controlling the illness through medication, through the alternative of institutionalization in humane—but secure—facilities.

(22) The criminal justice system should be seen as an interrelated, coherent system rather than as disparate parts in which the police were the eight-hundred-pound gorilla yesterday and

convictions and imprisonment are today. This results in starving vital but less sexy parts of the system, like defense attorneys, parole, probation, or treatment.

The list is by no means exhaustive, but it ought to serve as an imperfect guide to possibilities for discussion.

The sine qua non is the appointment of a President's Commission on Crime and Justice to gather experts to develop and discuss a cogent series of possibilities. We are in desperate need of such thoughtful measures, yet we wallow in an ocean of bromides and simplicities.

INTERNAL POLICE REFORMS: USEFUL AND OTHERWISE

There is no institution in our society in more need of oversight and control than that of the police. Theirs is the power to detain, arrest, question, search, seize, beat, and even kill. Simply on the basis of existing authority, they need to be held to account. But the catalog of terrible abuses cited in all forms of media, every day, lends real urgency to the issue of control.

And here, again, the issues are muddied by myths and cherished notions.

Reformers love civilian review boards, in which outsiders are charged with investigating and punishing police wrongdoing. The only problem is that, although tons of cities have one form of the genre or another, none works effectively, anywhere. The police have learned how to co-opt, resist, ignore, and defeat the workings of review boards with such dazzling efficacy as to render them a national nullity.

Residency laws meant to enlist ghetto dwellers into the ranks and make the police world more reflective of the community it serves haven't worked either. They clash with the prevailing wisdom in the core city, that the cops are the enemy and you just don't join their ranks. Residency requirements also limit the freedom of movement and are tacit and eloquent admissions that the city can't compete with the suburbs in providing suitable housing. Finally, and most compelling, these haven't worked either. New York long had residency laws and these were widely and successfully flouted as violators gave fictitious addresses—usually a compliant relative who could be counted on to support the lie. Although the idea is seductive, residency requirements ought to be scrapped.

Recruitment of minorities[22] will await the day that black leaders finally decide to encourage their youngsters into police careers. The efforts must, however, not only continue but be deepened and extended.

Members of the criminal justice system who are daily witnesses to perjury, evidence of abuse, frame-ups, and other wrongs by the cops would appear to be naturals for reform, but it doesn't work out that way. How many prosecutors or judges presided over the mendacities and frame-ups by the LAPD without questioning the integrity of the process? They stood unblinkingly by and accepted versions that might have collapsed under interested inquiry—yet scores were convicted, or pleaded guilty, despite being innocent. And what about those in prison, or even on death row, now being freed under the impetus of DNA findings that irrefutably establish their innocence?

No one asks how this could have happened.

No one examined the process for flaws.

And no one even suggests how procedures might be tightened to produce more just outcomes. The pressure is to convict and lock away.

The behavior of the system's witnesses to such egregious and obvious examples of police wrongdoing as "testilying" or the introduction of tainted evidence is nothing short of scandalous, yet no one is outraged. The system frees the wrongly convicted, compensates the aggrieved, and carries on with not a trace indicating any lessons have been learned. As to the question of punishing the malefactors of these wrongs, fuggedaboutit.

Civil service, as a reform tool adopted to attack the abuses of nepotism and cronyism in hiring and promoting, has now been twisted into an institution that protects wrongdoers through tenure, freezes incompetents and worse in place, and resists every effort to remove the clearly unfit or even criminal from the ranks. Civil services laws and the commissions enforcing the statutes have fallen prey to police union influence and, with the unions,[23] have become the central, critical foes of reform.

Political figures who play prominent roles in the selection and appointment of chiefs are just that—politicos who can, with such rare exceptions as the mayor of Minneapolis in the 1980s—be relied on to do the expedient thing. Even the few with real integrity lack the knowledge, or the desire to be informed, to make sensible choices.[24]

Model selection processes to choose police chiefs have been developed by national organizations in the police field, but the key politicians have seen their self-interest in preserving a status quo that frees them to select friends, relatives, compliant pets, or sycophants. It is only in such desperate straits as those of Los Angeles, Minneapolis, Baltimore, and, lately, Philadelphia that any effort at a meticulous selection approach has been attempted. These are rare enough to stand out vividly and usually come after so much harm that leading a reform effort resembles cleaning the Augean stables, a Herculean task.

Legislatures have simply ignored police reform altogether. They have contented themselves with mandated sentences, police officers' bills of rights, and similarly draconian or unwise measures. These bodies are attracted to catchy slogans with political appeal such as more cops, bigger prisons, and tougher laws. And they're addicted to the campaign contributions of the NRA or police unions. Complicated answers such as to be found in plea bargains, sentencing guidelines, treatment, education, prevention, or other out-of-prison approaches are usually scorned as political losers.

What, then, if anything, works?

THE CHIEF

The unforgettable lesson I learned in Pat Murphy's thirty months as the NYPD's police commissioner was the central importance of a determined, courageous, knowledgeable executive to police reform. I would, as a result of my exposure to this seminal period of change, put the selection of the police chief first on the list of must-dos. Yet in 2000, the only selection process I would describe as making a genuine effort to secure a top-flight executive was Philadelphia—which chose John Timoney,[25] a rising star, ironically, in the NYPD. In New York, the mayor made a safe choice, a man who was certain to remain in the wings while the star, Guiliani, took center stage, and repeated the act with his successor in 2000.

Elsewhere, there were journeymen and women (miraculously, they were beginning to surface at the upper reaches) or politically connected or compliant time servers. Some even came from union ranks. Mostly, though, they were—in the time-hallowed tradition of the genre—up-from-the-ranks survivors who seemed likely to be content to go along and get along.

It was still an uneven climb, as a high-ranking female member of the NYPD received a $1-million judgment for being forced out for failing to condone a cover-up in a sex harassment suit. Meanwhile in Hartford, Connecticut, a female chief was fired for "not performing" when an auditor released a report citing many deficiencies.

Political figures who appoint the nation's chiefs have a dismal record of selection, invariably opting for the safe, familiar, and predictable choices. Since they pay no price for this fecklessness there is no reason to expect they'll change anytime soon.

If I discovered nothing else in my peripatetic wanderings over the police landscape I found that every agency—without exception—had model written policies in place, calling for truth, beauty, and justice. Alas, these were honored more in the breach than the performance. The key variable usually proved to be the quality of the chief executives.

INSPECTOR GENERAL

Second to a talented chief, I'd push a new idea—the appointment, by the elected chief executive, of an outside inspector general (IG)[26] who would combine the tasks of Internal Affairs Division, outside auditor, and special prosecutor. As such, the IG would investigate charges of police abuses—especially corruption and brutality—and impose penalties.

The IG would be empowered to conduct inspections, audits, spot checks, polls, and other investigations to establish conformity with laws and policies and to gauge efficiency through such simple approaches as randomly questioning past callers to 911 to determine satisfaction with the service, or surveying motorists to detect such problems as racial profiling, sex harassment, or other abuses. The accuracy of crime statistics and customer/public satisfaction with the investigation would be another area of inquiry. Even convicts ought to be interviewed to detect such abuses as occurred in Los Angeles This IG model has been successfully used in the federal government for years. In smaller cities, the IG would serve as a watchdog over more—or even all—government agencies. Additionally, the IG would be empowered to prosecute wrongdoers in the entire criminal justice system—judges, prosecutors, cops, and so on. Subpoena power is central to this effort.

There is a caveat—it has to be acknowledged that New York City briefly flirted with a more limited special prosecutor model, with disastrous results.

The creation of such a post was the principal recommendation of the 1972 Knapp Commission's report. A special prosecutor was named and immediately launched a blizzard of indictments of judges, lawyers, and cops. The fur was flying but the zealotry was followed by disillusion as the charges resulted in humiliating dismissals and acquittals, all pointing to maximum zeal and minimum concern for orderly legal processes. It produced such an odoriferous result that the very title was redolent of opprobrium and rejection. The national experience proved at best only marginally better as Congress allowed the special prosecutorial law to lapse into oblivion in June 1999. Overzealousness was the cause of the demise in both cases.

A quarter century after the dismantling of New York's Special Prosecutor for the Criminal Justice System, the 1991 Warren Christopher Commission, examining the problems in the LAPD following the Rodney King fiasco, recommended the naming of a special outside investigator and prosecutor. He soon quit over his inability to overcome the police department's resistance to the effort. Obviously the potential risks are enormous, but the federal model—where outside monitors oversee the functionings of the agencies—seems to have worked reasonably well.

LITIGATION[27]

Third in terms of effectiveness comes the unlikely, recent, and chastening development of lawsuits. Multimillion-dollar verdicts—and Los Angeles now faces the ugly prospect of hundreds of millions in potential liabilities—have served to concentrate the minds of cities' parents wonderfully. There is nothing like the prospect of facing citizens with the prospect of higher taxes to pay for blatant and preventable acts of police abuse to get politicos to focus on real reforms. Thus far there have been no open rebellions over this colossal waste of treasure but, sooner or later, someone is going to make a campaign issue of it.

In the meantime, a long succession of costly outrages such as Rodney King and others, and the likely lawsuit hits in such others as the LAPD's massive scandal; the Louima, Dorismond, and Diallo cases in New York; and the many others all over the nation's landscape are bound to bring demands for reform. It is hard to see citizens uncomplainingly shelling out for these outrages ad infinitum.

The costs are, to be sure, indirect and not fully felt, but the sums—everywhere—are growing so fast as to ultimately concentrate the tax-payers' attention more forcefully. While New York City averaged 1,500 lawsuits a year around 1990, that number increased to almost 2,400 in 1999, and the cases involving large sums of money also seemed to be growing.

My experience as an expert witness in a clutch of such litigations persuaded me to the importance of federal courts in securing a just out-come. Brought under Section 1983, which protects the civil rights of cit-izens, the case is tried before jurists whose painstaking selection and life tenure carry a greater promise of wisdom and justice than the more raffish local courts, which are frequently so rank with the odors of political manipulations or, at best, considerations that are not always central to the question of dispensing simple justice.

THE PRESS

Altogether too many public figures see the press as the enemy and wage war against it. My repeated exposure to the Fourth Estate inclines me to side with Thomas Jefferson, who saw newspaper freedom as more impor-tant to democracy than even the existence of government.

Of course, the matter gets tangled with the very first question—what is news?

Well, it isn't that you've led a blameless life, unless you make it to the obituaries. News is most frequently a negative akin to gossip—except that hard evidence is required. Schadenfreude is news. Human nature secretly revels in the discomfitures of fellow beings.

It is more than likely that Americans are—at least in terms of the availability of information—the best-served people in history. Anyone can point to tawdry, meretricious, and mendacious examples, but the sheer depth and extent of the available information is nothing short of breathtaking.

The press has the psychic impact of the perennial eavesdropper who keeps the cynosure of such attentions honest—whatever the personal predilections or preferences.

Muckrakers and investigative reporters root about and unearth scandals. Reporters serve as something of a permanent band of inspectors general, always examining for wrongdoing. Most public figures take this personally and, instead of first looking within for the flaws, lash out at the media.

Look at any repressive society and find that its foremost enemies are the cellar pamphleteers who use truth and information as the most powerful weapons of an oppressed people. The press unearths secrets that are kept in the name of some form of national or community security, but which are mostly attempts at keeping the people from the truth. A free and untrammeled press is the greatest adornment of a free society and its strongest pillar.

THE FBI

The Federal Bureau of Investigation—always a clean and talented outfit, in terms of corruption (not abuse of power) and in the abilities of its members—has come a long way since shedding Hoover's stifling, even grotesque, controls. Free, and even prodded to pursue deeper interests, it has become the nemesis of organized crime. It has had, to be sure, internal problems over minority hiring and promotions but it has also become a powerful tool for racial and constitutional justice as it has been called into play when locals have failed.

Still, the agents are only too aware of their need for smooth relations with local police and prosecutors and tread warily in cases where they are called upon to intrude. Their involvement usually comes after an egregious miscarriage of justice and their participation constitutes an intrusion that will be resented.

The Diallo case in New York City is a prime example of the exquisite consternation such challenges bring. Another is the LAPD scandal in which the city council voted ten to one to ask the Justice Department to take over the investigation of corrupt acts, like frame-ups and the shooting of innocent citizens, from bickering local forces.

The FBI agents, with a highly educated, well-trained, thoroughly supported cadre, would be sure to conduct a meticulous, dogged inquiry with sharply enhanced prospects of success. They convicted six cops in the Abner Louima case, after all, and five in the New Jersey case in 2000. The question would center on whether they'd take up the challenge.

FBI MONITORING

In a dismaying development that threatened to remove one of the very few effective monitorings over police misbehavior—investigation and sanctions by the Department of Justice—then presidential candidate George W. Bush wrote, in May 2000, to a national police federation (union) that he didn't approve of the practice and, if elected, he'd discontinue it. Such controls as those imposed on the Pittsburgh and Los Angeles Police Departments, following blatant and egregious abuses, would be eliminated.

The threat of an FBI investigation indisputably inhibited wrongdoing by local cops. With only a very few arrows in the quiver of police oversight a candidate thoughtlessly cast one of the principal weapons aside and still failed to receive the endorsement he'd sought. The cops wanted more tangible benefits—in the form of economic promises.

The natural question is: Aren't the locals up to it? The answer is yes, but tossed and turned by political winds and extraneous considerations, they are fatally hobbled.

When a new special agent in charge was assigned to Minneapolis, he'd make a protocol call on the chief. At these meetings I always told him to investigate my agency without fear or favor. I'd welcome his intrusion, but, I'd add, I intended to beat him to every discovery. There was not a single FBI inquiry into the actions of the Minneapolis Police Department for those nine years, nor even any call for one.

The question and problems are vast and complex. The temptation—even to such talented folks as presidents—is frequently to pander to public expectations, rather than to examine the complexities and adopt effective—if, at first, unpopular—strategies. Therein lies a key dilemma: that many public difficulties require painful approaches that, in the immediate short term, often prove unpopular. This is one of the essential attributes of true leadership.

How, then, to develop the qualities needed for leadership?

As with the Greeks, it begins within.

21
SELF-IMPROVEMENT AND MANAGEMENT

I can remember three distinct events that shaped an urgent need to develop my mind. Two of them were humiliations, and from these I learned that most of my motivation in life would come from fear of failure rather than the glories of rewards or riches.

I was around seventeen when I made a new friend, and we found ourselves camping on a weekend and walking down a country road with two girls. The talk turned to opera and I found myself struck dumb. I searched desperately for an opening in the conversation, but found none and wound up in enforced, frustrating, ignorant silence. The universe of my knowledge was confined to the Brooklyn Dodgers–New York Giants rivalry.

The second occurred a year or two later when I'd just seen *The Fountainhead* and gushed enthusiastically over it. Another friend casually described the conflict between collectivism and rugged individualism. I discovered I'd missed the whole point. To me it had been a love story, with conflict between hero and villain, with the hero winning. I turned inwardly crimson with shame, said nothing, and moved on.

Around that time I was detained after class by my English teacher, Mr. Goldstone.

I had a job after school making Christmas decorations at the Paper Novelty Manufacturing Co. for sixty cents an hour, and resented being

266

forced to be late. I sat mopily for twenty minutes or so before Mr. Gold-stone called me up. He had a one sentence message for me: "You know, Bouza, you've got a good brain but you're too lazy to use it."

"Is that it, Mr. Goldstone?"

"Yes, that's it."

I sullenly slouched out, never offering a hint of the impact of the words. I was not, then, given to introspection. I was a stickball-playing New York Giants fan who hung out at the local ice cream parlor at the corner, another kid on the block—and I accepted my fate unquestioningly.

The three events shook me, though.

I now made a conscious choice to become "an intellectual" and joined the library and took out five or six classics every month, which I read. I had graduated, only just—from a really bad high school—with a 72 percent average that was inflated by high grades in four years of Spanish. In my final year I failed four out of five majors with one-third of the term to go. I stumbled to an undeserved diploma.

I joined the Great Books courses and met to discuss the week's tome with a group of about twenty at the New York Public Library. I went to the Salmaggi operas at the Brooklyn Academy of Music, and attended foreign films and as much theater as I could manage. My friends changed from the ball-playing, beer-drinking stalwarts on the corner to two guys heading for distinction—one as an engineer and the other as a scholar.

What was stunning in all this was how long I'd gone without the slightest clue of who I was, where I was heading, or why—or even what my potential might be. The incidents served as a harsh mirror suddenly popped in front of my psyche, cruelly reflecting the narrow confines of my view. From then on my life would be an unending search for growth and knowledge, accompanied by a certain sense of personal inadequacy that impelled me forward.

I taught myself to swim at twenty-four and had learned to drive only two years earlier. I was slow to arrive to every destination. But even in the army, a frisson of excitement swept over me, seeing my byline in the camp's newspaper. I read the *New York Times* every day and fought with a girlfriend's father, who adored Joe McCarthy.

I was not a liberal. I've always believed in aggressive policing, pun-ishment—up to and including the capital variety—and individual accountability and personal responsibility. But the times made me fear for our precious democracy. McCarthyism stirred the hot coals of American paranoia and created a miasma of suspicion and accusation that divided the nation dangerously.

Given momentum by Truman's phobia over communism and the growth of loyalty oaths and other paranoia, Senator Joseph McCarthy of Wisconsin was emboldened to ride the horse of Red-baiting to national power.

McCarthy saw betrayal everywhere. China had been sold out. Diplomats were spies. Near-sacred institutions like Harvard University and the U. S. Army were painted as vipers' nests of players and schemes. The man revered as the greatest American by President Truman—George C. Marshall—was vilified by McCarthy and abandoned by Eisenhower, who excised a defense of Marshall from a speech he delivered in Wisconsin.

Reds were under every cover. Lists abounded. Government agencies ran "name checks" to see if a prospective worker had ever signed a suspect petition, written an impolitic letter, attended a "fellow travelers" event, or otherwise expressed a view that might be labeled as un-American.

Subversives abounded. Artists lost their jobs; congressional bodies sent uncooperative witnesses to jail—some chose exile, often in Mexico. An entire industry grew up around the notion of cataloging suspect political actions and selling the information to such interested parties as employers, writers, or political enemies.

McCarthy seemed to take some very real concerns about a true menace—expansive, ruthless, Stalinist communism—and twist them into a grotesquely paranoical reaction in which, as in Salem, suspected witches fared badly, whatever the evidence.

I had had a curious encounter in the army with a lieutenant who laboriously plumbed my political beliefs in an extended conversation. At first flattered by a rare, friendly encounter with an officer, I later came to realize this was probably a loyalty check by army intelligence.

So, when I wrote Edward R. Murrow to commend him for his courageous attack on McCarthy, I did it with a certain sense of dread that my letter would wind up on a list that might prove an obstacle to entering the NYPD. I did it anyway, and was surprised to receive a gracious response—not from Murrow, but from a name I never forgot: Fred Friendly, his producer.

Many years later, as I attended a lecture at Harvard, I grew increasingly agitated over the speaker's assertions on policing. He didn't seem to know what he was talking about.

I turned to an associate and said I was going to take this guy on, and who was he?

"Fred Friendly."

I said nothing and he was spared a scolding.

There was a curious reprise in Madrid years later when I heard a judge lambast the cops for their fascist repressions, and so on. He was almost literally foaming at the mouth. I asked a Spanish police official who this guy was—I was going to attack his views—and the high-ranking cop answered this was a civil rights lawyer who'd been imprisoned for years and tortured by Franco.

I again learned the value of a studied silence and said nothing.

Entering the NYPD took care of my needs—psychic and economic—but the clear absence of both talent and interest fed into the low self-esteem that, with memory, may be the real legacy of poverty. My development as a culture vulture intensified even as I floundered in my job. I gradually sensed that I'd either grow into an administrator or simply be a time server waiting for a pension. I had no knack for police work.

Two events, both involving missing persons, illustrate the pointed certainty of my failures.

In one, a colleague persuaded me to see a psychic about locating a disappeared man. I had to get a personal item she could grasp and fondle. I produced an exercise stretcher and mentally recoiled as she closed her eyes and mumbled nonsense. My associate had been wrong to say there was no harm in it. There was. It was the surrender of science in the service of superstition.

In the other, I was assigned to investigate a stolen baby and actually encountered both the baby and the woman who stole it—but didn't know it. I hadn't bothered to really check the baby or to question the "mother."

Miraculously, another investigator discovered the pair and got a confession from her. She'd been pregnant, miscarried, and produced the neighbor's stolen baby as her own. A very kind commander who went on to become chief of detectives, James B. "Lefty" Leggett, covered up this blunder to protect me.

MANAGEMENT[1]

So what skills might I need?

Communication seemed central—the ability to speak to a group, write effectively, think clearly, and listen carefully. I sought opportunities to write—although here I basically became enamored of big, dead words and jargon, with really fatal results—and to speak.

Audiences often wanted to be entertained so I learned to inject humor into my talks and slip the enlightenment, such as it was, under their defenses.

Speeches, or even three- or four-minute talks to cynical cops, needed a beginning, a middle, and an end, and they had to be focused. Every audience was a different animal—hostile, friendly, cuddly, or crusty—and it was important to use the time preceding the talk to analyze it and to notice any features that might prove useful in the speech.

Repetition granted smoothness and mastery, but each event had to be followed by a critical examination of its flaws and a determined assessment of how it might have been improved.

The message needed to be a deeply felt truth—and risks had to be run. Each talk should, as if it were an essay, be seen as an opportunity to enlighten the audience and convert it to a deeply felt view. Passion matters.

Timing is important, particularly the pauses that lend pacing and drama and which prove essential to humor.

Surprise shocks audiences out of the lethargy of indolent thought. I gave a commencement speech to high school seniors whose peroration was my favorite poem:

> Beauty is truth.
> Truth is beauty.
> A rooty toot toot,
> And a rooty toot tooty.

Faculty was outraged. The kids loved it. All remembered it. I was not asked back.

I watched effective managers, went to school, and incorporated the thinking of artists—the true prophets of our age—into my administrative musings.

Curiously, civil service provided a clear set of rungs for us to climb—without regard to contacts, hooks, contracts, or rabbis—but it failed utterly to prepare managers. So the top rungs were clogged with executives who'd passed every test—and who had studied devotedly to master the information by rote—but who hadn't a clue about moving a group toward an objective, or even how to identify and define that destination.

So I proceeded on two tracks—the vocational one that prepared me for the very tough, competitive, and specific promotional exams, which measured knowledge of laws and mastery of arcane procedures; and the broader one of a general education that focused on liberal arts and administrative skills.

Recognizing the importance of balance between the physical and the intellectual (*mens sana in corpore sano*), I exercised daily.

As I moped about MBWA—management by walking around (Socratic, to be sure)—I learned a number of important things:

- Most people in an organization know what's wrong, what needs to be done, and how, but this usually entails high risks and deep effort.
- After a clutch of soundings, the same issues will repeatedly surface, even taking on priority forms.
- Everybody knows who the screw-ups are and their behavior becomes the lowest level of acceptable conduct.
- As the manager focuses attention on those evaluated at the bottom, numbers nine or ten—the foul balls—and punishes or ousts them, the level of performance is raised and the conduct of numbers seven and eight now become the lowest level of acceptable work.
- Workers hate change. But there can't be growth or reform without it, so it must be managed.
- Workers hate surprises. These can be avoided with preparation.
- Workers hate lies. Tell the truth.[2]
- Use the wisdom of the workers. They know a lot.
- Doing something to improve morale is nonsense. Morale should flow from the policies and programs of a vital organization. Morale is a product, not an end in itself.
- Personal loyalty subverts group goals. Loyalty must be to broad principles—such as, "The good of the people is the chief law."
- Base every decision on whether it helps the citizens served.

- Education and training are distinct but you can never have too much of either.[3]
- TV is the enemy of literacy and thought. Read, don't watch.
- Priorities should be constant and known. Too many executives shift to accommodate the convenience of the moment.
- Boredom leads to trouble.
- Hard work results in high morale, especially when the work involves service and is rooted in altruism.
- Integrity in all things. In a dishonest environment everyone figures out how to get theirs.[4]
- Keep it simple. Less paper. Few restrictions. Allow the allowable. Have sound reasons.
- Planning shouldn't be a straitjacket. It should be a road map into a defined future.
- Subordinates need to be nurtured and developed. Mentoring is a duty.
- Results matter. They need to be measurable and measured.
- Debate and discuss, but the executive also has to decide the key issues that demand action.
- As few secrets as possible.
- Require documentation of important acts and decisions.
- Workers have lives, needs, and problems and these impact on performance.
- The 1 to 2 percent of thumpers and meat eaters will set the tone, if allowed. Organizations abhor vacuums.[5]
- Ego is the enemy and must be fought every day. Humility and introspection are the weapons.
- Emotional insecurity leads to the temptation to surround yourself with sycophants—resist it.
- Painful opportunities to learn humility must be seized. The skin must be thickened. Issues shouldn't be taken personally.[6]
- Admit mistakes. Apologize when it is needed.
- When Pope John XXIII took over, he called for *aggiornamento*— the winds of change that bring us up to date. This is a constant organizational need.
- Socratically questioning and leading a team to its own discoveries is true leadership.

- Listening is critical. What is really being said? What is the true meaning?
- Planning means preparing for as much of the future as is clear at the time.
- Budgeting means getting things done effectively (the best way) and efficiently (at the lowest cost).
- Group cohesion can be a useful way of galvanizing a force and it might even be achieved through such negatives as coalescing around a common hatred of the chief.
- Artists are our prophets and seers. They understand human nature and wrestle with deep meanings. Their lessons are instructive to managers.
- Be equable, calm, and consistent. Bluster creates emotional short circuits. Be aware of your feelings and control them rigorously.
- The tougher the action, the softer the tone.
- The cop on patrol at 2 A.M., encountering an asshole, has to know how the chief will respond if he thumps him.
- Feedback—seek it and get it. Subordinates who depend on your favor will never provide it.
- Be crisp, clear, and concise. Avoid kaffe klatches and bullshit sessions. Manage time. Keep meetings short and to the point.

Everyone has their pet theories but those listed above did not come from a text, but from the hard crucible of experience.

The key reason there are so few effective managers at the helms of police departments is that the political figures that appoint them don't know what to look for, are driven by petty and narrow political aims, or seek safe choices. The odd thing is that cities promote informed, complex debates about selecting the football coach, but swallow the elephant of a police chief's selection without a blink.

Of course the only thing at stake is the public's safety, and what's that when compared to a Super Bowl?

I found that management matters.

The next caller to 911 doesn't know who he is but he'll want the cops to get there fast.

No one is ever going to fathom how she or her family were spared a traffic tragedy because of vigorous enforcement, but declining accident statistics certainly show these can be prevented even if they don't show the who. If you can bring down auto accidents and deaths—and you can, through tough enforcement—you still can't name those spared injury or death. This proves one of the great dilemmas of public service—measuring the benefits of precaution.

Effective investigations lead to the sequestration of menaces to society, but how do we identify the person *not* raped, mugged, or murdered as a result of selective interdictions? Focusing on recidivists, the real threats, and targeting them for selective incapacitation is the challenge.[7] We have so far failed to meet it.

Public safety is an abstraction, and to promote it is to work toward achieving an amorphous ideal, but it isn't at all foggy when the blows strike and the bullets fly and protesters riot. Maintaining order has the faint whiff of fascism about it that breeds suspicion. Conversely, when approached with patience, prudence, fairness, care, and an understanding of the constitutional issues, it doesn't.

Management isn't even that complicated. Everybody knows the main problems—and they usually aren't all that numerous. Even in the worst of places, everybody knows what must be done. As I wandered the halls of the Minneapolis Police Department in the early days of 1980, I was amazed to discover how the shortlist of problems kept being repeated, over and over.

And then comes the hard part—doing it.

That will probably involve ten or fewer major items that will require moral courage. Entrenched interests are there to defend the status quo. Few will thump your desk insisting on the changes—the "interests of the people" are rarely represented in power circles, but they must be. That's what public service means.

In the end, there is no satisfaction to equal the sense of having served faithfully and well. It is not a claim I would make, but I would say I tried. Reviewing my own past would result in my labeling my career a lucky one.

22
LOOKING BACK

I would define my thirty-six years in the police agencies as a love affair of heightening intensity. My belief in the mission grew as my admiration for the members blossomed.

FRONT-ROW SEAT

I felt admitted into an arena I'd never otherwise have been able to enter.

Besides exposure to the darker side of human nature I got to know such personages as Malcolm X, who struck me as both intelligent and a spellbinding orator; Fidel Castro, who argued with me about socialism versus capitalism and whose charm and charisma were irresistible; and hosts of others.

I was in the room when Nikita Khruschev rushed to embrace Indonesia's Sukarno, and waltzed the stunned general, briefly, around the Waldorf's floor. Later, I was somewhat outraged to see the Russian strongman thumping his shoe on a United Nations counter to protest a speaker's remark.

I watched De Gaulle and Nasser from close vantage points and once spent five days about ten steps behind First Lady Jacqueline Kennedy as she window shopped on Madison Avenue. On the last day, she was preparing to leave when the president showed up and I heard him ask her to remain to listen to his UN speech. She consented.

President Kennedy's visits were kinetic events. Once, we received word at about 1 A.M. that the president was going for a walk and only wanted one secret service agent and one cop along.

We trailed about ten paces back when he suddenly stopped and pushed a doorbell.

A window opened, about two floors above and a voice—it turned out to be Henry Fonda's—asked who it was.

I hoped he'd say, "The President of the United States," but he responded, "It's me, Jack, Hank," and was admitted. The president led a very nocturnal life.

When my wife emerged from a plane, having visited her father in Florida, I asked where Tony, our infant son, was.

"A little man insisted on carrying him."

When I saw who it was, I was stunned—Jose "Pepe" Figueres—the president of Costa Rica and a legendary promoter of democracy in Latin America.

I, like the character in the movie *Being There*, loved to watch. I got to see Nasser, Tito, and a host of Latin American presidents and dictators. I was waiting in the wings with England's Prince Phillip as he was being introduced at a huge dinner. He turned to me and said, "What do I do now, knock twice and ask for someone or other?"

Vice President Lyndon Johnson haggled with a shopkeeper over the cost of a dress for his wife and stormed off, upset at the $350 price tag. I regretted not going for a morning walk with former President Harry Truman, assigning someone else to do it because I was too busy.

But, my most satisfying moment was when President Ronald Reagan came to Minneapolis.

A group of anti-Contra demonstrators planned to protest the president's anti-Left policies in Nicaragua and asked to picket near the entrance of the hotel he was to visit. I was surprised I hadn't heard from the secret service on the route, knowing, from long experience, they'd try to shelter him from the protesters. In fact, I'd heard he'd never even seen a picket line in his years in office.

Finally I heard.

The secret service came by and changed the route, to circumvent the pickets. I thought it too tortured and insisted on his entering through the main street and front entrance.

Secret service offered to make me part of the motorcade—presumably a high honor. I demurred. There were calls to Washington and agitated discussions. They threatened to federalize the hotel—declaring it temporary government property—and supplant me as the person in charge. I said I'd see them in court.

They finally—after mutterings about dangers and security risks—reluctantly surrendered.

Reagan saw the hundreds of chanting picketers and I stood in front of the demonstrators to ensure order. It was a historic moment that went off without a hitch.

I derived inordinate pleasure from this little triumph.

FIRINGS AND OTHER DISAPPOINTMENTS

After choosing to repay this great nation for all the riches of education, wealth, and power it had showered on me and my family, I gradually came to recognize that this wasn't as simple as it appeared. There is some truth to the assertion that no good deed goes unpunished. Electing to serve the broad, amorphous interests of the people often meant having to deny the petitioner in front of me.

Therein lay a real dilemma.

People regularly trooped in and out of my office seeking something—and it was very rare that it was the people's good they were after. Hardly anyone, in fact, ever thumped on my desk demanding that I do what was plainly right. Usually the visitors sought some edge—for themselves or associates.

As the people slowly came to realize I was trying to serve them, as a body, they became affectionate, attentive, and supportive. Their backing gave me political power I could use—but only for their benefit, or it would be withheld.

I learned to be very careful to pursue issues that eloquently spelled reform before pushing hard. It became almost a given that reform meant strife and the creation of enemies. As I look back on what I'd call a very,

very lucky career, a number of stumblings stand out that illustrate the point.

The same commissioner who drove me to extend myself beyond what I thought possible—for me anyway—urged me to apply for chiefs' jobs in Boston; Montgomery County, Maryland; and Washington, D.C. In addition, both New Orleans and Seattle expressed more than a passing interest in me in the late '70s and I, driven by the simple need for a job after I'd been fired from the transit police in 1979, applied to several, including Dade County and Minneapolis.

I usually wound up among the finalists and came to understand the process of selection as being driven by either politics or desperation. I also came to an appreciation of rejection as a toughening and informing experience.

In later years I came to regret having passed on the New Orleans and Seattle possibilities simply because I was comfortably ensconced in the transit police. Comfort is the antithesis of progress. I realized, much later and almost too late to profit from it, that change is unnerving but that there is no growth without it. It seemed, in painful retrospect, as if all the important learnings—the deadening effects of familiarity and the restricting influences of safety—ran counter to human intuition. It was mostly the changes and challenges—and even the fears and crises forced on me—that contributed to my development as a police executive.

In 1972, I became one of two finalists for the job of chief of Boston's police. When I met with the mayor, I felt him recoil a bit when I said, "Mr. Mayor, I want you to know I think the department has serious corruption problems and I'm going to kick over the rock. I can't tell you what I'll find there—and can't guarantee I can even lick it—but I promise you I'm gonna kick it over."

He chose the other guy.

Three years later, I was a selection committee's choice (or so I was informally told) to head the Washington, D.C., police, but they chose an insider anointed by the outgoing chief who'd led the sweeps and round-ups that resulted in the illegal detention of thousands of Vietnam War protesters, who sued and won a whopping sum.

In 1975 came the job of police chief in Montgomery County, Maryland, where I was one of five finalists. Our collective consternation was great when, after a battery of competitive tests that mostly tested our relations with each other, we were told that the county manager had flown to Boston, fallen in love with the chief there (the very same guy I'd lost to three years earlier), and hired him on the spot.

It wouldn't be hard to guess my feelings when I was told this specter was one of the fourteen finalists for the Minneapolis job in 1979. He'd become my doppelganger.

Then came 1976 and Yankee Stadium and the police commissioner's invitation to depart my home—the NYPD. Although not fired, it was clear I had to go. In my next job, number two in the transit police, I was unceremoniously told to empty my desk and get out in five days—yet I had to formally resign. That was the protocol.

Now, out of work but not desperate, I taught a course at a New York college and discovered that a number of mostly black and Hispanic juniors could hardly write. The job paid $2,500 and that wasn't going to do much, but it gave me a place to go twice a week. I gave the students four small essays to write during the term and worked with them to first confront their true standing as scholars and, second, to prod them to work to improve.

I told these students no one would ever tell them they couldn't fashion a coherent sentence. They'd simply be flattered, fobbed off, and told, "We'll get back to you"—and never discover their unemployability.

The anger and resistance with which my tough grading and acerbic remarks were greeted frankly shocked me. Students came back with the essays I'd asked them to write and to which I'd appended critical evaluations, with notes from their English profs that announced, "This is perfectly acceptable work in my class and deserves a passing grade." The fobbing off had begun even earlier than I had surmised.

I applied for a number of chief's jobs and came close in Dade County, Florida. I had little hope for Minneapolis but flew in for a three-hour interview. I was one of fourteen finalists and the committee would interview two a day for a week. It was a frigid January and I felt as if someone had smacked my face with a frozen fish as I emerged from the terminal.

Minneapolis had a new mayor and he'd been elected on the promise of police reform. He had hired a personnel firm to do a search and I'd responded to their ad. A citizen's committee was created to scan the applicants and reduce the number to a workable figure they would inter-view at length.

I was so confident of losing that I casually graded papers as I waited and entered sans jacket for the interview. Months later one of my cham-pions on the committee—I didn't know anyone in the city, including her, having been there only once previously to address a conference of women in policing—said she liked me because I looked like I was ready to come in to work, in my shirt sleeves.

It got down to two finalists—me and a deputy chief from Cincin-nati—and each of us spent a weekend with the mayor, who talked to us and took us around to meet key groups and figures.

Finally the offer came and I gratefully accepted.

What I thought was a model search process (who, having been selected, wouldn't?) had, in fact, been driven by simple desperation. The loser rather ungraciously told the press I was the right choice if the city sought a "band-aid approach" to its problems.

Next came nine tough yet blissful years in Minneapolis—the only job I unequivocally left voluntarily, since I could look forward to reap-pointment again, with confidence. But I'd been there too long and the place needed the vigor of new leadership.

Notwithstanding such leftist outbursts as occurred at the 1999 World Trade Organization meeting in Seattle and the violence I observed at some "peace rallies," I viscerally believed the extremists on the Right were more murderously violent than those on the Left. The reaction of abor-tion foes to clinics and doctors performing those operations created the anomaly of violence to prevent the killing of fetuses. That these attacks are undertaken in the name of religious scruples only darkens the irony.

And the gun nuts always alerted my antennae to danger.

So, although I never rose to the exalted status of "gun grabber," the National Rifle Association initiated a phone tree that resulted in a flood of protests to Suffolk County, New York, leaders as I was announced as one of five finalists for the chief's job in the late eighties. They may not have been decisive in my defeat but they certainly didn't help my cause.

As I announced I'd leave Minneapolis in fourteen months, Jim Binger came to see me. He was formerly president of Honeywell and had married Virginia McKnight, heiress to the 3M founder's fortune.

Together, they oversaw the McKnight Foundation—a huge mountain of money doing great stuff.

His executive director was leaving in 1989; would I take over the McKnight Foundation?

I was deeply moved and grateful, and I accepted.

A year later he came to see me to tell me his daughter had taken over the foundation and wanted a younger director. The offer was withdrawn. It was blatant age discrimination, but I decided to wallow in self-pity for a bit, poop the bitterness out, and get on with my life.

I then became Minnesota's gaming commissioner and lasted seventeen months before a new governor essentially fired me. I recommended the job be abolished as I left, and it was.

From there I locked my house and moved with my wife to Washington, D.C., where I headed the Center to Prevent Handgun Violence. I lasted two weeks before I was fired—although, even there, they insisted on the protocol of a formal resignation, which suited me fine.

So my resume was free of the blemish of "fired" even though this had been, more than once, the truth.

By now I hoped I wasn't taking on the hue of a born loser.

When I interviewed with Mayor Goode in the mideighties in Philadelphia, he gave me a perfunctory audience and swiftly resumed his hectic schedule. He had been politically damaged by his razing a block of houses in an attempt to stamp out the militant group MOVE. I left with the distinct impression I was not the man's cup of tea.

The job I really lusted after was the NYPD's police commissioner.

Ed Koch came to see me, twice—once in the Bronx and once in Brooklyn—to seek my views on policing (the *New York Times*' October 16, 1976, front-page article captured a lot of attention). He was quoted as saying something to the effect of, "Tony Bouza is the type of person I'd look for in a police commissioner."

The other candidates also made the pilgrimage, except for Bella Abzug, who insisted I visit her and proceeded to regale me with advice on how police departments should be run. I hardly managed a full sentence. Koch's search committee had me as one of the select few to consider but I blew my chances when I gave a stupid answer to a good question. What would I do if I differed with Koch? I'd argue and do what he ordered, unless it was a question of principle, in which case I'd fight. The expected answer was that I'd quietly quit and make no fuss. My maverick tendencies spoiled whatever chance I might have had.

On Koch's election in 1977, he decided first on a white lawyer whose specialty was defending cops accused of wrongdoing, and whose appetite for internal reforms was not whetted by this experience. He carried the additional, heavy burden of no experience in the ranks, although his father had been a police executive. Koch later appointed the NYPD's first black police commissioner, an up-from-the ranks lawyer who experienced his own problems with the union.

I later interviewed twice for the job but never came close to getting it. My regret was in not confronting a group of enemies sitting on the selection committee in the early '90s, when Lee Brown was chosen. I'd at least have had the satisfaction of telling them I didn't think real reform was on their agenda.

At the Montgomery County, Maryland, finals we—the five survivors of the unnerving process—went through elaborate exercises designed to measure decision-making skills, teamwork, and problem solving. We all felt we'd been shabbily treated when the staffer had to admit the process had been undercut.

My only compensation was a conversation with a commander of California's Highway Patrol—a fellow contestant.

He was on his third or fourth wife and asked how many I'd had.

"Just one."

"Stick with her," he said ruefully. "They're all exactly alike. I would've saved a lot if I'd stuck with the first."

I thought it emblematic of the difference between California and New York.

In the early '90s a close friend pleaded with me to run for governor. When my wife and sons joined in, I said I'd think hard and let them know July 1, 1993. The election was in November 1994.

I thought about it, talked to some experienced pals and decided, on July 1, to do it.

Then came fifteen months of sweaty, undignified, rewarding toil. I'd long felt everyone should run for public office once, and remembered Sam Rayburn's rejoinder to Lyndon Johnson, when the vice president glowed about the distinctions of Kennedy's appointees—"Yes, but it would be nice if one of them had run for sheriff once."

Fortunately, I lost in the September primary on the Democratic ticket, gave a Lou Gehrig speech, and started writing a book, which died—fifteen months later—unheralded.

After my 1994 loss I was asked to serve on a small corporation's board. The president had invented a surveillance camera and my presence presumably lent security cachet. The chairman—who'd fronted the money—seemed to me to be in contention with the president. I sided with the latter and was soon asked to resign. I agreed to do it.

The board granted options to its members—essentially worthless, but who knew?

I walked out with a bunch. The firm went public but the shares hovered far below the $1.44 price, where I had the option to buy them.

My wife and I went to Europe for a month. On returning, I bought the *Wall Street Journal* at the airport and was dumbfounded to see the shares at twelve dollars.

I called a board member.

"Is this real?" I asked.

"Yes it is."

I immediately bought fifteen thousand shares at $1.44 and just as quickly sold them at twelve dollars, for a net profit of $160,000. There was tax hell to pay, but not a bad day's work.

Some firings work out better than others.

And there, more or less and excepting some painful reversals and wonderfully satisfying victories in court as an expert witness, ended my working life.

The really odd thing was that, even though all these fiascoes were matters of public record, I was generally regarded as a success.

REFLECTIONS

The police are, peculiarly and singularly, creatures of the larger society. They reflect the fears, hopes, and ambitions of our people—at their loftiest and basest levels. They are malleable instruments whose ostensible purposes are clearly delineated but who also receive subtle, tacit, unarticulated instructions that must, nevertheless, be obeyed.

In carrying out the darker missions, cops employ tactics that bring them into severe criticism from some quarters—such as the American Civil Liberties Union—that the larger segment of the public feels compelled to express shock at, because the actions are so clearly contrary to the society's articulated principles. But the approaches are not all that contrary to the unstated objective of control sought, and the police are powerless to point to the hypocrisy of being asked to keep the underclass under control and out of sight and then being punished for taking actions in furtherance of these objectives.

It is this dissonance between principles and Realpolitik that forms the basis of a continuing and seemingly insoluble dilemma for America's police.

At the near end, my life felt a lot like climbing a mountain. The higher I got, the slower I went, the more I strained, and the harder the breathing—but the view got broader.

Things I had mangled, stumbled over, or never understood became clearer. The petty jealousies and minor ambitions became indistinguishable dots far below.

The things left uncompleted or undone were more sharply etched and stood in silent rebuke of my failures.

It was the big questions—justice, truth, brotherhood, honor, dignity, and honesty—that seemed to stand in boldest relief.

To my successes, my humble desire is for my family, friends, colleagues, and the many people I've been fortunate enough to encounter in my life to remember me not only as a cop but as a public servant.

NOTES

CHAPTER 1: POLICE WORK

1. Arthur Niederhoffer, *Behind the Shield: The Police in Urban Society* (Garden City, N.Y.: Anchor Books, 1967).

2. Stuart Gellman, *The Making of a Cop* (unpublished, 1990).

3. David Bender and Bruno Leone, eds., *Criminal Justice: Opposing Viewpoints* (San Diego: Greenhaven Press, 1993).

4. Peter Maas, *Serpico* (New York: Viking, 1973).

5. Don Carlson, "Hiding behind the Blue Wall," *Ethics Roll Call*, fall 1997.

6. U.S. Census Bureau, *Statistical Abstract of the U.S., 1999* (Lanham, Md.: Bernard Press, 1999).

CHAPTER 2: A POLICE CAREER

1. "Men and Women of Letters: Tulsa, OK, Largest City to Adopt B.A. Requirement for Cops," *Law Enforcement News*, November 30, 1997.

CHAPTER 3: STREET CRIME

1. Dr. John H. Donohue III and Dr. Steven D. Levitt, "Legalized Abortion and Crime," *Law Enforcement News*, September 30, 1999; Anthony Bouza, *The Police Mystique* (New York: Plenum, 1990).

2. Christopher H. Wren, "Face of Heroin: It's Younger and Suburban," *New York Times*, April 25, 2000.

3. Richard Quinney, *Class, State, and Crime: On the Theory and Practice of Criminal Justice* (New York: Longman, 1977).

4. Tony Bouza, "NYPD Blues—Good, Lucky, or Both?" *Law Enforcement News*, January 31, 1997.

5. Tony Bouza, *Bronx Beat* (Chicago: University of Illinois Press, 1990).

6. John F. Heaphy and Joan L. Wolfe, *Productivity in Policing* (Washington, D.C.: Police Foundation, 1975).

7. Gary T. Marx, *Undercover: Police Surveillance in America* (Berkeley: University of California Press, 1988).

8. C. J. Chivers, "Another Cabby Slaying, and Another Set of Confounding Realities," *New York Times*, April 26, 2000.

CHAPTER 4: THE WAR ON DRUGS

1. "New York's Harmful Drug Laws," *New York Times*, May 12, 2000.

2. James Q. Wilson and George L. Kelling, "Police and Neighborhood Safety: Broken Windows," *Atlantic Monthly*, March 1982.

3. Julian K. Barnes, "Haitians Rally against Police," *New York Times*, April 21, 2000.

4. The Drug Policy Foundation, Washington, D.C.

5. Edward Behr, *Prohibition* (New York: Arcade Publications, 1996).

6. Peter Earley, *Super Casino* (New York: Bantam, 1996).

7. *Posse comitatus* (power of the country), passed June 18, 1878, prohibits the military from enforcing laws; Vincent T. Bugliosi, *Drugs in America* (New York: Knightsbridge Publishing, 1991).

CHAPTER 5: RACE

1. Studs Terkel, *Race* (New York: New Press, 1992).

2. James Sterngold, "Appeals Court Voids Ethnic Profiling in Searches," *New York Times*, April 13, 2000.

3. "Two Officers Cleared in Slaying of Colleague," *New York Times*, April 19, 2000.

4. "L.A.'s Ungovernable Police," *New York Times*, March 2, 2000.

5. "Does Third-World Torture Have a Place in Brooklyn?" *Law Enforcement News*, December 31, 1997.

6. William A. Geller and Michael S. Scott, *Deadly Force: What We Know* (Washington, D.C.: Police Executive Research Forum, 1992).

7. Andrew Hacker, *Money: Who Has How Much and Why* (New York: Scribner, 1997).

CHAPTER 6: CRIME FIGHTING AS MYTH

1. James A. Inciardi, *Criminal Justice* (New York: Harcourt Brace Jovanovich, 1987).

2. Linda Greenhouse, "Miranda Decision Has Its Day in Court," *New York Times*, April 20, 2000; "Saving the Miranda Rule," *New York Times*, April 19, 2000.

3. "STRESS," *New York Times*, March 10, 1972.

4. Geane Rosenberg, "F.B.I. Casts a Wide Net with Plenty of Tangles," *New York Times*, February 9, 2000.

CHAPTER 7: INTELLIGENCE OPERATIONS

1. Anthony V. Bouza, *Police Intelligence* (New York: AMS, 1976).

2. Robert D. McFadden, "Jailed in Malcolm X Killing, Man Is Given Mosque Post," *New York Times*, March 31, 1998.

3. "Undercover and Sensitive Operation Unit," Attorney General's Guidelines on FBI Undercover Operations, revised November 13, 1992; Richard Rosenthal, *Rookie Cop* (Wellfleet, Mass.: Leapfrog Press, 2000).

4. Karl Evanzz, *The Messenger: The Rise and Fall of Elijah Muhammad* (New York: Pantheon, 1999).

5. Howell Raines, "The Murderous Era of George C. Wallace," *New York Times*, April 26, 2000.

6. C. Eric Lincoln, *The Black Muslims in America* (Boston: Beacon Press, 1961).

7. Carl Bernstein, *All the President's Men* (New York: Simon and Schuster, 1974).

8. Anthony S. Ulasewicz, *The President's Private Eye* (Westport, Conn.: MACSAM Publishing, 1990).

9. Curt J. Gentry, *J. Edgar Hoover: The Man and His Secrets* (New York: Plume, 1992).

10. E. W. Count, *Cop Talk* (New York: Pocket Books, 1994).

11. Peter Maas, *Underboss* (New York: Harper Collins, 1997).

12. Selwyn Raab, "A Mafia Family's Second Wind," *New York Times*, April 29, 2000.

13. National Institute of Justice, *Understanding Police Agency Performance* (Washington, D.C.: Department of Justice, 1984).

CHAPTER 8: LEGAL ISSUES

1. Paul Chevigny, *Police Power: Police Abuses in N.Y.C.* (New York: Pantheon Books, 1969).

2. Laurie Goodstein and William Glaverson, "The Well-Marked Roads to Homicidal Rage," *New York Times*, April 10, 2000.

3. Nichole M. Christian, "Ex-Sailor Linked to Savage Slaying of Prostitutes Worldwide," *New York Times*, April 14, 2000.

4. Ford Fessenden, "They Threaten, Seethe and Unhinge, Then Kill in Quantity," *New York Times*, April 9, 2000.

5. James Sterngold, "Police Corruption Inquiry Expands in L.A.," *New York Times*, February 11, 2000.

CHAPTER 9: NYPD

1. Leonard Schecter with William Phillips, *On the Pad* (New York: Berkley, 1973).

2. David Chanen, "Police Chief Apologizes to Slain Man's Family," *Minneapolis Star Tribune*, January 13, 2000.

3. Edward S. Silver, D.A., *Report of Special Investigation by the District Attorney of Kings County and the December 1949 Grand Jury* (New York, 1954); James Lardner and Thomas Repetto, *NYPD* (New York: Henry Holt, 2000).

4. Mark Baker, *Cops: Their Lives in Their Own Words* (New York: Simon & Schuster, 1985).

CHAPTER 10: POLICE PROBLEMS

1. *Fighting Police Abuse: A Community Action Manual* (Medford, N.Y.: ACLU, 1992).

2. Samuel Walker and Betsy Wright, *Citizen Review of the Police, 1994: A National Survey* (Washington, D.C.: PERF, 1994).

3. "Talk About a Training Complex," *Law Enforcement News*, April 15, 1989.

4. Jane Fritsch, "Four Officers in Diallo Shooting Are Acquitted of All Charges," *New York Times*, February 26, 2000. See also articles on January 20, 24, 26, 27, February 1, 2, 3, 8, 9, 10, 11, 28, 29, and March 1, 3, and 5 of 2000.

5. David Barstow, "The Re-creation of a Firebrand," *New York Times*, April 28, 2000.

6. James Lardner, *Crusader: The Hell-Raising Police Career of Detective David Durk* (New York: Random House, 1995).

7. Lawrence W. Sherman and Richard A. Berk, *The Minneapolis Domestic Violence Experiment* (Washington, D.C.: Police Foundation, 1984).

8. *Bronx River Restoration: Preliminary Master Plan* (Bronx, N.Y., 1978).

9. Willy Stern, "Above the Law," *Nashville Scene*, October 21 and 28, 1999.

CHAPTER 11: MANAGING

1. James J. Fyfe et al., *Police Administration* (New York: McGraw-Hill, 1996).

2. Jerald Vaughn, *How to Rate Your Police Chief* (Washington, D.C.: PERF, 1989).

3. Chris Braiden, Supt. Edmonton [Alta.] Police Department, "Community Policing: Nothing New Under the Sun," *Problem Solving Quarterly* (summer 1990).

4. Malcolm K. Sparrow, Mark H. Moore, and David M. Kennedy, *Beyond 911: A New Era for Policing* (New York: Basic Books, 1990).

5. "Plenty of Parties Looking Over Police Shoulders," *Law Enforcement News*, December 31, 1997.

6. "Residency Rule Still Sits Poorly with Cops," *Law Enforcement News*, October 31, 1997.

CHAPTER 12: MANAGING TECHNOLOGY

1. *The Challenge of Crime in a Free Society: A Report by the President's Commission on Law Enforcement and the Administration of Justice* (Washington, D.C.: U.S. Government Printing Office, 1967).

2. Peter Maas, *Serpico* (New York: Viking, 1973).

CHAPTER 13: THE NATIONAL SCENE

1. Jan Golab, *The Dark Side of the Force* (New York: Atlantic Monthly Press, 1993).

2. David Burnham, "The FBI," *Nation*, August 1–18, 1997.

3. "Council to Ask U.S. to Head Police Inquiry in Los Angeles," *New York Times*, April 6, 2000.

4. Todd S. Purdum, "Washington Tries to Right a Stumbling L.A.," *New York Times*, May 15, 2000.

CHAPTER 14: SWEEPS, ROUNDUPS, AND OTHER ABUSES

1. Elaine Horscher and Marc Scadalone, "Hongisto Accused of Confiscating Gay Newspapers," *San Francisco Chronicle*, May 1992; Bill Mandel, "Hongisto in Trouble: Familiar Turf," *San Francisco Examiner*, May 20, 1992.

2. Archibald Cox, *Crisis at Columbia* (New York: Vintage Books, 1968).

3. Tape by Tony Schwartz, New York, 1975, involving Pres. Leonard Lief and Bronx NYPD C.O. Tony Bouza.

CHAPTER 16: POLICE UNIONS

1. Anthony V. Bouza, "Police Unions: Paper Tigers of Roaring Lions," in *Police Leadership in America* (New York: Praeger, 1985).

2. "Police Officers' Bill of Rights," *Subject to Debate*, June 1995.

3. Catherine Itzin, ed., *Pornography: Women, Violence, and Civil Liberties* (New York: Oxford University Press, 1992).

4. The mayoral election of the fall of 1979 was extensively covered by both the *Minneapolis Star* and the *Minneapolis Tribune*.

CHAPTER 17: INTERNAL CLIMATE

1. William K. Rashbaum, "Officers' Arrests Come As No Surprise on Street," *New York Times*, March 11, 2000.

CHAPTER 18: COPS: INDIVIDUALLY AND EN MASSE

1. Deborah Richardson, "Police Take a Beating on Spouse Abuse," *Law Enforcement News*, December 15, 1996; Judith Bonderman, "Why Are the Rules Different for the Police?" *Subject to Debate*, August 1995.

2. Steven A. Holmes, "A Civil Rights Crusader Unafraid to Challenge Anyone," *New York Times*, May 1, 2000.

3. Francis X. Clines, "Protesting by Angry Police Leaves Louisville Unsettled," *New York Times*, March 10, 2000.

4. "Study: Louisville Police Don't Fully Document Use of Force," *Louisville Courier Journal*, March 26, 2000.

5. "Grand Jury Indicts Four Indianapolis Cops," *Law Enforcement News*, December 15, 1996.

6. William Tucker, "How Rent Control Drives Out Affordable Housing," *Policy Analysis*, May 21, 1997.

CHAPTER 19: REFORMS WITHOUT AND WITHIN

1. Tony Bouza, "When Chief Says 'Shake' You Shake," *Minneapolis Star Tribune*, December 14, 1997.

CHAPTER 20: ISSUES ACROSS THE LANDSCAPE

1. John J. Donohue III and Steven D. Levitt, *Legalized Abortion and Crime*, unpublished.

2. Fox Butterfield, *All God's Children: The Bosket Family and the American Tradition of Violence* (New York: Knopf, 1995).

3. Richard Ford, "Armed but Not Alarmed," *New York Times*, March 21, 2000.

4. Donald J. Newman and Patrick R. Anderson, *Introduction to Criminal Justice* (New York: Random House, 1989).

5. Paul Mones, *Stalking Justice* (New York: Pocket Books, 1995).

6. "An Enduring Mystery's Lessons in Crime Scene Mishandling," *Law Enforcement News*, December 31, 1997.

7. Dirk Johnson, "No Executions in Illinois until System is Repaired," *New York Times*, May 21, 2000.

8. "Chicago Officials Complain of Too Many Sting Operations," *New York Times*, January 18, 1996.

9. Samuel Walker, *Sense and Nonsense about Crime: A Policy Guide* (Monterey, Calif.: Brooks-Cole, 1985).

10. *Young Black Males under Criminal Justice Control* (Washington, D.C.: Sentencing Project, 1998).

11. *The African-American Almanac*, 6th ed. (Washington, D.C.: Gale Research, 1994).

12. *U.S. Census Bureau: Statistical Abstract of the U.S.*, 199th ed. (Lanham, Md.: Bernard Press, 1999).

13. "A Closer Look at Rampage Killings," *New York Times*, April 13, 2000.

14. *Report of the National Advisory Commission on Civil Disorders* (New York: New York Times, 1968).

15. Alfred Blumstein, *Making Rationality Relevant—The American Society of Criminology 1992 Presidential Address* (Washington, D.C.: American Society of Criminology, 1993).

16. William Spellman et al. *Repeat Offender Programs for Law Enforcement* (Washington, D.C.: PERF, 1990).

17. Kevin Flynn, "In Tough Reply, Police Call Racial Profiling Report Recklessly Unfair," *New York Times*, May 16, 2000.

18. From a speech by Cornelius J. Behan, PERF, Washington, D.C., May 5, 1993.

19. Jacob R. Clark, "A Day Late, A Dollar Short," *Law Enforcement News*, April 15, 1997.

20. Steven R. Donzinger, ed., *The Real War on Crime: The Report of the National Criminal Justice Commission* (New York: Harper Perennial, 1996); *FBI Uniform Crimer Report: U.S. Department of Justice*, Washington, D.C.

21. Matthew Purdy, "For Too Many Judges, Drug Sentences Mean Having to Say You're Sorry," *New York Times*, May 21, 2000.

22. Sam Walker, *Employment of Black and Hispanic Police Officers, 1983–88: A Follow-Up Study*, Center for Applied Urban Research, University of Nebraska at Omaha, February 1989.

23. "P.B.A. Lawyers, Others in Kickback Scheme," *Law Enforcement News*, February 28, 1997.

24. *The Police Chiefs*, PBS Documentary, aired July 31, 1990.

25. Samuel Hughes, "The Empirical Light of Lawrence Sherman," *Gazette* [University of Pennsylvania], March and April 2000.

26. "The Case for a Police Monitor," *New York Times*, April 30, 2000.

27. Barry Meier, "Bringing Law Suits to Do What Congress Won't," *New York Times*, March 26, 2000.

CHAPTER 21: SELF-IMPROVEMENT AND MANAGEMENT

1. Edward J. Tully, "Misconduct, Corruption, Abuse of Power: What Can the Chief Do?" *Beretta USA Leadership Bulletin*, December 1997.

2. Sissela Bok, *Lying: Moral Choice in Public Life* (New York: Vintage Books, 1989).

3. Lawrence W. Sherman, *The Quality of Police Education* (San Francisco: Jossey-Bass Publishers, 1985).

4. Carol W. Lewis, *The Ethics Challenge in Public Service* (San Francisco: Jossey-Bass, 1991).

5. Bonnie Szumski, ed., *Police Brutality* (San Diego: Greenhaven Press, 1991).

6. Edwin J. De Lattre, *Character and Cops: Ethics in Policing* (London: University Press of America, 1989).

7. Peter Greenwood, *Selective Incapacitation* (Santa Monica: Rand, 1982).

INDEX

295